Devolution
in Britain today

MANCHESTER
UNIVERSITY PRESS

Politics Today

Series editor: Bill Jones

Devolution
in Britain today

Colin Pilkington

Manchester University Press
Manchester and New York

distributed exclusively in the USA by Palgrave

Copyright © Colin Pilkington 2002

The right of Colin Pilkington to be identified as the author of this work has been asserted
by him in accordance with the Copyright, Designs and Patents Act 1988.

Published by Manchester University Press
Oxford Road, Manchester M13 9NR, UK
and Room 400, 175 Fifth Avenue, New York, NY 10010, USA
www.manchesteruniversitypress.co.uk

Distributed exclusively in the USA by
Palgrave, 175 Fifth Avenue, New York,
NY 10010, USA

Distributed exclusively in Canada by
UBC Press, University of British Columbia, 2029 West Mall,
Vancouver, BC, Canada V6T 1Z2

British Library Cataloguing-in-Publication Data
A catalogue record for this book is available from the British Library

Library of Congress Cataloging-in-Publication Data applied for

ISBN 0 7190 6075 3 *hardback*
     0 7190 6076 1 *paperback*

First published 2002

10 09 08 07 06 05 04 03 02   10 9 8 7 6 5 4 3 2 1

Typeset in Photina
by Servis Filmsetting Ltd, Manchester
Printed in Great Britain
by Biddles Ltd, Guildford and King's Lynn

Contents

Preface

The number of perspectives through which the student is expected to study British Government and Politics is constantly increasing. There was a time, not so long ago, when we used to stress that the subject must be studied from both a national and local viewpoint, given that many students tended to ignore local government. Then, in the late 1980s and early 1990s the European dimension was added to the national and local. Since 1997 a fourth perspective has been added and, thanks to the growing importance of devolved government, students are now told to consider the subject at national, local, European and regional levels. This broadening of perspective is reflected in the new A-level syllabuses that were introduced as of 2000, as well as in numerous introductory courses at universities offering political studies.

There is, however, very little that has been written about devolution for the general student. There is Vernon Bogdanor's book, of course, and the excellent work of the Constitution Unit of the University College of London, but the former was written before the devolved governments were installed and the latter is written from a highly academic standpoint that is a little off-putting to the student coming new and unprepared to the subject. The book which follows is an attempt to take a wider view than was possible for Bogdanor and does so, moreover, in a more accessible language than that used by the UCL team. This view of devolution has been written in the aftermath of the 2001 Westminster general election with the first-time student particularly in mind.

I am afraid to say that any politics text suffers from the fact that politics is in a state of constant flux and a writer is always aware that what he or she writes today can be completely out of date tomorrow. This speed at which one's words become outdated is magnified out of all recognition by the time it takes to get a book into print. As far as devolution is concerned, this refers particularly to the situation in Northern Ireland since the on–off nature of devolution to Stormont means that here more than anywhere the nature of the settlement becomes history even as it is being written about. This book comes with a health warning: Chapter 8 dealing with the Good Friday Agreement and its aftermath was completed in mid-August 2001, while the Northern Ireland executive was suspended, as it continued to be until November. Similarly, the resignation of Henry McLeish as first Secretary of Scotland also took place long after the book was complete. Although attempts have been made to update the relevant passages in the light of events, the reader should be aware of the continued fluidity of the situation. It is hoped that the judgments I have made and the implications I have drawn as a result of the devolution settlements are equally as valid no matter what form has since been adopted by the devolved structures.

What I am saying therefore is that this is a history book, tracing the reasons for and development of devolved government for parts of the United Kingdom, rather than a fixed contemporary picture of the status quo. And, having mentioned history, might I mention at this point the subject of Chapter 2? This chapter traces the history of how the various disparate regions came together, not just to form the UK but to form the component parts of the UK like England and Scotland. This analysis goes rather far back in history and many readers might feel that it is irrelevant to what is, as the title suggests, a study of 'devolution in Britain today'. Anyone who feels like that is free to omit the chapter altogether. However, I hope that they will not because for me it is important that the reader should appreciate how the strains that have produced demands for devolution, if not independence, today were in fact built into the system in the way that different and often conflicting cultures were forced together into political entities. It seems to me, for example, to be amazingly significant that the division of Wales into those who voted 'yes' or 'no' to the devolution referendum mirrors exactly the thirteenth-century division between lands ruled by the Norman Marcher lords and those ruled by Welsh princes.

The usual guilty parties are lined up to be thanked. To Dr Bill Jones, series editor, my thanks for his constant support and encouragement. To Tony Mason and Richard Delahunte of Manchester University Press for their tolerance and understanding when the wayward behaviour of Ulster Unionists and Sinn Fein kept altering the date at which I could regard the book as complete. To Dennis Harrigan, my colleague, whose Northern Ireland contacts proved invaluable, and to those friends of mine living in Scotland and Wales, the Methvens and the Thorpes in particular. To Glynis Sandwith of the Politics Association Resource Centre for all the help given in finding those odd facts. Finally I should like to express my own appreciation of the help that is now given to researchers by the internet and the World Wide Web. The bibliography includes a list of the more valuable sites, without which I could not have written this book and which the reader might well find invaluable for keeping the record up to date.

Colin Pilkington

List of abbreviations

AMS	additional member system
BIC	British-Irish Council
BIIGC	British-Irish Intergovernmental Conference
COR	Committee of the Regions
DfEE	Department for Education and Employment
DUP	Democratic Unionist Party
FCO	Foreign and Commonwealth Office
FPTP	first past the post
GLA	Greater London Authority
GLC	Greater London Council
GM	genetically modified
GO	government office
GOL	government office for London
MLA	Member of the Legislative Assembly
MSP	Member of Scottish Parliament
NAAG	National Assembly Advisory Group
NICRA	Northern Ireland Civil Rights Association
NIUP	Northern Ireland Unionist Party
NIWC	Northern Ireland Women's Coalition
NSMC	North–South Ministerial Council
NUT	National Union of Teachers
OFMDFM	Office of the First Minister and Deputy First Minister
OMOV	one member one vote
PC	Plaid Cymru
PPP	public–private partnership
PR	proportional representation
PUP	Progressive Unionist Party
RDA	Regional Development Agency
RIC	Royal Irish Constabulary
RUC	Royal Ulster Constabulary

SDLP	Social Democratic and Labour Party
SF	Sinn Fein
SNP	Scottish National Party
SPCB	Scottish Parliamentary Corporate Body
SQA	Scottish Qualifications Authority
STV	single transferable vote
TEU	Treaty on European Union
UDA	Ulster Defence Association
UKUP	United Kingdom Unionist Party
UUAP	United Unionist Assembly Party
UUC	Ulster Unionist Council
UUP	Ulster Unionist Party
UVF	Ulster Volunteer Force
WLGA	Welsh Local Government Association

1

Introduction:
the meaning of devolution

Sovereignty

The issue of devolved power is at the very heart of a whole cluster of constitutional devices, each of which impinges upon and influences the others. At the heart of this tangled knot of political arrangements is the key concept of the nation state and the means by which the political, legislative and administrative integrity of that national polity might be assured against both internal and external threats. In order to understand devolution it is therefore necessary to examine closely the concept of national sovereignty and the related topics of nationhood, nationality and subsidiarity.

A dictionary definition of the word sovereignty is 'supreme and unrestricted power residing in an individual or group of people or body'. More precisely it is the legislative or judicial entity that has no superior body able to override legislative or judicial decisions made for the territory over which it is sovereign. In the United Kingdom, Parliament is held to be sovereign because no other body but Parliament has the right to pass and implement laws. So jealously does Parliament guard the right to be the only legislative body that other governmental or quasi-governmental bodies which need to pass laws, rules and regulations, such as local government authorities or transport undertakings, can only do so through the device known as delegated legislation. Through delegated legislation, Parliament grants to other bodies the facility to pass laws, but only laws specifically related to the jurisdiction of the authority concerned. In strict legal parlance they are not laws, but by-laws. As the nineteenth-century constitutional writer, A. V. Dicey, himself an ardent opponent of Irish Home Rule and dedicated upholder of the Union Parliament, put it: 'The sovereignty of Parliament is the dominant characteristic of our political institutions . . . [Parliament] has, under the English constitution, the right to make or unmake any law whatever, and, further, that no person or body is recognised by the law of England as having a right to override or set aside the legislation of Parliament' (Adonis, 1993, p. 8).

With a view to what we shall be discussing later, it is worth bearing in mind the way in which Dicey used the expressions '*English* constitution' and 'the law of *England*' in the passage quoted above. Dicey was of course talking about the sovereignty of the United Kingdom Parliament in Westminster but, by equating Britishness with Englishness, he manages to ignore the claims of Scotland, Wales and Ireland to a share of that sovereignty in what after all has been claimed to be a 'multi-national' Britain. There is a hint of imperial arrogance in this statement of English superiority which suggests that the Scots, Welsh and Irish are all subordinate nationalities, subject to an overriding English sovereignty. It has long been an argument put forward by unionists that Britain can be regarded as a nation for no other reason than that most of the people living in Britain speak English (Budge *et al.*, 1998, page 140).

For a word in regular use by politicians and political commentators, sovereignty is very difficult to define with any precision, simply because it can mean different things to different people at different times. And that imprecision over the meaning of 'sovereignty' implies that a skilled politician can make the word mean whatever he or she wishes it to mean. However, according to elementary political theory the many and varied meanings can be summarised under just two headings, distinguished as:

- **Legal sovereignty**, which is usually vested in the legislature but which in federal states is usually said to rest in a sovereign constitution. British parliamentary sovereignty is typical of the former, while the governance of the United States is typical of the other.
- **Political sovereignty**, which is vested in a person or persons. At one time the monarch was sovereign but with democracy has come the belief that sovereignty is vested in the *demos* or people.

The outward manifestation of political sovereignty is the referendum, which is a Swiss invention of the nineteenth century, devised to match a provision of the Swiss constitution of 1874 which states that, if 30,000 citizens can be found to sign a petition against an act of the Federal Assembly, then that act must be voted on by the entire electorate. Following that early example many states now have provision for referendums written into their constitutions for when legislation threatens to alter it. Consider, for example, the six or more referendums held in Denmark over the years concerning Danish membership of the European Union (EU). Denmark is not alone, however, since Austria, Denmark, Finland, France, the Republic of Ireland and Sweden of the fifteen EU member countries all require referendums before changes are made to their constitutions.

In Britain sovereignty is said to be vested in 'The Crown in Parliament', in which the term 'Crown' no longer refers to the monarch but to the body which now exercises the royal prerogative on behalf of the monarch: in other words, 'the crown' equals 'the government'. It is only fair to say that what is called by ministers *parliamentary sovereignty* might be rather more accurately described as *executive* or *governmental* sovereignty. It has been claimed that this blurring of distinctions is the 'contradiction at the heart of the British Constitution: the principle of parliamentary sovereignty being used by executives to minimise their accountability' (Judge, 1993). The claim made by upholders of parliamentary sovereignty is that referendums are unnecessary, under the principle of representative democracy, 'since everyone has a representative in parliament and those representatives can be mandated on policy matters through election, there is no need to undermine the sovereignty of parliament by approaching the electorate direct' (Pilkington, 1997, page 127).

Despite this clinging to the principle of parliamentary sovereignty, the major political parties have been forced in more recent years to align with much of Europe and concede the point that any legislation which affects the constitution of the United Kingdom, such as the devolution legislation of 1998 (or any future British decision to join the single currency), has to be submitted to the public in a referendum. It is a concession that has been bitterly resisted by those jingoistic, unionist politicians who see such alien imports as yet another decline in the status of the nation state.

However, all nations in the modern world are inevitably having to surrender some aspects of their sovereignty because of the multinational nature of life at the start of the twenty-first century. The demands of a global economy mean that a cutback in oil production by the OPEC countries can alter fuel prices worldwide and may precipitate a recession in America or Western Europe. The developed nations are economically interdependent and there is no doubt that, even while Africa and Asia were seeing the birth of new nations, even as the old powers relinquished sovereignty over former colonies, and even as the fragmentation of the USSR spawned a plethora of independent states, there was nevertheless a commensurate marked decline in the nature and status of the nation state elsewhere in the world.

For the United Kingdom the concept of a nation state raised upon the solid foundation of parliamentary sovereignty is becoming increasingly more difficult to sustain as the unitary nature of parliamentary sovereignty is squeezed between the conflicting demands made by the pooling of sovereignty represented by the EU and the sharing of power demanded by devolution to the regions. Under attack from two different directions the unitary nation state would seem to be in terminal decline. And, as the nation state has declined in the developed world, so too have the more chauvinistic elements of what the people understand by the terms 'nationality' and 'sovereignty'.

The nation state

In medieval Europe the concept of a politico-geographical entity composed of people with a common ethnicity, religion, language or culture was unknown. Everyone paid lip-service to a vague concept known as Christendom, within which the Emperor represented secular power and the Pope spiritual dominion. Within that dual hegemony, loyalties and allegiances were personal, made up of the reciprocal oaths, duties and obligations of the feudal system. When the nation state began to emerge, as early as the fourteenth century, it was largely due to a breakdown in feudal relationships through disputed allegiances.

The dispute between France and England over the overlordship of Aquitaine known as the Hundred Years War transformed a feudal quarrel between two kings into a bitter war between two countries, each of which developed a strong sense of national identity as a result. All the early examples of nation states came about through war, revolution, or the expulsion of an alien power. For example, England, Scotland and France discovered their national identities by fighting one another in a series of wars spread over more than two hundred years, while Spain and Portugal emerged from the rise of those Christian kingdoms who took joint action to expel the Moors from the Iberian peninsula.

Yet, although a handful of nation states existed as early as the fifteenth century, the development of the nation state to the point at which it was perceived to be a part of the natural order of things, is a fairly recent development. Essentially it can be claimed that nationalism as we understand it today was created by the French Revolution. In a post-Napoleonic Europe the oppressive Austro-Hungarian Empire or the crumbling Ottoman Empire led to the rise of liberal nationalism in the nineteenth century among their subject peoples in Italy and the Balkans, leading to outcomes such as the independence of Greece and the unification of Italy, in the creation of what Mazzini called 'a sovereign nation of free and equal beings'. Basic Liberal ideology in the nineteenth century naturally included a belief in national self-government and this implied support by the Liberal Party for national independence movements abroad and Home Rule for Ireland and possibly Scotland in Britain (Coxall and Robins, 1995, page 69).

The heyday of the nation state, however, undoubtedly came after 1918 when the collapse of the Austro-Hungarian, Russian and Ottoman Empires created a wealth of new nations in Central Europe and the Middle East. That was followed by the many newly-independent states created by the period of decolonisation that followed the Second World War; with even more to come after the collapse of the Soviet bloc in 1989. As Peter Alter said in a survey of Europe taken at the time of Maastricht in 1993:

Between 1870 and 1914 there were only about 50 sovereign states in the world, 16 of them in Europe. The figure barely fluctuated over the period. By the end of the First World War the community of nations had grown by 10 as new states emerged in Europe. When it was founded in 1920 the League of Nations had 42 members: its successor the United Nations, was established in 1945 with a membership of 51. By 1960 this figure had grown to 82; by 1973 it was 135 and in 1992 it stood at 183. (Keegan and Kettle, 1993)

It would be convenient if all those political entities we generically call countries, states or nations were homogeneous in having populations that are religiously, ethnically, linguistically or culturally united, within clearly defined geographical boundaries. Unfortunately, this is almost never the case since most countries, whether by conquest, amalgamation, annexation or mutual interest, are made up of divergent and sometimes conflicting groups: there are Catholics and Protestants in Ireland; Serbs, Croats, Bosnian Muslims and Kosovan Albanians in the former Yugoslavia; Flemings and Walloons in Belgium; Jews and Palestinian Arabs in Israel; Kurds in Turkey or Iraq and so on. Virtually every state in the modern world has significant minorities within its borders that are so different ethnically, linguistically or culturally that they could well form separate national entities themselves.

Many of these so-called multinational or multicultural states have sections of the population, usually the majority sections, which regard themselves as superior to the rest of the population. As we have already stated about the English in the United Kingdom these feelings of superiority can lead to attitudes that are virtually colonial and oppressive in nature. The lesser or minority groupings in this situation naturally resent being placed in an inferior position and this in turn leads to feelings of resentment and alienation on the part of the minority groups. And it is these feelings that have helped create those nationalist parties that take up the cause of separatism in an attempt to achieve autonomy, self-determination and freedom of domination by the 'superior' nation. Often these groups work to achieve their aims through political, democratic or parliamentary means but, in some instances, as with the Basque separatists in Spain, the Palestinians in Israel, the Kurds in Turkey or the IRA in the UK, these nationalist groupings can employ violence to pursue their ends in the so-called 'military option': whereupon these nationalist activists become 'terrorists' to their enemies and 'freedom fighters' to their friends.

One of the problems created by an upsurge in national self-determination is that it is like a set of Chinese boxes: when one is opened, another is revealed within. Minority groups seeking separation from the larger body may well achieve that separation only to discover that they too have minorities within themselves, also clamouring for separation. Consider the problem of Ireland, where a section of the population sought independence from Britain, only to find when they achieved that independence that there was a Protestant minority in the north-east which wanted to preserve the union with Britain and who were willing to fight to maintain that union. And then, when the Protestants were granted their own unionist state in Northern Ireland, they in turn discovered that a Catholic nationalist minority was unwilling to accept the authority of Stormont and they too were ready to take up arms against the majority (Budge *et al.*, 1998, page 141).

One of the principal functions of a constitution is to counter such fragmentations by reconciling the different social, ethnic and political groupings living within the state or other sovereign body. There are largely two ways of creating a political union out of a regional cultural diversity, these two ways being known as unitary and federal systems.

Unitary systems

In a unitary system there is one sovereign authority with the sole ability to legislate, administer and adjudicate for the whole of the state or society. If power is devolved to the regional components of that society it is with the consent of the central authority, which supervises such devolution *and can revoke it*. Various areas or districts of the country can pass and administer their own local laws but those secondary laws can only be passed because the national legislature has delegated that right to the local authority.

There are those politicians, like Margaret Thatcher, who think of themselves as unionists, who campaign vigorously against what they see as the break-up of the union in movements towards nationalism or devolution and to whom any hint of federalism is anathema. At the end of the nineteenth century the fervently unionist A. V. Dicey believed that 'the nations of Great Britain have historically expressed a desire for unity and a sense of common interest and national feeling' (Evans, 1999, p. 45). To unionist politicians like Dicey or Lady Thatcher the United Kingdom is the perfect example of a unitary state, with one sovereign parliament controlling all aspects of the governance of Great Britain and Northern Ireland. And it is a defining feature of a unitary system that it should have one sovereign body made up of just one executive, one legislature and one judiciary. In 1997, when framing the bill which would create a devolved parliament in Edinburgh, a clause was included which related to the importance of preventing the fragmentation of the Civil Service in Scotland by stating that, 'this ensures that all the staff of the Scottish Administration should be civil servants in the Home Civil Service. Maintaining a unified Home Civil Service is considered to be essential for the preservation of the Union.' The same White Paper, describing the nature of the Scottish Parliament, stated quite clearly that 'the United Kingdom Parliament is and will remain sovereign in all matters' (White Paper, 1997). In the actual Scotland Act which followed, it was made clear that the Scottish parliament's legislative powers 'do not affect the power of the Parliament of the United Kingdom to make laws for Scotland' (Scotland Act, 1998).

A problem does exist in that a unitary state imposed on disparate groupings, some of whom are willing to join but where others are reluctant to do so, has great difficulty in seeing itself as a united entity and thereby engendering a sense of national consciousness and identity. Within the United Kingdom there are those who can readily identify themselves as being Scots, Welsh or Irish; some who somewhat less eagerly see themselves as being English, but very few who readily answer a question as to their nationality by admitting to being British – except for those who say 'British' when really they mean 'English'.

Federal systems

In a federal system the component provinces or regions within the national state each possess their own supreme authorities which have legislative and executive jurisdiction within their areas of competence; the central authority or federal government merely retaining the most important functions like economic planning and defence. To maintain relationships within the conflicting interests of federal component states means that a federal system must be regulated by a written constitution and controlled by a Supreme Court. It is these regulating bodies which decide the dividing lines between federal and subsidiary authorities; which apportion responsibilities, and which determine the extent to which the component states of a federal body have the right to pass their own primary laws.

The problem for a federal government is where the component states are very different in size, population, wealth and power. In such a situation the representatives of the smaller and less powerful states feel oppressed and overwhelmed by their colleagues from the larger and more powerful states, while the larger states in their turn feel frustrated and held back by having to consider their smaller colleagues. In the immediate aftermath of the American Revolutionary War, before the constitution was written, the United States was a confederation of states the Congress of which had a unanimity rule for the passing of legislation, which meant that just one state, albeit a state as small as Rhode Island, could frustrate the wishes of states such as New York or Virginia by vetoing the desired legislation. The larger states wanted to replace the unanimity rule by a Congress in which members of both houses were elected according to a system based on proportionate populations. It was an analogous situation to the Council of Ministers of the European Union, whose decision-making process was originally subject to a unanimity rule that amounted to being a national veto, and which meant that Luxembourg, with a population of half a million, could veto the decisions of states such as Britain, France or Germany. The national veto is still used and can still generate controversy but, on the other hand, in recent years the EU has increasingly turned to the device of qualified majority voting, under which system the member states have differing numbers of votes, weighted according to population size (Pilkington, 2001).

In the United States the anomalous situation was resolved by Federalists like Alexander Hamilton who, when they drew up the constitution, created a Congress in which members of the lower house, the House of Representatives, are elected to represent geographical constituencies of approximately equal population, while the upper house, the Senate, represents the interests of the States, with each and every state having two senators, regardless of size, the confederation thereby becoming a federation (Brogan, 1985).

The union state

Despite fulfilling the criteria of a unitary state, the United Kingdom is, strictly speaking, neither unitary nor federal but rather what is known more simply as a union state:

- Like a unitary state it has a single sovereign parliament but that parliament did not originate as a single body but grew from the merger of previously separate assemblies, as the English parliament united with the councils, assemblies or parliaments of Wales (1536), Scotland (1707) and Ireland (1801). Compared with a federal structure, therefore, the component parliaments within a union state have surrendered their jurisdiction and sovereignty and, even where some devolution of power has occurred, as was the case with the Stormont government in Northern Ireland, the devolved assembly can be no more than quasi-federal in that it remains subordinate to the national parliament and can be suppressed, as indeed was the case when direct rule was imposed on Northern Ireland in 1972.
- Unlike a unitary state, on the other hand, the component nations of the UK continue to possess pre-union rights and institutions peculiar to themselves, which maintain some degree of autonomy. This is even reflected in the constitutional terms given to the component parts of the union: England and Scotland being kingdoms, Wales a principality and Northern Ireland a province. The most obvious example of differing political institutions is the Scottish legal system, which is distinct from the English system in enacted law, judicial procedure and the structure of the courts. There are also other factors, as with the Scottish banks issuing their own banknotes or an education system so different that someone with an English teaching qualification cannot automatically work in Scottish schools. In Wales there is legislation ensuring that the Welsh language has equal status with English in the courts, schools and local administrations. Northern Ireland is the one part of the United Kingdom which up to now has regularly used proportional representation in elections and which has its own distinct Civil Service. And these three national entities within the UK have had their own government departments for some time in the Scottish, Welsh and Northern Ireland Offices, providing administrative devolution in a number of discrete areas. For these and other reasons, the UK cannot be regarded as ever having been a single monolithic structure.

It is interesting to compare the United Kingdom's status as a union state with two other European states that were created in the nineteenth century by a process of unification: Germany and Italy. Germany grew out of the merger of the North German Confederation and, the southern principalities like the Kingdom of Bavaria and, although the act of unification was the result of machinations by the Prussian Chancellor, Otto von Bismarck, the German Empire proclaimed in 1871 was essentially an association of separate kingdoms which chose to recognise the king of Prussia as emperor. It therefore possessed a federal constitution from the start and the structure put in place at that time can still be recognised in the Federal Republic of Germany that we know today. Italy on the other hand was unified by the merger of various states with the Piedmont-centred Kingdom of Sardinia, under King Victor Emmanuel II. The other Italian states were either annexed and absorbed, as was Lombardy after the Austrians had been expelled by Franco-Sardinian forces; or they voted to join Piedmont in a plebiscite of the people, as was done by the Grand Duchy of Tuscany or the Kingdom of the Two Sicilies. Ultimately the united Kingdom of Italy was proclaimed in 1861, the parliament of the Kingdom of Sardinia became the parliament of the Kingdom of Italy and Turin, capital of Piedmont, became the capital of Italy. Italy therefore, like the United Kingdom, is a union state, created by merger and absorption (Taylor, 1954).

The German, Italian and British states have one thing in common: all three have formed a union of peoples within which one particular people is dominant. One is reminded of the final slogan proposed by Orwell in *Animal Farm*, 'All animals are equal but some are more equal than others.' Alternatively it is possible to consider the position of the English within the United Kingdom in the context of a term borrowed by Tom Nairn from the world of natural history and speak of the UK as 'consociational'; a term which means a community of animals living together in which one species of animal is dominant (Nairn, 2000, p. 155 ff.).

Devolution or subsidiarity?

Devolution is quite simply defined as 'the transfer of powers from a superior to an inferior political authority (Bogdanor, 1999, p. 2), although the best defini-tion was probably given by the Irish nationalist leader, John Redmond, who, in defining Home Rule in a speech of 1883, said: 'The idea at the bottom of this proposal is the desirability of finding some middle course between separation on the one hand and over-centralisation of government on the other' (quoted in Bogdanor, 1999, p. 20). The original concept of devolution was put forward by Edmund Burke at the end of the eighteenth century and formed part of his solution to the problems of the British government in dealing with the revolu-tionary American colonists and the Irish Catholics who were disenfranchised by the 1801 Act of Union. He based his ideas on the fact that the Westminster parliament had two functions – as a legislature for the United Kingdom and as an imperial parliament for all British territories. If these two functions were sep-arated so that the various British possessions such as America or Ireland had their own local legislatures while owing overall allegiance to the imperial par-liament in London, then the circle could be squared (Bogdanor, 1999, p. 23).

In terms of national governments it can be seen as the process by which political power is transferred from the centre to local or regional bodies, which thereby carry out governmental functions while leaving sovereignty in the hands of central government.

There are, however, three forms of devolution:

- **Executive devolution**, which devolves the power to make decisions, and is typified by the Welsh Assembly,

- **Legislative devolution**, which devolves the power to make laws, and is the form of devolution represented by the Scottish Parliament,
- **Administrative devolution**, which devolves the power to carry out specific functions, and which was practised by the Scottish, Welsh and Northern Ireland Offices, as well as the various English regional government offices and the Greater London Authority.

Devolution is a dispensation of governmental powers that appeals to the British public outside London, a public which largely resents the domination of south-eastern England and which feels alienated as a result. It is an alienation that is particularly true of the national regions of Britain like Scotland, a separate country until 1707, and Wales, with its own language and culture: although it is a reaction not unknown in parts of England such as Cornwall or Tyneside who feel just as equally distant and alienated from a political culture based in the south-eastern corner of the island. Since alienation of this kind can be a powerful force in the generation of unrest it has been the practice of successive British governments to use devolution as 'a policy instrument . . . to assimilate the demands of nationalist movements within the 'nations' seeking greater autonomy' (Evans, 1999, p. 47). Vernon Bogdanor puts it rather differently, seeing devolution as being central government's way of avoiding trouble from militant separatists when pressure for regional autonomy becomes intolerable. 'If there are these powerful centrifugal forces at work in Britain today it might well be that the best way to strengthen national unity is to give way to them a little' (Bogdanor, 1999, p. 297).

Devolved government is not new in the UK:

- When Ireland achieved home rule in the 1920s, six predominately Protestant counties in the north-east formed a separate province still subordinate to the British Crown and with MPs in the Westminster parliament, but where most executive, legislative and administrative matters were devolved to a Northern Ireland parliament at Stormont which lasted until 1972.
- Administrative devolution as manifested by the Scottish, Welsh and Northern Ireland Offices has been with us for some time and the sidelining of local government during the 1980s led to an increased awareness of the gulf between decision makers in London and the general public. In England, in 1994, as part of a programme of administrative devolution that hopefully would defuse demands for political devolution, the Major government created ten Government Offices for the Regions, merging the regional offices of the Departments of the Environment, Employment, Transport and Trade and Industry. These integrated offices served the same administrative functions for the English regions as the Northern Irish, Scottish and Welsh Offices have done for the national regions. In 1998 the Labour government followed the lead set by the Conservatives and these ten regional offices were reinforced by eight Regional Development Agencies, which John Prescott as the

then Minister for the Regions, and an enthusiast for devolution to the English regions, would have liked to see as embryo strategic authorities, if not actual regional governments.

A political concept often associated with devolution is subsidiarity which, as a term, has been in use for some time. However, it came to have a specific application in the negotiating sessions leading to the Treaty on European Union (TEU) (Maastricht) when a particular interpretation of subsidiarity was developed in order to counter British fears of what was seen as the pro-federalism of the Maastricht agreement. In Britain, unlike the rest of Europe, federalism was equated with centralism, giving rise to fears of a powerful federal administration in Brussels imposing its will on the member states, with no regard being paid to the wishes of national parliaments. What was developed at Maastricht therefore was a form of subsidiarity, defined in the Treaty as being when, 'decisions are taken as closely as possible to the citizen . . . In areas which do not fall within its exclusive competence, the Community should take action, in accordance with the principle of subsidiarity, only in so far as the proposed action cannot sufficiently be achieved by the Member States and can therefore, by reason of the scale or effects of the proposed action, be better achieved by the Community' (TEU, Title II, article 3b, 1992).

Although the term subsidiarity has largely been used in the context of politicians arguing about the relative sovereignty of national governments within the decision-making process of the European Union, hoping thereby to counter the over-centralisation of the EU in Brussels, it is a two-edged sword which can also be invoked when action by national governments may be considered as inappropriate when compared to regional or local action. Certainly, the Scottish National Party adopted the concept of subsidiarity with enthusiasm, going into successive elections under the slogan of 'Scotland in Europe', meaning that, in matters of importance to Scotland, there need be no intervening English body between Brussels and a Scottish parliament. This has been particularly relevant in recent years as the Committee of the Regions (COR) has become a major institution of the European Union, allowing the regions of EU member countries to have a significant say in the decision-making and legislative processes of the European Communities.

There are, however, two forms of subsidiarity; divided between the 'bottom-up' and 'top-down' versions. Originally the term derived from the Latin word *subsidiarii*, which referred to the auxiliary troops used by the Romans to strengthen and support the legions. In this interpretation the larger organisations are helped and supported by the smaller subsidiary groups. Neunreither has compared this 'top-down' subsidiarity with the Catholic Church, in which power and the control of dogma is entirely in the hands of the church hierarchy. In contrast, Neunreither states, there is Calvinism, in which the thoughts of the individual or congregation are more important than the *diktats* of cardinals or bishops and where the individual can communicate directly with God without the use of a priestly intermediary. This is the 'bottom-up' version of subsidiarity in which 'a larger unit only assumes functions in so far as the smaller units of which it is composed are unable or less qualified to fulfil their role. Starting from the individual, civil associations, communes, regions to national states and beyond, each larger unit has only a subsidiary role' (Cooper, 1995, p. 179). It is this 'bottom-up' version that provides the model for devolution from a central government to regional parliaments or assemblies.

Catering for regional autonomy

As has been said, there are two main solutions to the problem of unifying a multinational state under one government and they are broadly defined as the alternatives of either a federal or a unitary constitution. The unitary states are further sub-divided according to the degree of devolved autonomy they give their regional components and there is also the additional complication of the union state which accepts diversity of administrative or judicial practices within a unitary system and which usually possesses a degree of administrative devolution for its component parts. In Europe the need for some means of reinforcing unity has been made more urgent by an awareness of what happened to the federal state of Yugoslavia once the influence of President Tito and the Communist Party was removed. The complete fragmentation, inter-state warfare and ethnic cleansing which followed set a dreadful example to any government that had minority populations within its borders, particularly when those minorities were asking for some form of autonomy if not outright separatism.

There are just three examples of federal constitutions in Western Europe. The earliest of these is that of Switzerland, where the Helvetian Confederation has more or less existed since the three forest cantons of Uri, Schwyz and Unterwalden signed a pact of mutual assistance against their erstwhile Habsburg overlords in 1291; although it was the beginning of the sixteenth century before Swiss independence of the Holy Roman Empire was widely recognised. Originally it was a loose confederation of cantons, each of which zealously guarded the right to have its own state institutions, currency, postal service and customs. The 22 cantons then existing changed their constitution in 1848 to a more federal system, after a dispute between Protestant and Catholic cantons had almost led to a complete breakdown of the confederation. It is that constitution, as revised in 1874, which still exists today and which has proved so successful in binding together such a disparate group of peoples as the Swiss, who have four official languages and a deep religious divide, not to mention the immense communication and transport problems posed by the Alps. Even the neutrality of the Swiss, which has been recognised since 1648, arose from a desire not risk internal divisions over whether to support the French or German, Protestant or Catholic side in a European war.

Most divisions within so-called nation states are created by either conflict over religion or disputes hinging on language and it was the inherent conflict between linguistic communities which created the federal state of Belgium in 1981. The division of Belgium into the linguistically-based provinces of Flanders and Wallonia gave rise to three regional community assemblies each with its own executive council. The Flemish Community Assembly is responsible for Flanders and the Flemish-speaking population of Brussels; the Walloon Regional Assembly is responsible for the French-speaking provinces of south-eastern Belgium; while the French Community Assembly is responsible for the French-speaking population of Brussels and certain matters in Wallonia. Apart from these three there is a German-speaking Community Assembly based at Eupen, granted autonomy in 1984, and a Brussels Regional Council with a five-member executive that was created in 1989. The linguistic differences are so great in Belgium that even the political parties are divided into separate Flemish and Walloon organisations so that we have, for example, a division of the Greens into *Ecolo* (the Francophone Ecology party) and *Agalev* (the Flemish Environmental party).

The federal nature of Germany is a fairly recent construct but, as has already been said, it is based on the merger of the North German Federation and the South German principalities which formed the Second German Empire in 1871. The present Federal Republic of Germany was formed in 1949 out of the three western zones of occupied Germany and consisted of ten states or *länder*, two of which – Bremen and Hamburg – were in effect city states. In 1991, after the fall of the Berlin Wall, the re-unification of Germany meant the accession to the federal republic of Berlin and the five *länder* that had formed East Germany (the DDR). Like the United States, the two houses of the German parliament are divided into a lower house (*Bundestag*) with more than 650 representatives elected on the basis of proportionate populations and an upper house (*Bundesrat*) composed of 68 delegates for the *länder*. The *länder* are very varied and include three cities and their surroundings (Berlin, Bremen and Hamburg), the remainder ranging from the very large, such as North Rhine Westphalia with a population of 16.9 million, to the comparatively small, such as Saarland with 1.1 million.

Apart from these three federal states the remainder of the countries in Western Europe are at least nominally unitary. In most cases there is no need for the devolution of power because the population is homogeneous and there is little if any alienation within the state. Denmark, Finland, France and Portugal have all devolved autonomous governmental powers but in each such case devolution is to communities beyond the national metropolitan territory. Denmark has granted almost complete autonomy to the Faroe Islands and Greenland, to the extent that neither territory is a member of the European Union despite the continued membership of Denmark itself. Finland maintains the Aaland Islands as a tax-free zone with the right to issue their own postage stamps. As far as France is concerned, the regions of the country already possess considerable autonomy but a much fuller autonomy, including the right of the territories to have their own parliament and government, has been granted to Corsica and the four overseas departments of French Guiana, Guadeloupe, Martinique and Réunion. Portugal similarly has locally elected parliaments and governments for the two island regions of Madeira and the Azores. The relationship between these four countries and their external regions is rather like that which exists between the United Kingdom and the Crown Dependencies of the Isle of Man and the Channel Islands, the dependent territories being fully self-governing except for foreign affairs and defence.

Two countries have reformed their constitutions to permit a considerable amount of devolution to their constituent regions. They can therefore provide a useful model for any devolution proposed for the United Kingdom since they, like Britain, are also union states and wish to satisfy the demands for self-determination of minority nationalities within their borders before those demands become separatist in nature. Furthermore the two countries in question both apply a system of asymmetrical devolution, in that different regions get different levels of devolved powers and have a differentiated representation in the national parliament, arrangements that might well provide useful guidance for the different versions of devolved government suggested for Scotland, Wales and Northern Ireland as well as providing a possible solution for the so-called West Lothian question. The two countries are Italy and Spain.

In 1970 Italy was divided into fifteen regions with extensive powers of local government but devolution to certain regions has a much longer history. Italy rejected its monarchy in 1946 and a new republican constitution was drawn up, coming into force in 1948. That constitution allowed for the existence of five autonomous regions, each with its own assembly and having primary legislative powers in economic, social and cultural matters. The autonomous regions set up at that time include the two islands of Sardinia and Sicily, the French-speaking Valle d'Aosta, the German-speaking Trentino Alto Adige and Friuli Venezia Giulia, which is on the borders of Slovenia and where the people speak Friulian, a form of the Alpine language Romansch, although much corrupted by Venetian dialect.

When a new constitution was drawn up for Spain in 1978, after the death of Franco, the country was divided into seventeen autonomous communities, each with its own parliament and government. Seven of these regions – Andalusia, the Canaries, Catalonia, Euskadi (Basque country), Galicia, Navarre and Valencia – have additional powers over health, education and policing. There are several parallels between the situation in Spain and that in the United Kingdom which have a specific relevance for any discussions of devolution in Britain. There are areas that have their own language such as Catalonia, Galicia and the Basque country. And, in the Basque country Spain has a province similar to Northern Ireland where a separatist movement has proved ready to use violence and extremist measures in their struggle for full independence. It was very noticeable that, ever since the 1970s, when the

British political establishment first acknowledged the possibility of introducing devolution at some future date, the position of Catalonia within Spain became the template for any British proposal for Scottish or Welsh devolution. Spain in general and Catalonia in particular became the chosen destination for a whole series of British parliamentary delegations investigating the possibility of devolution. Tom Nairn wrote about the way in which the experience of Catalonia was a sound indication of the future prospects for a Scottish parliament. 'In fact President Pujol came to Scotland to rub the point in, and shortly thereafter Donald Dewar went out to Barcelona to confirm it. The official message is that there is no reason why the Scots should not follow the Catalan example, as a non-state autonomous region' (Nairn, 2000, p. 291).

Conclusion

The main thrust of the argument in this chapter seems to suggest that the principal reason for power to be devolved is the need for a unitary state to find the means of evading any threat to its integrity that might be posed by nationalism and separatism; particularly the sort of separatism that is backed by violent action. In that context the issue of devolution becomes like any other policy adopted by political parties for self-interest, electoral benefit and convenience. Yet the commitment to devolution that was exhibited by the Labour government elected in 1997 also recognised that any decision to devolve power had wider implications that would affect far more than just how Wales or Scotland might be governed. As a leading commentator on Scottish affairs put it, the process of devolution which began in 1997

> has the potential to generate a new style and substance in British politics that constitutes a break with the notions of adversarial politics, one party government, parliamentary sovereignty and central control of party organisations. The broader impact of devolution points towards greater consensus politics, power sharing, proportional representation, co-operation between different levels of government and changes to the membership and functioning of the House of Commons. (Lynch 1997/98, p. 96)

Devolution then is not simply the description of yet another political process but is instead a major and fundamental shift in the political structure of the British state and the engine by which the constitution is completely reformed.

Part I

Foundation and origins

2

The making of
the United Kingdom

This chapter contains a great deal of early history that some might find irrelevant and the reader might well skip the chapter without much loss. Nevertheless I would recommend a quick look at what follows since, if we are to understand the process of devolution, we need to look at the way in which the United Kingdom was created and to consider the nature of the union state thus established. For, while the United Kingdom is a union of four different 'nations', each of those four is itself a composite: a mongrel construct of diverse peoples. Uniting the component parts was long and slow but the very process tells us a great deal about power relationships existing within the union state.

Britain first became a united political entity under the Roman Empire, but Roman Britain never included Ireland, never extended further into Scotland than a line from the Clyde to the Forth, and included no more than one tribal territory in south-east Wales. When the Romans left Britain in AD 410, the abandoned Romano-Britons were left to face Germanic invaders who infiltrated the river valleys of southern and eastern England in a westward expansion that the British were unable to resist, given the inability of Celtic peoples to organise their own defence. Writing about the British in his *Life of Agricola*, Tacitus said that 'nothing has helped us more in war with their strongest nations than their inability to co-operate. It is but seldom that two or three states unite to repel a common danger' (Mattingley, 1948, p. 62).

England

These Germanic invaders are known as Anglo-Saxons, after the Angles, Saxons and Jutes who inhabited the North Sea coast of Europe between Flanders and Jutland. An interesting insight into the nature of these people is provided by the names by which they are known. In speaking of themselves, they nearly always used the word *Angli* – English – but to their enemies they were Saxons. Even today the Gaelic word for English speakers is *Sassenach*, while the Welsh call them *Saesneg*, both words meaning Saxon.

The English formed themselves into small political units based on the ships in which they came to England. The captains of those ships, having become local chieftains, gave their allegiance to powerful warlords or kings. By the year 600, England had become a patchwork of kingdoms: most prominently Northumbria, Wessex, Mercia, East Anglia, Kent, Sussex and Essex. These seven are customarily known as the Heptarchy[1].

Northumbria began a century of dominance between 600 and 615, when Æthelfrith extended his rule north into the Lothians, and attacked the British in Chester to the west. This latter action drove a wedge between the Celtic peoples of Wales and their cousins elsewhere, helping to create Wales as a separate entity and completing the work begun by the battle of Dyrham near Bath in 577, by means of which West Saxon expansion had cut land communications between Wales and the Celts of Devon and Cornwall.

In 736, the Mercian king Æthelbald was the first to style himself *Rex Britanniae* – King of the British. Murdered in 757 he was succeeded by Offa, who maintained Mercian dominance for almost half a century, annexing the kingdoms of Kent, Sussex and Wessex and acquiring London and Middlesex from Essex, while Offa completed the making of his kingdom with the addition of East Anglia in 794. Offa styled himself both *Rex Anglorum* (King of the English) and *rex totius Anglorum patriae* (King of all the English lands). Offa's important contribution was the construction of Offa's Dyke to separate Mercia from Powys. This long earthwork, running from near Wrexham to a point on the Wye near Chepstow became accepted as dividing England from Wales.[2]

After 825 England was divided into the four kingdoms of Northumbria, Mercia, Wessex and East Anglia but only Wessex remained English after the Danes, or Vikings, had established a permanent army on English soil in 865. However, Alfred, who succeeded to the throne of Wessex in 871, forced the Danes back into what became known as the Danelaw, behind a line drawn from London to Chester. In 911 Alfred's son Edward the Elder gained control of Mercia and went on to occupy all Anglo-Danish lands south of the Humber, at the same time receiving homage from Hywel Dda, prince of western Wales. In the north the Danes of Northumbria were replaced by Norse-Irish from Dublin who set up the Kingdom of York in 919. In a northern campaign Edward enforced submission on the king of Scots, the king of York, the king of Strathclyde and the Northumbrian lordship of Bamburgh.

Athelstan succeeded Edward and, in 927, received the homage of Scotland, Strathclyde and Bamburgh as well as occupying York. He also dealt with his western borders, receiving homage from Hywel Dda and other Welsh princes, fixing the border with Wales on the Wye and the border with Cornwall on the Tamar. Ten years later, in 937, Athelstan and his brother Edmund defeated an allied army of Irish-Norse, Scots and Strathclyde British, setting the seal on the unity of the kingdom. There is no accepted date for the unification of England but there is a good case for regarding 973 as significant. In that year Edmund's son Edgar became the first English king to open his reign with a coronation. Crowned at Bath in 973, he then went by sea to Chester and received the submission of several British princes.[3]

After Edgar the English state remained virtually unchanged, despite an interlude under Danish kings. The most significant change of direction came with the conquest of England by Duke William of Normandy in 1066. It was a unified England that William conquered and, although the Normans contributed a sense of organisation and administration to consolidate English unity, it was a unification already completed. From 1066 onwards the main aim of the English state became the gradual absorption of Wales, Scotland and Ireland.

The unification of England is not just about geography but concerns the union of peoples. First and foremost among those peoples are the so-called Anglo-Saxons who first assumed the name of *Angli*, living in *Angle-land*. However, the English by no means replaced the indigenous Celts. Dismissed slightingly as *weallas* ('Welsh' – meaning 'foreigners'), there was a large-scale Celtic survival in England, as witness the number of Waltons (meaning 'Welshtown') to be found in almost every English county and the frequency with which rivers, hills and other features of the landscape are given Celtic names. The rulers and political institutions were English but most of the ordinary people were of Celtic descent.

Norse and Danish incomers after 800 had no difficulty in integrating with the English, their origins and languages being sufficiently close as to make them almost indistinguishable. In certain parts of the country the use of Scandinavian personal and place names persisted for some centuries while differences in language created a difference in dialects and accents between the Anglo-Danish north and Anglo-Saxon south. The Norman-French who followed Duke William in 1066, and further French immigrations under Henry II and Henry III, played an important part in the development of language and administration for the ruling classes but the ordinary people were hardly affected. The Normans came as conquerors, securing lordships for themselves but outnumbered by the people they had conquered: a Norman-French élite ruled, but most people were a mixture of English, Dane and Celt.

The creation of the English state, as we have seen, was the product of conquest and coercion, imposing the rule of one part of the population over the rest and the actual unity of England was originally secured by the forceful expansion of Wessex. One of the factors influencing calls for devolution in our own time has been the fact that Englishness has often been associated with arrogance and feelings of superiority, not only of the English over the Scots, Welsh and Irish, but also of the southern English of the Wessex homeland over the northern and western English of the Danelaw.

Wales

Wales never achieved union in the same sense as did England. The propensity of the Celts for arguing among themselves, already noted by Tacitus, allied to the mountainous terrain in the interior of Wales, meant that the territory they called *Cymru* was geographically and politically fragmented throughout the Middle Ages. From time to time Welsh princes such as Hywel Dda or Llywelyn ap Gruffydd succeeded in uniting the Welsh principalities, only to have the unity fall apart on the prince's death. Unlike England, Wales had no memory of political union in the Roman period. Romans occupied Wales militarily but the only civil settlement was in the south-east, where the Emperor Hadrian decided that the Silures deserved self-government, a new tribal capital being built and named Venta Silurum (now Caerwent), which gave its name in turn to the post-Roman kingdom of Gwent.

Wales only became a separate politico-geographical area after the English reached the west coast; the men of Wessex reaching the Severn estuary in 577 and the Northumbrians gaining the Irish Sea in 603. After that time the British inhabitants of Wales were isolated and forced to develop separate political and cultural institutions. Within the confines of modern Wales a number of king-doms developed, with names that were to appear again in the local government reforms of 1974: names like Gwent and Powys.

In the immediate post-Roman period a prince named Cunedda was uprooted from the area around Edinburgh and resettled in Caernarfon for defensive reasons, thereby founding the kingdom of Gwynedd, while in the south-west the kingdom of Dyfed was founded by Irish immigrants, becoming important in the early Middle Ages as the home of the Welsh Church founded by St David. To the north of Dyfed and separating it from Gwynedd was Seisyllwg, a kingdom formed by the merger of Cardigan and Carmarthen.

After 920, Hywel Dda (Howell the Good) united Seisyllwg, Dyfed and Brecon to form Deheubarth. Acquiring Gwynedd and Powys later he can claim to be the first ruler of a united Wales. In the face of Viking threats he did homage for his lands to Edward the Elder (918) and Athelstan (927), thereby creating England's claim to suzerainty over Wales. Hywel was much influenced by English practices; minting silver pennies after the English model and codifying Welsh law. The Laws of Hywel Dda remained valid in Welsh courts until 1536.

After the time of Hywel Dda there were essentially four kingdoms in Wales: these being Gwynedd, Deheubarth, Morgannwg[4] and Powys. Powys was the weakest of the four since it occupied the area between Dee and Severn later known as the Welsh Marches and, unlike Gwynedd or Dyfed, constantly con-fronted the English.

The Norman conquest marked the beginning of the end for Welsh independence. In order to defend his borders William I established the first Marcher lordships in 1067, his most effective followers receiving the lordships of Hereford, Chester and Shrewsbury. Other gifts followed until a line of Anglo-

Norman lordships stretched the length of Offa's Dyke, from Denbigh to Chepstow. In 1070 the Marcher lords merged the kingdom of Gwent with the lordship of Newport to form Monmouthshire while, in 1090, Robert Fitzhamon moved from Gloucestershire to form the lordship of Glamorgan in southern Morgannwg, building a castle in Cardiff, and gaining palatine powers. Most prominent of the early Marcher lords was Arnulf of Montgomery who went on to establish the lordship of Pembroke in the south-west. The Anglo-Norman occupation of Pembroke replaced the native Welsh so completely that the area was known until comparatively recently as 'Little England beyond Wales'!

The Marcher lordships were free of royal authority and able to make and administer their own laws. In many cases, former Welsh principalities divided their allegiance between the Marcher lords on the coast and native Welsh princes in the hills. Two systems of law, known as the Englishry and the Welshry, co-existed and reflected the lowland-upland division.

The expansion of the Marcher lords ended in 1169 when the Anglo-Normans of Pembroke became involved in Ireland, but even before that the Welsh kingdoms of Gwynedd, Powys and Deheubarth had consolidated themselves to resist the Anglo-Normans. The final century of Welsh independence belongs to the supremacy of Gwynedd, under the rule of three men.

Owain Gwynedd became king in 1137 and, during the anarchy created by the struggle for the English throne between Stephen and Matilda, extended his borders to Cardigan in the south and Flint in the east. In 1157 he paid homage to Henry II and survived unchallenged. His grandson, Llywelyn ab Iorwerth (Llywelyn Mawr), succeeded in 1203 and was recognised by King John. Shortly thereafter he quarrelled with John and went on to profit from civil war in England. siding with the rebel barons and earning a number of concessions in Magna Carta, acquiring Cardigan, Carmarthen and Powys.

Llywelyn ap Gruffydd, grandson of Llywelyn Mawr, was recognised as Prince of Wales by the Welsh lords. Like his grandfather he exploited the troubles of the English king, joining the rebel barons under Simon de Montfort. After the death of Henry III, Llywelyn was accused by Edward I of failing to fulfil his feudal obligations and, in 1276–77, was faced by a massive English invasion. Edward was determined to make an end of an independent Wales and, under the terms of the Statute of Rhuddlan in 1284, a Principality of Wales under English rule was established. Gwynedd as it had existed under Llywelyn was divided into the shire counties of Anglesey, Caernarvon and Merioneth, with Deheubarth becoming the counties of Cardigan and Carmarthen. The counties were shires in that each had a sheriff and coroner to represent royal authority. Criminal law was English law but civil cases remained Welsh under the laws of Hywel Dda.

Wales was now divided. Shires of the north and west together with Flintshire were crown lands held by the king and dispensing the king's justice. The east and south was given over to a patchwork of Marcher lordships, independent of the crown and each other. Ironically it was the half of Wales directly ruled by

England that remained most Welsh, while the Marches had an increasingly English character. Seven hundred years later it is interesting to consider the devolution referendum of 1997 when, apart from Glamorgan and the valleys, the former Marcher lordships all voted 'no', while the old crown lands of Gwynedd and Deheubarth all voted 'yes'.

The first real bid for Welsh independence or devolution came after a century. There was resentment because English merchants in Welsh towns had commercial privileges denied the Welsh, while Welshmen were said to be excluded from office in church and state. These resentments motivated the actions of Owain Glyndwr who proclaimed himself Prince of Wales early in the reign of Henry IV, rising in rebellion and gaining considerable success in mid and south Wales in alliance with English rebels like the famous Hotspur. He called an assembly in Machynlleth which demanded an independent principality, a Welsh church independent of Canterbury, a university and a civil service. He was defeated at Shrewsbury and gave up after Harlech had surrendered and his wife and children were taken prisoner.

Glyndwr's rebellion had no real effect on relations between England and the principality but it did call into question the autonomy of the Welsh Marches and the Marcher lords. Edward IV countered the independence of the Marches by calling a Council for Wales in the Marches, a body that was recalled by Henry VII and later still by Thomas Cromwell during the reign of Henry VIII. It was a wish on the part of Cromwell to cut back the separate jurisdictions of the Marches rather than any desire to curb the independence of the Welsh which motivated the so-called Act of Union.

At the time it was not called an Act of Union since it was held that the act merely confirmed an existing state of affairs that had existed ever since Hywel Dda and other Welsh princes had done homage for their lands to the king of England. Wales was said to be: 'a very member and joint of the English realm, as it rightfully is and ever hath been' (quoted in Bogdanor, 1999, p. 6). There were two Acts. The first, setting out the principles of union, was agreed in 1536, while the administrative details of union were laid out in an Act of 1543. The delay between the two Acts enabled Welsh MPs, elected as a result of the former, to be present in the House of Commons to debate the passage of the latter.

The main provisions of the Acts of 1536 and 1543 were:

- The Marches were abolished and replaced by the shire counties of Monmouth, Brecon, Radnor, Denbigh and Montgomery, together with the palatine counties of Pembroke and Glamorgan.
- English law replaced Welsh law, although it was administered in separate Welsh courts with Welsh justices – a system that lasted until 1830.
- Each Welsh county elected one MP (Monmouth had two) and each county town (except Harlech) chose a burgess as MP.
- Four judges' circuits were set up. There was, however, doubt as to whether

Monmouth was Welsh or English and that county was attached to the Oxford circuit.
- English administrative practices, including the appointment of justices of the peace, were introduced throughout Wales.
- English became the only recognised language of administration and the law.

The union was accepted by the Welsh without difficulty and might be regarded as a success. In 1775 Edmund Burke even used the union with Wales as a good example of how the British government should treat the American colonists. When Wales became enamoured of nationalism in the twentieth century, that nationalism was not so much concerned with political independence as with a desire to reassert a distinctive culture and way of life based on the Welsh language.

Bearing in mind the linguistic division created by the Statute of Rhuddlan, it is interesting to note that Plaid Cymru has always been strongest in Gwynedd and Ceredigion and that the first Plaid Cymru MP was elected for Carmarthen. Similarly, the areas voting 'no' to devolution in the referendum of 1997 match almost exactly the anglophone territories of the Marcher lordships. As with the unification of England, the union with Wales carried the seeds of devolution into the moment of its creation.

Scotland

Scotland is as much a mixture of peoples as England and just as fragmented politically as Wales, making the union of peoples extremely complex. And, as was the case with Wales, the process of unification with England carried with it the seeds of future disunity.

In the aftermath of the Roman occupation the peoples of Scotland could be divided into the pre-Celtic Picts north of the Antonine Wall and the Brythonic Celts between there and Hadrian's Wall. Very little is known about the Picts other than that their name, which was given them by the Romans simply means 'painted people'. From the sixth century on they shared the lands north of the Forth with groups of Goidelic Celts[5] known as Scots who came from Ireland. The Scots settled in Kintyre, Lorne, Argyll and the Western Isles, naming their new homeland Dalriada after the lands in Ulster from whence they had emigrated.

South of the Antonine Wall the North British tribes formed two loose confederations. To the west was Strathclyde, extending from the Clyde to the Mersey while in the east was Manaw Gododdin, named for the Votadini tribe. These lands as far north as the Forth were infiltrated by Northumbria after 500, putting the Lothians under English control. For nearly 200 years the four peoples – Picts, Scots, Britons and English – coexisted in Scotland, fighting endless wars with each other, and often tied in flimsy temporary alliances.

A fifth people came to Scotland in the ninth century when Norsemen occupied Orkney, Sutherland, the Hebrides and Galloway and attempted to take Moray. In 839, they killed a leader of the Scots, Alpin of Gabhran, at the same time wiping out the Pictish army together with their king. The son of Alpin, Kenneth MacAlpin, used his mother's Pictish ancestry to claim the throne of Pictland and was named High King over all of northern Scotland. Originally the united kingdom was called Alba but its ruler was known as the King of Scots.

Between 921 and 973, a king of Scots accepted English overlordship at least three times. On the most famous of these occasions Kenneth II did homage to Edgar at Chester. In return Kenneth received the Lothians and was granted suzerainty over Strathclyde.

In 1040 King Duncan, a descendent of MacAlpin, was beaten in battle by Macbeth, the ruler of Moray, but in 1057 Duncan's son, Malcolm, returned to avenge his father's death, taking the throne as Malcolm III.[6] Malcolm was little more than a barbarian chieftain but during his seventeen years' exile he had married an English princess, Margaret, as his second wife. A very pious woman, recognised in Scotland as a saint, Margaret initiated many changes, overthrowing the independent Celtic Church and subordinating it to Rome. She was also the first to invite Norman knights and churchmen to journey north and become the sixth of Scotland's peoples.

The sons of Malcolm and Margaret were more English than Scots. The court moved from Dunfermline to Edinburgh, the English dialect known as Scots replaced Gaelic as the language spoken at court and the legacy of the sons of Canmore caused Scotland to turn its back on its Gaelic-Pictish heritage, forming a nation sharing much of its culture with its southern neighbour. The greatest of Malcolm Canmore's sons, David I, personally invited large numbers of Normans to accept major land holdings in Scotland, resulting in a Scottish nobility more than half made up of Norman families such as Sinclair, Bruce, Seton or Balliol.

Despite a crushing defeat at the Battle of the Standard in 1138, David I received Cumbria and Northumbria from King Stephen during the English anarchy. However, David's grandson, Malcolm IV, known as 'The Maiden', surrendered the two counties to Henry II in return for the earldom of Huntingdon. This became the cause of many of Scotland's ills since, when the Scottish king was obliged to do homage to the English king, it was never clear as to whether that homage was in respect of Huntingdon or of Scotland.

In 1266 Alexander III defeated Haakon of Norway at Largs and the Treaty of Perth which followed ensured the unification of Scotland by ceding Man and the Western Isles to the King of Scots. In 1286, after the premature accidental death of Alexander III and the subsequent death of his six-year-old granddaughter, the Maid of Norway, the future of the kingdom fell into the hands of Edward I of England who was named Lord Paramount of Scotland in order to arbitrate between rival claimants to the throne.

Edward, who had crushed the last independent Prince of Wales, now saw his chance to subordinate Scotland to England as well. He nominated John Balliol as king but repeatedly humbled him by treating him as a vassal. When Balliol rebelled, Edward invaded Scotland and subjugated the kingdom: a subjugation symbolised by removing from Scone the Stone of Destiny, on which Scotland's kings had been crowned since the days of the Picts.

Reaction to Edward's occupation of Scotland most famously came with the action of William Wallace, a Strathclyde Celt who killed the Sheriff of Clydesdale, William Hazelrig, and then took arms in support of a rebellion led by Bishop Wishart of Glasgow and James FitzAlan, the Steward. For a time Wallace was successful against the English but his followers were finally beaten by the long-bow, and Wallace, captured after a period on the run, was hanged, drawn and quartered by Edward, a punishment for treason which implied that Wallace was not a patriot but a rebellious subject of the English king.

Wallace was a man of the people but he was not part of the establishment. The real contenders were the Anglo-Norman families who formed the aristocracy of both England and Scotland. John Prebble has described the conflict between Robert Bruce and Edward Plantagenet as 'a civil war within the Anglo-Norman state' (Prebble, 1971, p. 57). Bruce's success did no more than ensure that Scotland was ruled by Scots-Normans rather than Anglo-Normans.

In the two centuries that followed Bruce's victory at Bannockburn, Scotland developed as a nation, the royal administration running ever more smoothly under the system of sheriffdoms that were introduced throughout the lowland east and south.

It was largely a time of peace because England was preoccupied first with the Hundred Years War with France and then with the Wars of the Roses and therefore had no time for 'the problems of conquering and then controlling, from London, a country whose farther reaches were geographically both remote and difficult' (Falkus and Gillingham, 1981, p. 90).

Scotland finally joined England, not by conquest but through dynastic marriages, the two crowns merging in the person of James I and VI in 1603. The political centre moved south with the king and for some time Scotland was ruled largely through the Scottish Privy Council, especially during the reign of Charles I. Yet, despite the accession of a Scottish king the culture of the royal court was essentially English and Charles I attempted to force bishops on to the Church of Scotland, a move resisted by the National Covenant in the armed conflicts known as the Bishops' Wars. In the course of these struggles episcopacy was swept away by the Covenanters and the Scots Parliament became the effective ruler of Scotland.

The Covenanting army allied itself with the English parliament during the Civil Wars and was of decisive assistance at the battle of Marston Moor. But the execution of Charles I was regarded as an insult, since the English had in effect killed a Scottish king without consulting the Scottish people. Charles II was crowned King of Scots and a Scottish army invaded England in 1651, only to be defeated at Worcester. Between 1651 and 1660 Scotland was ruled by the New Model Army under General Monck and the two countries were united in 1654.

After the Restoration the situation reverted to a union of the crowns, with the two countries retaining their own parliaments, laws and institutions. James II and VII then made himself unpopular by his advocating episcopacy for Scotland and, after his flight from England, the Scots Parliament declared him deposed on the grounds of his tyranny.

William and Mary who followed him were confirmed on the throne of England by the 1689 Bill of Rights which created a constitutional monarchy by subordinating the monarch to Parliament. However, in North Britain it was hard to see how a monarch subordinated to an English parliament could rule Scotland. In 1701 the Act of Settlement fixed the succession to the English throne on the House of Hanover but no provision was made for the Scottish throne to pass to Hanover along with the English throne.

The reign of William III and II saw the start of a process designed to reduce the independence of the highland clans: a process that included what is popularly known as the Massacre of Glencoe when government soldiers from Clan Campbell turned on their Clan Donald hosts. William was very unpopular in Scotland and, unlike Northern Ireland where he is the heroic 'King Billy', the flower named after him is known to the Scots as 'Stinking Billy'. It began to look as though England and Scotland might drift apart after the death of Queen Anne. The English even passed an act in 1705, declaring that all Scots in England were to be treated as aliens.

In the midst of these fears negotiations began which led to the 1707 Act of Union. The Scottish commissioners agreeing the union managed to obtain recognition for an unaltered Scottish legal system and the Scottish Kirk. But, while a strong case was made out for a confederation of the two countries in which the two parliaments would be equal in status and power, this was seen as impractical and the Act in its final form suppressed both parliaments, replacing them with a single Parliament of Great Britain. In fact the English Parliament continued virtually unaltered and, with 45 Scottish members as against 513 from England, the House of Commons left the Scots under-represented and in a minority.

Under the terms of the treaty:

- Scotland was granted 45 Commons seats and 16 elected representative peers.
- Scotland retained the Presbyterian Kirk as the established Church of Scotland.
- Scotland retained its own courts and legal system.
- The royal burghs retained their privileges and self-governing status.
- All hereditary offices and jurisdictions were retained.

Many of the safeguards vouchsafed to the Scots were short-lived. The Scottish Privy Council was abolished in 1708 and, while Scotland's own legal system was independent it was nevertheless subject to the House of Lords in Westminster as a final court of appeal. In 1747, after the '45 rebellion, the Abolition of Heritable Jurisdictions Act did away with the power of Scots lairds and clan chieftains. In the same period the laws against the use of tartans and Highland dress reinforced the view that Englishness was being imposed upon the Scots.

Although the union was favoured by the lowland legal and business establishment as an economic necessity, eased by the payment of bribes and inducements, it was greatly disliked by most of the Scottish people. There was a sense of betrayal that was summarised in the Jacobite ballad 'We are bought and sold for English gold.' As was the case in Wales the act of union carried the seeds of discontent with it.

Ireland

Of the four nations making up the United Kingdom, Ireland was the last to join and the first to leave. What is more, the whole concept known as the devolution of powers has its origins in the Home Rule for Ireland Movement of the nineteenth century, just as the first example of a devolved parliament in the United Kingdom was to be found at Stormont.

Ireland never knew a Roman presence and was never united except under foreign rule. In the post-Roman period, Ireland's Celtic art, literature and system of laws mixed with a devout and evangelical Christianity to evolve into a cultural golden age for Ireland in what to the rest of Europe was known as the Dark Ages. However, Ireland was united culturally but never politically; rule of the island being divided between literally hundreds of 'kings', of whom there were three classes. Each village and its surrounding area had its own 'king' or chieftain, who deferred in turn to a regional over-king. Over them came the kings of the four main provinces of Ireland – Ulster, Leinster, Munster and Connaught. There was also a fifth province, Meath, in which Tara, seat of the *Ard Righ* or High King, was located.

The office of *Ard Righ* was most important during the Viking invasions when the duty of the High King was to lead resistance against the invader. The Norsemen almost conquered the island before the best known of the High Kings, Brian Boru, defeated them in 1002. After their defeat the Vikings settled down and were assimilated by the native population, often becoming 'more Irish than the Irish'. Nevertheless, the Norsemen changed the nature of Ireland since, as merchants and traders, they established market towns and ports such as Dublin, Wexford and Cork in what had been a purely pastoral society. The chief Norse town, Dublin, grew to be so important that it replaced Tara as the symbolic capital and the Lord of Dublin effectively became the 'King of Ireland'.

The independent and liberal beliefs of the Irish Celtic Church were in constant conflict with the doctrines of the Roman Church. In 1155 the English

Pope, Adrian IV, issued a papal bull for the reform of the Irish Church, known as *Laudabilitur* and passed it to Henry II of England for execution. Nothing happened for ten years and then, in 1166, the High King, Rory O'Conor, drove out the king of Leinster, Dermot McMurrough. Dermot looked to Henry II for assistance and it was at his wish that Richard de Clare, Earl of Pembroke ('Strongbow') invaded Ireland at the head of a Norman-Welsh force, followed in 1169 by the king himself.

Intermarrying with the Irish nobility and part-assimilated by Irish culture, the Norman lords conquered and brought under English suzerainty something like two-thirds of the island. Henry II was confirmed as 'Lord of Ireland' by the Pope and the island was absorbed into the Angevin Empire. However, English power did not last long and a decline set in with the Scottish invasion by Edward Bruce in 1325. By the end of the fifteenth century, the direct influence of the king was restricted to Dublin and its hinterland, in the territory known as the Pale. Beyond the Pale the great Anglo-Irish lordships of Ormond, Desmond and Kildare were as independent of the English crown as were the Marcher lords in Wales.

Any movement towards separatism by the Irish was halted by Poynings' Law of 1494, when the Lord Deputy, Sir Edward Poynings, ruled that the English Privy Council must approve the summoning of an Irish Parliament and any legislation of that parliament. The Law was re-affirmed in 1719 and stated, '[Ireland] is and of right ought to be subordinate unto and dependent upon the imperial crown of Great Britain' (Cannon, 1997, p. 767).

This movement against Irish separatism continued under Henry VIII when, after the rebellion of Thomas Fitzgerald in 1534, the English king smashed the power of Kildare and the Geraldines, taking Ireland under direct rule and dividing the country into shires after the English model. In 1536 Henry was declared to be head of the church in Ireland. Finally, in 1541 Henry became the first English king to be known as 'King' rather than 'Lord' of Ireland.

Throughout the sixteenth century Connaught and Ulster remained outside the Pale and gave rise to a series of anti-English, anti-protestant revolts. The most serious rebellion was led by Hugh O'Neill, third Earl of Tyrone between 1594 and 1603 which involved an anti-English alliance between Ireland and other Catholic countries which led to landings at Kinsale by the Spanish. Once the rebellion was put down, the government of James I and VI intensified the policy of imposing Protestant settlers on Catholic areas in what were known as 'plantations'. Between 1603 and 1640, some 30–40,000 Scottish and English Protestants were placed on plantations in Ulster, thus leading to the north–south religious divide which still exists.

The massive plantation programme which dispossessed so many Catholic farmers and peasants led to the great Irish rebellion of 1641 in which thousands of Protestants were killed by Catholics, and were then avenged in a number of savage reprisals. The mixture of religious, political and economic factors which fanned the rebellion laid down a heritage of hate and suspicion that is still remembered today and can be regarded as the start of 'the Irish Question'. The rebellion was viciously put down by Cromwell and Ireton, who massacred the Irish at Wexford and Drogheda. Attempts were then made to imitate the Cromwellian union of England and Scotland with a union of Britain and Ireland. Bills to this effect were introduced in 1654 and 1656 but both failed.

War between the Catholic and Protestant populations resumed in 1689, when Irish Catholics espoused the Jacobite cause of the deposed James II and VII. But James fled from Ireland after the Battle of the Boyne and the whole affair petered out in the following year. The Treaty of Limerick promised religious freedom for Catholics but the promise was never honoured and there was instead a series of anti-Catholic laws. Catholics were excluded from the Irish parliament in 1692 and disenfranchised in 1727. 'In Ireland, the king and the English state were associated with alien Protestant settlers . . . in Ireland the political nation was the Protestant nation' (Bogdanor, 1999, p. 16).

During the American War of Independence British troops were withdrawn from Ireland and fears grew that Ireland might be used as the springboard for a French invasion and moves to pacify the Catholic population were introduced. A pro-independence paramilitary force, the Irish Volunteers, was set up, anti-Catholic laws were relaxed in 1781 and Poynings's Law was repealed in 1782, creating a de facto parliamentary independence.

When the war with revolutionary France broke out in 1793, fears grew as to French involvement in Ireland, since Wolfe Tone of the United Irishmen appealed to France for help and there were two unsuccessful French landings. The French threat led the authorities to a fierce repression of those Irish nationalists suspected of helping the French and in reaction to the brutality of that repression the United Irishmen rose in 1798. The rebellion was easily put down but an Anglo-Irish problem obviously existed. As a solution, the Prime Minister, William Pitt, proposed to unite the Irish and Westminster Parliaments. Originally the proposal failed because of Protestant hostility but a campaign of persuasion and bribery won over the waverers and the Act of Union was passed in 1800, coming into force on 1 January 1801.

The Act of Union provided for a complete shake-up of Irish political, religious and administrative arrangements:

- The Irish Parliament was dissolved.
- 28 Irish peers were elected for life to serve in the Westminster House of Lords.
- 300 members of the Irish lower house were replaced by 100 MPs in the UK House of Commons.
- Irish Westminster seats were divided into 64 for the counties, 35 for the boroughs and one for Dublin University.
- There was also a union of the Churches of England and Ireland, four bishops of the Church of Ireland serving in the Lords.
- A customs union was formed between Ireland and Great Britain.

In one way the Act of Union can be said to have succeeded in that its provisions remained unaltered for 120 years. However, it is fair to say that the Union was flawed from the start. In order to encourage the Catholic population to vote for the measure, Pitt had effectively promised that Catholic emancipation would be granted alongside the Act of Union. But this proposal met with strong opposition from the devoutly Protestant George III and, although Pitt resigned and his government fell over the issue, emancipation was not granted until 1829. Unlike Scotland, where the Presbyterian Kirk of the majority population was recognised as the established Church of Scotland, the Catholicism of the majority Irish population was ignored and the Anglican Church of Ireland was imposed on the country. Aided by memories of massacres during the 1641 rebellion the causes of Catholicism and Irish nationalism became inextricably linked. As a distinguished professor of Irish history has said, 'The Union formulated on January 1st 1801 was not (as Pitt had envisaged) between Britain and Ireland but between Britain and the Irish Protestant élite' (Jackson, 2001, p. 21).

In one other way the union with Ireland was vastly different from the situation existing elsewhere in the UK. It was only the Irish Parliament that was suppressed under the act and an Irish administration remained in Dublin under the Lord Lieutenant and the Chief Secretary for Ireland, who was a cabinet minister. Ireland also retained its own Privy Council, complete with judges and law officers. Ireland therefore had an executive and judiciary of its own but no independent legislature. By this measure Ireland was obviously a subordinate country ruled by the British rather than the Irish. 'Scotland had been treated as a partner after the union, but Ireland seemed a dependency' (Bogdanor, 1999, p. 20).

Conclusion

The union of parliaments in 1801 created the last stepping-stone in the creation of the United Kingdom but, in recognising the achievement of melding together what Gladstone called 'a partnership of three kingdoms, a partnership of four nations',[7] it has also to be said that the process of unification carried within itself inherent flaws that would lead to tensions and resentments, which would lead in turn to pressures for fragmentation.

- Although the Acts of 1707 and 1801 spoke of the union of parliaments as though it were a happy marriage of equals, it is obviously the case that both the Scottish and Irish parliaments were swallowed up and subordinated to the English parliament at Westminster.
- Similarly, the union was created by the supremacy of an ascendant people over a subordinate people. This is obviously the case in Wales, Scotland and Ireland, where an Anglo-Norman élite triumphed over a Celtic majority, but even in England the Norman-Saxon south gained the upper hand over the Anglian midlands and north.

- Incidents from the confrontation of the Celtic peoples by the Anglo-Norman ascendancy set off points of difference that have rankled through the years. The theft of the Stone of Destiny by Edward I caused resentment with the Scots for over six hundred years and ultimately led to the stealing back of the Stone by Scottish nationalists in 1950, not to mention the efforts made by Michael Forsythe, Scottish Secretary in the dying years of the Major administration: attempting to curry favour with the Scots by the ceremonial return of the Stone to Edinburgh.
- Attempts to take back power from England have a long history when it comes to the creation of the union. At around the time he was elected First Secretary in Wales, Rhodri Morgan wrote an article in which he said that one had to understand Owain Glyndwr to understand Welsh aspirations. 'Owain Glyndwr wanted a country united in a properly organised society with representation from all parts of Wales. He envisaged a Welsh future in a European context . . . Six centuries later we are starting to think in those terms again' (quoted in Hazell, 2000, p. 41).[8]
- There was an economic dimension to the union and this also was divisive, with wealth-creating mining and manufacturing located in the north and midlands of England, southern Wales and central Scotland, while the management of that wealth in capitalism, trade and service industries was concentrated in London and south-eastern England.
- Small peasant, or subsistence farmers, particularly in the Celtic fringes of the union state, were neglected and often, as was the case with the Highland clearances or the Irish potato famine, so mistreated that they were forced to abandon the land and emigrate.
- Religion was a factor in Wales, where the majority were chapel-going non-conformists, and Ireland, where the majority were Catholic.

These factors, and particularly the issue of religion in Ireland, began to loosen the ties of the union from the very moment that the union came into being.

Notes

1 The Heptarchy was not always made up of seven kingdoms, and they were not always the same seven.
2 It is interesting to note that the present-day border between England and Wales very closely mirrors the line of Offa's Dyke.
3 In a symbolic act, Edgar was rowed on the Dee by rowers who included Kenneth, King of Scots, Malcolm King of the Cumbrians (Strathclyde), Maccus, Lord of the Isles, and Iago of Gwynedd (Stenton, 1947, p. 364). The historic reality of this event is questionable but the political reality of what it symbolises is very real. From that time on English sovereignty was fully recognised and from the submission of the British princes came all later claims for English suzerainty.
4 Morgannwg was situated in the South Wales valleys and occupied an area similar to that occupied by Glamorgan today.

5   The words 'Gael' or 'Goidelic' come from the Welsh word *Gwyddel*, meaning 'Irish'.
6   Malcolm III, King of Scots, is more commonly known as Malcolm Canmore ('Canmore' = 'Bighead').
7   Gladstone speaking to the House of Commons in August 1892.
8   The comment by Rhodri Morgan appeared in the Western Mail, 17 April 2000, and referred to an exhibition in the National Library of Wales where a letter from Glyndwr seeking a French alliance was exhibited.

3

Home Rule –
precursor of devolution

The nineteenth century was the century of liberal nationalism and, as a result, saw not only the rise of Irish nationalism but also the first stirrings of Scottish and Welsh nationalism. However, the nationalism that was so admired by the liberal establishment was very different from the Irish nationalism that began to emerge mid-century. Liberal nationalism welcomed the creation of new nations by the liberation of their component parts from an imperial power and the assimilation of those parts within a nation state: the great achievements of the nineteenth-century nationalist movement being the unifications of Italy and Germany. To that kind of nationalist the great achievement of British nationalism would have been the creation of the United Kingdom as outlined in the previous chapter, while the fragmentation of that union into autonomous units was out of key with the mood of the times.

It is worth noting that, in all his years of negotiating for Irish Home Rule, Gladstone never once mentioned 'Irish nationalism' but instead always referred to Irish 'nationality'. An Irishman, Welshman or Scotsman might have a 'local patriotism' to Ireland, Wales or Scotland but 'it does not follow that because his local patriotism is keen he is incapable of Imperial patriotism' (Bogdanor, 1999, p. 22).[1]

For the most part, the inhabitants of the British Isles were content with the union as it existed in 1801, or at least they were not particularly excited at the idea of political separatism. Any concerns over the union were largely material and involved the fairness or otherwise of the distribution of wealth between the component nations. For Scotland and Wales this meant that the concerns of the people were largely left to the existing British political parties most concerned with social issues: first with the Liberal party and later with Labour. In Ireland a nationalist answer to social and economic issues began to emerge after the potato famine of 1848, encouraged by the widespread European revolutions of that year.

For Wales and Ireland, however, the main dispute with the union state was religious in nature. In Wales an overwhelmingly nonconformist, chapel-going population sought the disestablishment of the Welsh church. In Ireland, as has already been mentioned, the issue which most detracted from the Act of Union was the failure to include Catholic emancipation in its provisions. Between 1801 and 1842 the initiative in Ireland was taken by the repeal movement which, as the name suggests, wanted repeal of the Act of Union but whose primary concern was to gain emancipation for Ireland's predominantly Catholic population.

Catholic emancipation and the Young Ireland Movement

After 1800 there was a movement towards Catholic emancipation in Britain as a whole but the English establishment, faced with a mere 60,000 Catholics in 1780, did not view the matter with quite the same urgency as it was seen in Ireland, with its majority Catholic population running into millions (Steinberg and Evans, 1970, p. 63). For the first thirty years of the union the main issue in Irish politics was that of Catholic emancipation and the leading figure working for emancipation was an upper-class Catholic lawyer called Daniel O'Connell whose success was such that he was later nicknamed 'the Liberator'.

In 1823 O'Connell formed the Catholic Association in order to bring pressure to bear on the government by such acts as electing Catholic MPs. Organised among the ordinary population through a network of parish priests, the association was immensely popular.[2] In 1825 it was dissolved before it could be suppressed by the government but it was instantly reformed. In 1828 O'Connell was elected as MP for County Clare, although he was unable to take his seat because of the Test Act of 1673 which prevented him from taking the oath as a Catholic.[3] At the same time the British government was becoming disturbed by the level of disaffection in Ireland and both Wellington and Peel feared an outbreak of civil war that the government would not have the military resources to subdue. In that light the government moved, despite intense opposition from the Conservatives and George IV, first to repeal the Test Act in 1828 and then pass the Catholic Emancipation Act of 1829. The act made it possible for Catholics to serve as MPs and to accept any public office with the exceptions of becoming Lord Chancellor or Lord Lieutenant of Ireland.

The Catholic Association was dissolved for the second time in 1829 since it was felt that it had achieved its aim in having secured Catholic emancipation. But the attention of the people had turned from the question of religion towards those social and economic concerns that now became more important, especially as regards questions of land tenure. As unrest grew, agitation for repeal of the union resumed after 1829. O'Connell founded the National Repeal Association in 1841 and started the journal *The Nation* a year later in order to promote Irish nationalism. One result of his work was his imprisonment in 1843 for conspiracy.

Many in the Association deplored the willingness O'Connell had shown during the 1830s to work with the Whig government in London and he lost much of his influence. Under the leadership of two Protestants, Smith O'Brien and John Mitchel, a Young Ireland Movement was started in imitation of Mazzini's nationalist 'Young Italy' and, in 1846 the more militant members of Young Ireland split with O'Connell on the issue of how willing the movement should be to use force and violence to achieve its ends, forming the Irish Confederation. After O'Connell's death in 1847 the militants gained in influence and in 1848, inspired by the spate of revolutions that were sweeping Europe, the more revolutionary members of the Confederation promoted a peasant's revolt in Tipperary that was easily put down in a few days. O'Brien and Mitchel were both arrested and transported to Australia.

The growth of nationalism

The critical event of the nineteenth century, an event that is crucial in understanding Irish alienation from British rule, was the potato famine of the 1840s. Traditional Irish laws of inheritance meant that land was not passed as a whole to the eldest son but was divided between all a man's sons. Over the generations a small farm was divided time and time again until the average Irish cotter's family possessed about as much land as would make a large garden. Needing a crop that could feed a family with the highest possible yield from a small area the Irish became almost totally dependent on the potato: so dependent that, if the potato crop failed, the family starved. In 1845 about half the total crop became diseased and rotted in the fields. In 1846 there was a total crop failure. There was a partial recovery in 1847 with a fair harvest but in 1848 there was a total failure again. As an immediate effect of the famine about one million people died in Ireland and three million emigrated to Britain, about two million of whom went on to the United States.

Initially the crisis was handled well by Peel's Conservative government but they lost the election in 1846 to a doctrinaire Whig administration. After initial aid the partial recovery of 1847 persuaded the government that the crisis was over and aid was suspended. Anger in Ireland was fanned by the British government continuing to export meat and grain from Northern Ireland to Great Britain while hundreds were starving in the south and west of the island. The combined lack of sensitivity, complacency and maladministration shown by Britain had no immediate consequence but the famine and consequent emigration was of lasting importance to Irish nationalism. The reason why support for Irish nationalism has always been so strong in the United States is because over two million immigrants went there after 1848, each of them handing on bitter and resentful memories of British treatment.

A secret society called the Irish Republican Brotherhood, better known as the Fenian Movement, emerged in the years after the famine. They encouraged rebellion and in 1867 succeeded in promoting a Fenian Rising; although it was fairly easily put down by the authorities. Many of the Fenians taken prisoner during the uprising were defended by Isaac Butt who, despite coming from a protestant and Orange background, had become interested in the nationalist movement when he defended a number of Young Ireland members after the 1848 rising. Claiming to believe that Ireland's problems could be mitigated by the existence of a subordinate parliament in Dublin, Butt went on to found the Home Government Association in 1870, renamed as the Home Rule Association in 1873.

The aim of the movement was not separatist, but wanted a return to the 1783 constitution, having both a legislature in Dublin and a token Irish presence at Westminster. In the first elections held after the Ballot Act had introduced the secret ballot and effectively outlawed the bribery and intimidation that had so dominated Irish elections previously, the Home Rule Association successfully elected 59 Irish nationalist MPs in 1874. But Butt was generally regarded as ineffectual and the nationalist movement remained in the doldrums under his leadership until the advent of Charles Parnell and the Land League in 1879.

By demonstrating the shortcomings of those inheritance laws which resulted in divided holdings, the potato famine of the 1840s had highlighted just one of the many agrarian problems faced by Ireland. The real difficulties lay with absentee landlords, a lack of tenants' rights and the questions of eviction and coercion. The government tried to remedy the situation with Gladstone's Land Act of 1870 which provided compensation for eviction and improvements by tenants. But it did not go far enough since there was no compensation for eviction because of unpaid rent and there was no security of tenure. It was this which led to the formation of the Land League in 1879 and provided the Home Rule Movement with a cause it could espouse with vigour.

Charles Parnell and the first Home Rule Bill

Coming from Co. Wicklow, Charles Parnell was an Anglo-Irish Protestant, like so many in the Irish national movement and was elected as MP for Meath in 1875. He was associated with the Home Rule Association group in Parliament but was one of those who were disenchanted with Butt's moderate policies. In 1878 he split with Butt and formed a group known as the New Departure, in alliance with former Fenians, Irish American sympathisers and land reformers.

In 1879 when the socialist Michael Davitt formed the Irish Land League to fight against the worst offences of landlordism, Parnell became its president. Under his guidance Parnellite MPs began their disruptive tactics in Parliament[4] and this, allied to agrarian unrest in the countryside and the Boycott campaign of 1880, forced Gladstone to concede a revised Land Act in 1881. The act did not go far enough since it did not deal with the question of rent arrears and the agitation continued, as a result of which Parnell and two other MPs were arrested in October 1881 and sent to Kilmainham prison. They were released in May 1882 by the terms of the so-called Treaty of Kilmainham. Agreed between Parnell and Gladstone and brokered by Joseph Chamberlain, the 'treaty' required Parnell to renounce violence and restrict himself to parliamentary action in return for Gladstone's promise to introduce a new Arrears Act.

In 1882 the new Irish chief secretary, Lord Frederick Cavendish, was murdered by a terrorist gang in Phoenix Park, Dublin. In reaction the government clamped down on nationalist supporters in an exceptionally severe coercion act.[5] Refusing to be provoked into violent action, Parnell obeyed the Kilmainham terms and devoted himself to political action, organising his Irish national party in Parliament and beginning his campaign for home rule.

In the 1885 election a total of 86 Irish nationalist MPs were returned while the number of Liberal MPs was so reduced that Gladstone could only form a government with the assistance of Irish members. Parnell used a combination of the Irish party's strength in Parliament together with this Liberal alliance to persuade Gladstone to accept the necessity of Irish Home Rule – a bill to bring that about being placed before Parliament in 1886. Unfortunately, Parnell and Gladstone had underestimated the extent of hostility to home rule on the part of Ulster Protestants and a significant number of Liberal MPs. Sufficient dissident Liberals, the most prominent of whom was Joseph Chamberlain, voted to defeat the bill on its second reading in the Commons. The same dissident Liberals, by leaving the Liberal party to form the Liberal Unionists and ultimately making common cause with the Conservatives, caused the Liberal administration to collapse, replaced by a pro-union Conservative government.

In the light of that failure the Irish national party languished and Parnell's career went into decline. In 1887 Parnell was accused of complicity in the Phoenix Park murders. The accusation was investigated by a parliamentary commission but, although Parnell was cleared of the charge in 1889 he was then plunged into scandal. Cited as correspondent in the O'Shea divorce case, Parnell's affair with Kitty O'Shea became public property, offending both the non-conformist conscience of the Liberal party and the sensitivities of Catholic Ireland. Without Parnell the Irish party split and was totally eclipsed between 1890 and 1900.

The Home Rule issue, 1890–1914

The Liberals regained power in 1892 and a second Home Rule Bill was introduced, differing from the first in that it allowed for the retention of Irish members at Westminster. This time the bill was passed by the Commons but was thrown out by the Lords. Home Rule as an issue faded from view; particularly after the Conservatives returned to power in 1895. For the next ten years the Conservatives continued a policy begun by Arthur Balfour when he had been

Irish chief secretary in 1891. Balfour had been so severe in his application of coercion acts that he was known as 'Bloody Balfour' but he mitigated the harshness by a generous and enlightened social policy. The Conservative administration between 1895 and 1905 pursued just such a generous social policy, permitting tenants to buy land and investing in schemes intended to benefit rural communities: schemes that ranged from light railways to new strains of seed potatoes, in a campaign that was said to be 'killing home rule with kindness'.

The Irish parliamentary party made something of a comeback in 1900 under the leadership of John Redmond but it did not have the popular support it had enjoyed in Parnell's heyday. The younger and more radical elements were not enthused by Redmond's cautious policies and tended to go far more extreme solutions such as were represented by Sinn Fein.

Redmond's main hope came after 1910. In that year the Liberals, campaigning on the issue of reforming the House of Lords in response to the Lords' rejection of the 1909 budget, were returned as a minority government in the first general election of 1910. A second general election only produced two more Liberal MPs and the government needed the support of Irish MPs in order to pass the Parliament Act of 1911. In return the Irish party expected and received a third Home Rule Bill which this time passed both houses, even though its main provisions were badly mauled.

As with Parnell and Gladstone in 1886, Redmond and Asquith underestimated the extent of Protestant opposition to Home Rule. Opposition from Edward Carson and the Orange Order in Ulster and a mutiny by British army officers at the Curragh Camp meant that implementation of home rule was shelved for two years. And of course, the end of those two years saw Britain embroiled in the First World War and it became understood that nothing would be done in Ireland until the war was over.

Redmond supported Irish involvement in the war and also the widespread recruitment of Irishmen for the British Army, moves that cost him popularity in exactly the same proportion as the war itself became unpopular. When the Irish Republican Brotherhood and Sinn Fein promoted the Easter Rising in 1916 Redmond failed to condemn the harsh treatment of the republican leaders by the British. Compared with Sinn Fein's preparedness to take direct action, Redmond and the Irish national party lost all credibility with the mass of the people and the 1918 election turned into a landslide for Sinn Fein, with the Irish national party vote totally collapsing. When Lloyd George tried to resume negotiations on home rule the mood had changed and the British were faced with an armed insurrection and had to negotiate with persons very different from the moderate, constitutional party founded by Charles Parnell.

The principles of home rule were then applied to the settlement which led to partition between the Irish Free State and a government of Northern Ireland at Stormont. The intention of those promoting the idea of home rule was to find a formula within which nationalist and separatist feelings could be satisfied without breaking up the union state of the United Kingdom. Northern Ireland has been paying ever since for the failure of the original home rule intentions.

The nature of, and problems posed by, home rule

The Liberal government under Gladstone was forced to consider the option of home rule by the parliamentary tactics of the Irish MPs but, quite apart from that, Gladstone had himself become convinced that repressive coercion acts had had their day and could well become counter-productive. There was also the purely pragmatic point to be made that a continued denial of legitimate demands for self-government might well lead the protesters to attempt taking that self-government for themselves by means of armed rebellion, as had happened to the American colonies. If Burke's solution to American complaints had been adopted would the Revolutionary War have happened and would the colonies have been lost?

Once the decision had been made to grant some form of home rule the central dilemma facing the government was how to reconcile the legitimate demands of the Irish for self-government with the overriding importance of maintaining the sovereignty of the Westminster Parliament. To resolve this dilemma Gladstone turned again to the writings of Edmund Burke as they related to the Irish and the American colonists.

Burke had claimed that the Westminster parliament had two functions:

1 as a local legislature for Great Britain and Ireland;
2 as an imperial legislature for the constituent countries of the British Empire.

He believed that the two functions should be separated with the power to legislate on local issues being devolved from the imperial parliament to the local. In this way two political structures could coexist; one of them supreme and the other subordinate.

Gladstone was able to cite the union of Norway and Sweden and the formation of Austria-Hungary as examples of supranational polities currently existing that had a centralised executive but twin legislatures. Moreover, Gladstone was able to point to the more recent example of the British North America Act of 1867 which set up the Confederation of Canada. Under that Act *all* the legislative powers of the imperial parliament in Westminster had been devolved to the Canadian federal government, under the control of the Governor-General and the judicial committee of the Privy Council.

However, Canada had to make many decisions for itself simply because distance made it difficult if not impossible for London to deal with them. Ireland on the other hand was closer geographically to the London parliament and therefore neither needed nor wanted its own foreign or defence policy. It was proposed that only domestic matters would be devolved to Dublin and for that reason all matters for legislation were divided between the **devolved powers** that a Dublin parliament would deal with and **reserved powers** that would remain the responsibility of the Westminster parliament. Here too Gladstone found a precedent in the Canadian legislation because, although virtually total power had been devolved to the federal government by London, that government reserved certain powers for itself when devolving local matters to the governments of Canada's constituent provinces.

The first Home Rule Bill of 1886 was modelled directly on the British North America Act, even to the extent of using the same wording. The reserved powers of the imperial parliament were said to be:

- matters relating to the Crown, the armed forces and defence;
- foreign and colonial relations;
- trade protection and customs dues.

With the central dilemma resolved, the framing of the three Home Rule Bills of 1886, 1893 and 1912 posed two further major problems, which proved very difficult to resolve and which are both relevant today since much the same questions faced those responsible for framing the devolution legislation of 1997. The questions arise over:

- **Representation**: how was Ireland to be represented in the Westminster Parliament after a devolved parliament had been established in Dublin?
- **Taxation**: how should taxation be raised in such a way as to produce equity between the UK and Irish exchequers?

With regard to representation, the first Home Rule Bill of 1886 excluded Irish members from Westminster in the first of three possible solutions that were proposed on the representation issue:

1 There should be no Irish representation at Westminster once an Irish Parliament had been established. This was a solution that appealed to non-Irish members since the disruption caused by Parnell's tactics after 1880 left many English, Welsh or Scottish MPs feeling that the sooner they were rid of the Irish members the better. The proposal was unpopular with the Irish, however, and many others were less than enthusiastic. The point was that the exclusion of Irish MPs meant that the Irish would have no say whatsoever in the raising and spending of taxation. Everyone was very aware that the clarion call of the American colonists had been 'no taxation without representation'!
2 The so-called 'in and out' option under which Irish MPs would attend Westminster when Irish or United Kingdom matters were in dispute but would not participate in English, Scottish or Welsh matters. Apart from the obvious practical difficulties the in-and-out solution had the ability of creating a constitutional crisis. The British constitution provides that the leader of the party who can command majority support in the House of Commons should be nominated as prime minister and asked to form a government. Yet,

in the light of voting patterns in the late nineteenth century, it was easy to envisage the situation where Irish nationalist MPs held the balance of power so that, with the Irish MPs present, the government would be in the hands of a Liberal-Irish national coalition, while the absence of Irish members would automatically hand over government to the Conservatives.

3 There should be continued Irish representation at Westminster but in reduced numbers to compensate for so much Irish business being done in Dublin. In many ways this seemed to be the obvious solution but it raised the question as to whether it was right for Irish members to discuss English, Scottish or Welsh affairs when English, Scottish or Welsh MPs were unable to vote on matters affecting Ireland. Ninety years before Tam Dalyell asked in a similar context why the member for West Lothian should be able to discuss the affairs of West Bromwich when the MP for West Bromwich was prevented from discussing West Lothian, here is the original anomaly that later became known as the West Lothian Question and which still exists as 'the English Question'.

In the first Home Rule Bill Gladstone chose the first of these options and if the bill had been passed Irish members would have been excluded from the Commons. This aspect of the proposal met with such objections that the Prime Minister recognised that changes would have to be made before the second bill was submitted in 1893. Gladstone briefly toyed with the in-and-out option but met with sufficient opposition as to force a change of plan. The 1893 bill, repeated in 1912, included proposals for a continued Irish presence at Westminster but with the number of Irish members reduced by 20 per cent to 80 MPs instead of 103.

The question of finance was equally as difficult and controversial. The main point is that there were some heavy expenditures that were an imperial responsibility; the most obvious of them being defence. Since the Irish would benefit from the role of the army in defending the whole United Kingdom then it was thought only right that Ireland should contribute towards the cost of that army. The amount of money needed to pay for the army and all such similar responsibilities was known as the Imperial Contribution. Out of the total amount of money going into the Irish exchequer, a substantial proportion would represent the Imperial Contribution, with the remainder set aside for the day-to-day expense of running Ireland. The question was whether the Imperial Contribution ought to be the first charge on the exchequer, running the risk of not having enough resources left to run Ireland. Or should the money to govern Ireland be paid first with the Imperial Contribution taking whatever was left.

In 1886 it was proposed that the Imperial Contribution should be a fixed sum representing one fifteenth of total imperial expenditure at the time the act became operative and that this sum should be the first charge on the Irish exchequer. The fixed sum of money determined in this way would remain unaltered for thirty years because the government was determined that fiscal policies should not disadvantage Ireland when there were no Irish MPs present at Westminster to debate fiscal matters and scrutinise the economy. One of the main complaints raised to this arrangement was that it made the Imperial Contribution seem too much like a levy by an imperial power on a subject people.

In 1893 it was proposed that one third of Irish customs dues should go to the Imperial Contribution, with Ireland taking the remainder. A commission under Hugh Childers reported that a fixed sum Imperial Contribution would not have worked. But, by 1912, everything had changed, thanks to the reforms of the Liberal government elected in 1906. In what is seen as the origin of the welfare state the government had introduced national insurance, unemployment benefit and old age pensions. This massive increase in public spending on welfare meant that the Irish budget was operating in deficit, the Imperial Contribution could not be afforded and a totally separate Ireland would not be viable unless it gave up the welfare benefits. It began to look as though Ireland could only continue with a British subsidy.

Home rule for Scotland and elsewhere

We have concentrated in this chapter on the question of Irish Home Rule because that is where it began and the term 'home rule' when it is used in a nineteenth-century sense is generally taken to mean the series of confrontations between the British government and the Irish National party between 1880 and 1914. There is also the point that, although not the intended outcome, a form of home rule and the first devolved government in Britain did emerge in Ireland. Nevertheless we need to acknowledge that the agitation in Ireland did provoke echoes of nationalist leanings in Scotland and Wales, both countries becoming involved with thoughts of home rule after 1880.

The Act of Union was initially very unpopular in Scotland and there was widespread criticism that consent had only been obtained through widespread bribery and corruption. For a generation there was unrest, culminating in the Jacobite rising of 1745, followed by the repression of the Highlands. The repression involved in suppressing the Highland way of life, with the banning of tartan and Highland dress, was as harsh as the coercion acts in Ireland and the enforced evictions and mass emigrations to Canada involved in the Highland clearances carried echoes of the injustices practised during the Irish potato famine. But in Scotland it was not the English who were responsible for the destruction of the Highland clans but rather it was the work of Lowland Scots, while those enforcing the clearances were the clansmen's own Anglicised lairds.

In the last quarter of the century, however, there was a golden age for Scotland outside the Highlands, with a cultural renaissance in the arts, literature, philosophy and education. It was a time when the neoclassical New Town was built in Edinburgh and that city became known as the 'Athens of the

North'. Alongside the cultural flowering there was a growing prosperity in industry, agriculture and commerce and it was clear that both Scotland and England were benefiting from the union. '. . . the happy investment of English capital in the Scottish industrial renaissance brought a tolerant acceptance of an ancient enemy' (Prebble, 1971, p. 312). As well as the growth in prosperity there were new openings for the Scots in the growth of British imperialism: the history of the British Empire providing a rich roll-call of Scottish names acting as soldiers, explorers and administrators in imperial expansion.

Unlike the Irish, the Scots seemed to have gained a great deal from the union and, although a certain amount of resentment was felt at what was seen as English arrogance there was not the anger and frustration that was felt in Ireland. This lack of resentment was aided by the fact that Scotland still retained its own institutions in the Kirk and the Law.

At the time of the French Revolution there was unrest among the lower middle and working classes and revolutionary clubs known as the United Scotsmen were founded in an attempt to emulate Wolfe Tone's United Irishmen. The riots and demonstrations, however, were not the result of any anti-English or anti-union feeling but were much more a class matter, with anger directed at the prosperous middle classes, the factory owners and the landlords, who in most cases were themselves Scottish.

During the first half of the nineteenth century, early English tourism and the writings of Sir Walter Scott, coupled with the enthusiasm of Queen Victoria and Prince Albert, led to a complete transformation of the English view of Scotland. The English might patronise the Scots and romanticise the Scottish way of life into a culture of tartan and bagpipes but the English grew to respect the Scots in a way that they never did the Irish.

When Scotland came to consider calls for home rule it was a movement without overt hostility to the idea of being British. The aim was not to separate Scotland and England but to give Scotland equality with England in constitutional law and it was pointed out that while Scotland had retained its own legal system in the union, it was now in the unusual situation of having an independent judiciary with no legislature to support it.

At the time of the first Irish Home Rule Bill in 1886 the Scottish Home Rule Association was formed and, under its auspices no fewer than thirteen home rule proposals were placed before the House of Commons between 1890 and 1914, gaining the support of a majority of Scottish MPs on eleven of these occasions. The nature of these proposals can be seen from the text of a resolution passed by 180 votes to 170 in 1894, saying: '. . . it is desirable, while retaining intact the power and supremacy of the Imperial Parliament, to establish a legislature in Scotland for dealing with purely Scottish affairs' (Mackie, 1964, p. 368).

There was no real passion underlying these home rule proposals, merely a feeling that, if Ireland could have home rule, so too should Scotland. Despite the sympathy of the Liberal party and support from future Labour leaders like Keir Hardie and Ramsay MacDonald, none of the proposed measures got past the committee stage in the Commons. The most determined effort came with 20 MPs forming a Scottish National Committee in 1910, under whose auspices the Commons voted in 1912 to treat Scotland like Ireland, proposing a separate Scottish Parliament of 140 members. A Scottish Government Bill was prepared and presented but no room in the parliamentary timetable was found for 1913 and in 1914 the outbreak of the First World War ensured that any such bill was postponed indefinitely.

In the meantime, a more significant event for the future of devolution in Scotland was the beginning of administrative devolution in 1885 with the creation by Lord Rosebery of a Scottish Office. At first the Scottish Secretary had very little to do, but he was always a cabinet minister after 1892 and the job grew in importance. In his short term as Prime Minister Rosebery followed up his institution of the Scottish Office with the formation in the Commons of the Scottish Grand Committee, formed of all Scottish MPs and expected to give special attention to legislation affecting Scotland.

Wales

As was the case in Scotland, the English were disliked in Wales but without any real animosity. Wales had been a part of England since 1536 and had never been united as a separate state before that time so that there were certainly no separate specifically Welsh institutions, as was the case in Scotland where the Scots were clearly seen to have their own particular legal system. Another factor distinguishing the Welsh situation was that, unlike Ireland, there was no class of absentee and alien landlords. The landlords and squirearchy of Wales were themselves Welsh-speaking and part of the same community as their tenants.

Wales did, however, differ from the rest of the United Kingdom in that the people were overwhelmingly nonconformist in religion and radical in politics. Where Ireland was hostile to the British presence in all its forms, the Welsh were opposed to specific institutions like the Anglican church and the Conservative party. The Liberal landslide in the general election of 1868 made Wales the least Conservative part of the United Kingdom and as such it remained. In 1881 that combination of Liberalism and nonconformity, allied to the temperance cause, led to the Sunday Closing (Wales) Act, the first parliamentary act that applied only to Wales and not to England: a form of devolution in itself!

Another factor that made the situation in Wales very different to that in Ireland was the growing industrialisation in the valleys of South Wales. This had two outcomes:

- Unlike Ireland and Scotland where an existing over-population had been made so much worse by the potato blight and the highland clearances that it could only be rectified by wholesale emigration abroad to the United States or Canada, the dispossessed of rural Wales could remain in the principality by going to live and work in the valleys.

- The evils of industrialisation, in working and living conditions, made for a new divide in Wales that had nothing to do with nationality. The Welsh people had always been radical in their political opinions; now they became ardent in class conflict between the workers and the forces of industry and capital.

When the movement for Irish Home Rule began to gain strength there was a movement towards home rule in Wales similar to that in Scotland but, again as was the case in Scotland, this was simply a feeling that if Ireland could have home rule so too should Wales. In 1866 a society calling itself *Cymru Fydd* (Future Wales) was founded, but its aims and interests were more cultural than political. Much was done to improve Welsh education, including founding the University of Wales, and efforts were made to stem the decline in the use of the Welsh language. In the political field the efforts of *Cymru Fydd*, along with the Liberals, were devoted to reforming the structure of Welsh local government.

As far as Welsh nationality was concerned the members of *Cymru Fydd* did not look for separation from England. They looked instead for equality; refusing to accept that Wales might be regarded as being in the second rank and somehow inferior or subordinate to England. On the other hand they had difficulty with the notion of a Welsh nation because Wales was rife with inequalities and divisions. The north distrusted the south; the former principality distrusted the former Welsh Marches; rural north and mid-Wales distrusted the industrial south; Welsh-speakers distrusted English-speakers and vice versa while the large counties claimed a greater say in Welsh affairs than the smaller counties were willing to grant them[6]. Apart from the divisive nature of these rivalries and suspicions, rooted in the past history of Wales, there were communication problems created by the Welsh mountains which in essence cut off the north from the south and make it easier for many Welsh people to travel to London for a meeting than to make their way to Cardiff. Even the university was founded on three separate campuses at Bangor, Aberystwyth and Cardiff, while meetings of all-Welsh committees were held in Chester, Shrewsbury, Hereford or Ludlow.

Cymru Fydd collapsed in the 1890s, after which Labour replaced the Liberals as the party of protest in the valleys: the South Wales coalfield becoming one of Labour's heartlands, providing huge and safe majorities for Labour and providing a base for Labour leaders from the earliest times when Keir Hardie was the MP for Merthyr Tydfil. The Labour party inherited from the Liberals all the great radical issues, although the issues were much more about class, the treatment of the workers and the distribution of wealth than it was about the peripheral issue of home rule.

For Labour just as much as for the Liberals the great national issue in Wales was the disestablishment of the Anglican church. Figures from a survey carried out in 1906 showed that something like 74 per cent of the Welsh people were nonconformist and chapel-going by religion (Steinberg and Evans, 1970,

p. 399) and yet the Church of England was the established church in Wales, a church which the Welsh regarded as remote from the concerns of their daily lives. As was the case in Ireland the vast majority of the people belonged to a religion that was not the established church of the state. And, again as was the case in Ireland, people were penalised for not being of the right religion: in the middle of the nineteenth century Welsh tenant farmers were expected to pay a 'tithe' to a church of which they were not members and widespread unrest was caused by the so-called 'tithe wars' when farmers refused to pay up.

The Church of Ireland was disestablished in 1858 and, with a Liberal land-slide occurring in the same year, it might have been expected that the Liberal government would take up the cause of Welsh disestablishmentarianism with equal enthusiasm. Gladstone did not approve, however, and did not want to see the Liberal government diverted away from the cause of Irish Home Rule. As a result, the cause of disestablishment could not succeed while Gladstone remained the leader of his party. The cause also failed under Rosebery and it was not until the second Liberal term under Asquith that a measure to disestablish the Church in Wales was finally put before the Commons. Disestablishment was granted in 1914 but was yet another casualty of the outbreak of war and it was 1920 before the Church in Wales separated itself from Canterbury.

While efforts were being devoted to disestablishmentarianism the home rule issue had been forgotten and, by the time disestablishment was granted in 1920 things had changed so much that it seemed the forgetfulness might last for ever. The Labour party had gained its ascendancy in South Wales and the burning issues had become social issues such as poverty, living conditions, education and pay. In 1922 there was a proposed conference on devolution but it failed for lack of interest.

Home rule all round

Alongside the proposals for home rule for Ireland, Scotland and Wales there was an alternative advocated by some politicians which envisaged a federal structure under which Scotland and Wales, as well as Ireland, and together with either England or the English regions would each gain their own legisla-tures, although all these assemblies would subordinate to the federal parlia-ment in Westminster. The main point to remember about the proposed federal structure – or 'home-rule-all-round' as it was known – was that it provided an answer to certain difficulties that had emerged in home rule legislation and which are still relevant to devolution today.

The federal plan would:

• provide for fair and equal treatment for each component part of the UK;
• equalise fiscal matters since each legislature would have its own taxing powers;

- encourage unity, as the devolved legislations combined could bring others into line.

The federal plan was first put forward by Earl Russell in 1872 and gained sufficient support for the 1912 Irish Home Rule Bill to be renamed as the Government of Ireland and House of Commons (Devolution of Business) Bill since it contained proposals that would have provided for English, Scottish and Welsh Grand Committees. The federal aspects were dropped from the bill but they were known to have had the support of Asquith and other frontbench spokesmen (Bogdanor, 1999, p. 45).

The inherent problem in any federal solution is that England, Ireland, Scotland and Wales are very different places with very different needs, and could never be fitted into a uniform pattern. Moreover the real sticking point – and this is still very relevant today – is that while Scotland, Wales and Ireland could all produce good reasons why they should have their own distinct legislature the same is not true for England.

Advocates of home rule thought that federalism was irrelevant and little more than a trivial diversion. Unionists on the other hand saw federalism as a great threat to the union which would lead inevitably to the break up of the United Kingdom.

Irish unionists were ironically in favour of federalism if it meant a federation of regions rather than of nations. Under such an arrangement it would be possible to have separate legislatures for the Protestant north and the catholic south. Irish nationalists on the other hand were equally as certain that Ireland was a nation, whole and indivisible, for which only a national solution was acceptable. In this way the federal argument was laying the groundwork for that resolution of the Irish question which would involve partition.

After the First World War in 1919, a Speaker's Conference was called to consider devolution and the possibility of a federal solution. But the conference failed to resolve the contentious issues and the whole home rule project collapsed. Discussion was overtaken by events as the Irish question moved to confrontation and the armed struggle.

Notes

1 This is a quote from a speech made by Gladstone to the House of Commons, 8 April 1886.
2 An indication of the size and popularity of the Catholic Association can be gained from the fact that a membership subscription of only one penny a month (known as the 'Irish Rent') could produce a revenue of £1,000 a week (Steinberg and Evans, 1970, p. 63).
3 The Test Act of 1673 required all holders of public offices to be communicants in the Anglican church, who were expected to renounce publicly the doctrine of transubstantiation in a way Catholics would find impossible.

4 The favourite weapon of the Irish nationalist party was the filibuster by which Irish MPs would speak at length, one taking over from another as the first tired, and thereby prolonging debates beyond their designated time, 'talking out' the bill and seriously disrupting government planning. One side effect of Irish nationalism was to introduce various devices such as the guillotine into the Commons by which time-wasting debate could be cut short.

5 Coercion acts by which the government sought to control unrest and potential revolution were a permanent feature of life in Ireland during the nineteenth century and half a dozen acts between 1814 and 1891 sought to control the population through measures such as suspending trial by jury, martial law, banning of public meetings, increased powers of search and arrest etc. The Royal Irish Constabulary was founded in 1836 as a semi-military force to enforce the coercion acts. Always the target of Irish nationalists the coercion acts continued until recent times, continuing to be used in Northern Ireland under the name of 'emergency powers' after 1969.

6 An idea of the inequalities can be gained from the fact that well over 50 per cent of the Welsh population lived in just the two counties of Glamorgan and Monmouth.

Part II

Preparing for devolution

4

Scotland and Wales –
devolution resurgent

When the Irish question was settled at the end of the First World War it looked as though the issue of home rule for Scotland had become irrelevant and would shortly be totally forgotten. As late as 1924, during the first Labour government, the Scottish Liberal Federation had proposed that Scotland should have a parliament to deal with Scottish affairs, and George Buchanan, MP for the Gorbals, proposed yet another Home Rule Bill that was talked out by the opposition. But these were ideas and proposals that belonged to the old Liberal party, albeit with Labour support and, by 1924, the Liberals were already fading from the scene, to be replaced by Labour at a time when Labour was becoming as much of a unionist party as the Conservatives.

Labour, having supported home rule since the days of Keir Hardie, cooled on the issue as the slump and unemployment of the late 1920s seemed to show that the problems of Scotland were primarily problems of class. According to the Labour viewpoint, the English, Scottish and Welsh working classes were equally disadvantaged and righting any wrongs was best done on a UK-wide basis, seeking a fairer solution through working-class solidarity, for which one strong central government was required, not one that was fragmented regionally. Labour was already cooling on the idea of home rule and when a group of MPs, some local authorities and the Convention of Scottish Royal Burghs formed the Scottish National Convention in 1924 to campaign for home rule the idea got nowhere.

In 1928 the Scots National League was formed to agitate for an independent Scotland. It was a cultural as much as a political movement, based on a sort of Walter Scott, pipes and tartan kind of Scottishness, typified by wearing the kilt, learning Gaelic, eating haggis and reading the novels of Compton Mackenzie. It was a fringe party made up of students, romantics and eccentrics, but it had a minor success in 1931 when Compton Mackenzie was elected Rector of Glasgow University on a nationalist ticket.

The deep depression of the 1930s introduced an economic element and the remnant of those who had supported home rule for Scotland formed themselves into the Scottish Party which advocated devolution rather than separate independence. In 1933 the National League and the Scottish party merged to form the Scottish National Party (SNP) under John MacCormick, who had left the Labour party while still at Glasgow University in order to campaign for Scottish devolution. The SNP contested local and parliamentary by-elections throughout the 1930s without any significant success but during the Second World War MacCormick was ousted as leader and the party became more militant and separatist in its aims.

The newly assertive SNP took advantage of the fact that during the war the main parties had declared an electoral truce and did not contest elections while the fighting continued, maintaining the pre-war status quo. The SNP, however, decided that they would fight any by-election in Scotland, always putting up a candidate against whichever party held the seat. As a result Dr Robert McIntyre became the SNP's first ever MP in the Motherwell by-election of 1945, only to lose it three months later when normal political activity resumed in the first postwar general election.

It was the SNP's only success for some time but, although all of Britain suffered years of austerity and hardship after 1945, there were still those who believed that Scotland was suffering disproportionately from the neglect of Westminster. In 1949 two million Scots signed 'a Scottish Covenant' calling for a home rule Scottish Parliament within the United Kingdom and John MacCormick, founder of the committee organising the Covenant, was elected as Rector by the students of Glasgow University, as Compton Mackenzie had been before him.

At that time the Labour government was too concerned with the creation of the Welfare State, the nationalisation programme and planning the Festival of Britain to spare any thought for such parochial matters as Scottish devolution, and Attlee refused to meet MacCormick to discuss the Covenant. It must be remembered that a substantial part of Labour representation at Westminster was founded on the party's Scottish seats and no one in the party was likely to do anything that might reduce the number of Labour seats north of the border and thereby weaken their position. The trade unions also believed that only a UK-wide national wages policy could protect the level of pay in Scotland. In 1950 a report on financial links between England and Scotland stated that 'the economies of the two countries are so closely-related that disentanglement was well-nigh impossible' (Mackie, 1964, p. 369).

One event that did raise public awareness of nationalism for a time was the theft of the Stone of Destiny from the Coronation throne in Westminster Abbey by a group of nationalist students. It was stolen in December 1950 and recovered in Forfar the following April. For four months Scottish pride and separatism dominated the front pages of the British press. As one nationalist-inclined commentator said: '*This* was what stirred the quiescent Scotland of 1950–51 – not the plans for the coal industry, Stafford Cripps's budget or Ernest Bevin's Cold War foreign policy' (Nairn, 2000, p. 105). Memories of that stunt lingered over the years and was reflected in Scottish Secretary Michael Forsythe's act of 1996 in returning the Stone to Edinburgh in an attempt to curry favour with the Scottish people.

Meanwhile in Wales

Wales has always been very different from Scotland in the way that devolution has been perceived. As we have seen, Wales was never united as a fully indepen- dent state as Scotland had been and whereas the conflict for Scotland was with England, the divisions were internal for Wales. Even after the day of the native Welsh princes had passed, Wales was still divided between the lands conquered by Edward I and under royal jurisdiction on the one hand and the semi- autonomous Marcher lordships on the other. Equally as important over the years since then have been the deep and abiding divisions between north and south, church and chapel, industrial and agricultural, Welsh-speaking and English-speaking.

To the Welsh people the struggle was economic rather than political and the intense loyalty of Wales first to the Liberals and then to Labour was based on the belief that they were the parties that could obtain the best possible eco- nomic outcome for Wales. In 1922 those who believed that the Welsh them- selves should influence what was done in Wales attempted to organise a conference on devolution in Shrewsbury which failed for lack of response, most notably through the actions of Glamorgan and Monmouthshire both of whom failed to send representatives, even though these two counties by themselves contained virtually 50 per cent of the Welsh population. It is also indicative of the internal tensions inherent in Wales that a conference on Welsh affairs should have to be convened in an English town like Shrewsbury because a loca- tion in Wales equally acceptable to all parties could not be found.

As has been mentioned, there was a nationalist Liberal group in the nine- teenth century known as *Cymru Fydd* (Wales of the Future) but the movement collapsed in the 1890s and was never revived, as the Liberal party went into decline after the First World War. A sort of Welsh National party was founded in 1925 in the form of *Plaid Cymru* (Party of Wales) but it was essentially a party which saw Wales as being differentiated from England by the Welsh lan- guage and bardic culture rather than economic and political deprivation.

Labour might have been expected to be sympathetic to the problems of Wales but the position they adopted was that the problems of poverty and unemploy- ment would best be met by socialist solutions and they could only be applied by a strong central government. In 1945 the Labour Home Secretary, Herbert Morrison, in rejecting the idea of Wales having a Welsh Office on the same lines as the Scots had a Scottish Office, declared: 'The proper remedy for Wales, as for Scotland, is to ensure that they both form part of a single economic plan for the whole country' (quoted in Evans, 1999, p. 51).

During this period *Plaid Cymru* (PC) was largely disregarded by the majority of the Welsh people, although the issue of the extent to which Wales was exploited by the English was kept alive by such high-handed actions of the British government as the proposal to flood the Tryweryn Valley in Merionethshire to provide drinking water for Liverpool, drowning the village of Capel Celyn and dispossessing 67 Welsh-speaking families. Nevertheless, until 1959, PC put up candidates in only a few constituencies and then only in Welsh-speaking areas. Before that date, for example, no PC candidate had ever been put forward in the populous counties of Glamorgan and Monmouth in the south-east. In the 1959 general election, however, in the face of growing unease at what was seen as English exploitation, PC put up 20 candidates and polled over 77,000 votes.

In the 1960s there was a growing Welsh language movement in *Cymdeithas yr Iaith Gymraeg* (the Welsh Language Society) that showed itself ready to take direct action to support its cause. Most direct action was fairly innocuous and involved vandalising road signs and posters worded in English but there was a more extreme wing that developed during the agitation surrounding the flooding of Capel Celyn and culminated in the student protest year of 1968. A handful of activists, the most formidable of whom were known as the Free Wales Army, showed that they were prepared to burn down holiday cottages and second homes belonging to English owners, while several English-language radio and television transmitters belonging to the BBC were blown up or threatened. The investiture of the Prince of Wales at Caernarfon Castle in 1969 was the excuse for a number of disruptive acts by extremist groups and which ended with the arrest of a Welsh nationalist accused of planting a bomb. Activists like the Free Wales Army did not have the support of more than a small minority of the population and therefore the situation in Wales was never comparable to the troubles of Northern Ireland. In 1968, *Plaid Cymru* sought to distance themselves from the more extreme language activists by declaring PC to be bilingual.

The Welsh language did, however, gain the recognition that was sought for it in the 1960s. *A report on the Legal Status of the Welsh Language* was issued in 1965 and the Welsh Language Act was passed by Parliament in 1967 giving Welsh equality of status with English in the courts, as well as requiring legal documents to be issued either in both languages separately or as bilingual documents. The speaking of Welsh, which had been in decline, began to recover, especially among the young. Welsh-language schools were developed and the ability to speak Welsh became a required qualification for teachers in most local authority areas. In the world of popular culture a number of pop groups emerged who performed in Welsh and, when Channel 4 was set up in 1982, its Welsh equivalent, *Sianel Pedwar Cymru* (S4C), was created as a largely Welsh language television channel.

Administrative devolution

In 1892, seven years after the Scottish Office was created, an attempt was made to set up a Welsh national body on the same lines to assume responsibility for local government, the Poor Law, public works and the Charity Commission. The attempt failed because there was no agreement as to how representatives should be chosen for the new body: whether each county should have equal representation, which would give parity to Glamorgan and Anglesey, or whether it should be proportionate to the population of the various counties. Glamorgan, as the most populous county, wanted representation to be based on population but the effect would have been to give Glamorgan alone 25 of the body's 59 places.

Special Welsh departments and administrative units were set up within Whitehall. In 1907 a Welsh department was set up in the Board of Education and was responsible for many innovations, not least initiatives establishing the place of the Welsh language in the curriculum. In 1911 a Welsh commission was set up to administer the National Insurance Act in the principality and in 1919 the Board of Agriculture, Food and Fisheries acquired a Welsh Office. By 1950 there were no fewer than seventeen such administrative units in Wales but still the government refused to appoint a Welsh Secretary.

The Conservative party always opposed the idea of a Welsh Office and a succession of Tory governments rejected any such proposals. Labour was not so clear-cut and, after Morrison's outright rejection in 1945 a split developed among Labour's Welsh MPs between those, led by James Griffiths and Cledwyn Hughes, who favoured the appointment of a Welsh Secretary and those, led by Aneurin Bevin and George Thomas, who were implacably opposed. Unlike Scotland with its own particular legal and education systems, Wales had never been treated as a separate administrative unit and since 1536 had been seen as an integral part of England, leaving no justification for a Welsh Secretary. In the early 1950s an all-party campaign advocated a Welsh parliament but although a petition asking for this received half a million signatures, it was ignored by both government and opposition, while Cledwyn Hughes was disciplined by the Labour party's National Executive Committee (NEC) for his support of the proposal.

In fact it was Winston Churchill's Conservative government which finally set up a Ministry of Welsh Affairs in 1951, but as an integral part of the Home Office rather than a separate department. In 1957 Harold Macmillan transferred the responsibility for Wales to his Minister of Housing and Local Government, Henry Brooke, since it was felt that Welsh affairs were more a matter of local government than a responsibility of the Home Office. Brooke began well but destroyed his own credibility by approving the flooding of the Tryweryn Valley by Liverpool Council, an act opposed by 27 of the 36 Welsh MPs (Bogdanor, 1999, p. 159).

In 1954 the Labour party, persuaded by James Griffiths, decided in favour of the appointment of a Secretary of State for Wales and, following this decision the promise of a Welsh Office appeared in the party's election manifesto for both the 1959 and 1964 general elections. The success of Harold Wilson in 1964 meant that Labour was at last able to fulfil its promise and the Welsh Office was created in October of that year, with James Griffiths as the first Secretary. But the Office as then constituted was very limited in its powers, being restricted to the control of housing, local government, roads and planning. Over the years that followed the powers of the Welsh Office were expanded; health being added to the remit in 1968 and schools in 1970. Ultimately the Welsh Office acquired almost as much power and control as the Scottish Office, growing to ten times its original size in terms of staff and budget, although never reaching parity with the Scottish Office.

It was always intended that, in an ideal world, the Secretary of State for Wales should be Welsh and that the Welsh Office should be staffed by Welsh MPs. For twenty years this worked well enough. There were no problems in periods of Labour government but, just as was to be the case in Scotland, the decreasing number of Conservative MPs who were elected for Welsh seats meant increasing difficulty in filling ministerial positions in the Welsh Office and the numbers were often made up, not just by Welsh MPs sitting for English seats but by English or Scottish MPs who had no connection with the principality. In 1987 the position of the Conservatives in Wales had deteriorated to the point that: 'the Conservatives could no longer find any suitable MPs from Wales or with Welsh connections who wished to be or were thought capable of being, Welsh Secretary' (Deacon, Griffiths and Lynch, 2000, p. 91). Only Nicholas Edwards (1979–87) of the six Conservative Welsh Secretaries actually sat for a Welsh constituency. Of the English Secretaries, Peter Walker (1987–90) was moderately successful, at least in terms of attracting industry to the principality, but others like the Thatcherite free-marketeer, John Redwood (1993–95), were a disaster from the Welsh point of view. The Welsh verdict on Redwood is epitomised by an embarrassing television shot, often repeated, which shows the Welsh Secretary looking desperate, opening and shutting his mouth in a vain attempt to persuade viewers that he actually knew and was singing the words of *Hen Wlad fy Nhadau*, the Welsh national anthem known in English as 'Land of my Fathers'.

Growth of nationalism, moving towards devolution

In the 1955 general election the SNP put up just two candidates who gained 0.5 per cent of the Scottish vote between them. By 1966 the number of candidates had risen to 23, who accounted for 5 per cent of the vote. Until 1959 the majority of seats in Scotland coincided with the party forming the UK government but certain factors were changing in Scottish voting patterns and, in 1959, whereas Conservatives had previously had a majority of seats in Scotland when there was a Conservative government in London, Labour became the largest party in Scotland, despite the Conservative government. That lead not only continued but increased, until the 1997 election which saw no Conservatives at all elected in Scotland.

In the mid-1960s a major change took place in the nature of party alignment in Britain, leading to growing successes for the SNP and *Plaid Cymru*. It was a time when a growing volatility in voting behaviour reflected the fact that voters rapidly became disenchanted with governments and would register their disapproval by delivering a protest vote in mid-term by-elections. A protest vote usually means a vote against the governing party but, at the same time, voters usually cannot bring themselves to vote for the main opposition party. That is why, during times of Conservative government, disillusioned Tory voters turn to the Liberals. Faced with a Labour government, however, those Scottish and Welsh Labour voters who wished to protest could vote for the SNP or PC, thus not only delivering a protest but making the point that the protest was primarily against the English orientation of the government, whichever unionist party was in power. As the psephologist, David Butler, has said: 'The accident of by-elections undoubtedly shaped the pattern of successive Liberal and Nationalist revivals since the 1960s' (Cook and Ramsden, 1997, p. 11).

In 1966, in a breakthrough for PC, Gwynfor Evans won a by-election in Wales's largest constituency, Carmarthen, caused by the death of Megan Lloyd George. For the time being Carmarthen was the solitary seat actually won by the nationalists but, in May 1967, PC came very close to winning a by-election in Rhondda West, cutting the Labour majority to 9.1 per cent in a constituency where the smallest Labour majority previously had been 55 per cent. In July 1968 PC went on to fight a by-election at Caerphilly, where they reduced the Labour majority from 59.7 per cent to 5.2 per cent, pushing the Conservatives into third place and costing them their deposit.[1] The significance of these by-elections is that, although Carmarthen is a largely rural seat in a Welsh-speaking area and a strong *Plaid Cymru* possibility, both Rhondda West and Caerphilly were typical South Wales mining communities that were almost entirely English-speaking and traditionally rock-solid Labour.

In the March 1967 Pollok by-election the SNP gained 28.2 per cent of the vote in a Labour marginal, letting in the Tory. Eight months later Winnie Ewing won her famous by-election result in Hamilton, until then Labour's ninth safest seat in Scotland, gaining 46 per cent of the vote in a seat not even contested in the general election eighteen months previously (Cook and Ramsden, 1997, p. 185). It was a toe-hold for the SNP that they never really lost thereafter. In 1968 the SNP won nearly 100 places in local government elections, depriving Labour of an overall majority in Glasgow. During the period of the 1966–70 Parliament the average SNP vote in by-elections was 29 per cent while, after 1970, the SNP share in general elections rose from 11 per cent to 30 per cent as the party chose to stand in every Scottish constituency. In October 1974 the SNP won 11 seats, passing the Conservatives to become the second largest party in Scotland.

In the two general elections of 1974 PC picked up a total of three parliamentary seats: Caernarfon and Merioneth were won in the February election, while the party regained Carmarthen in October. These successes encouraged many people to believe that the nationalist vote was growing as fast in Wales as it was in Scotland but this was not necessarily the case. The first-past-the-post voting system favours political parties that are geographically concentrated. The vote for PC was increasing, but only in Welsh-speaking West Wales where the three seats were won, while the PC vote actually fell back elsewhere.

The Kilbrandon Report

To understand the surge of support for the SNP and *Plaid Cymru* in the late 1960s one must appreciate that the boom years of the 1950s, which had given birth to the vision of an 'affluent society', allowing Macmillan to fight the 1959 election under the slogan 'You've never had it so good!', had ended in disillusionment. In Scotland the slowdown in the standard of living was seen to be disproportionate, with the Scots doing far less well than the English, because traditional industries like mining, steel and shipbuilding were going into decline. The Scottish people were inclined to blame Labour for not doing more to halt this decline and electors began to abandon their traditional support for Labour while refusing to vote Conservative, seeking instead the party likely to do the most for Scotland.

The message promoted by the SNP was that the Conservative, Labour and Liberal parties were all UK-wide parties and their instinct would always be to look after the majority grouping in the UK, which was the English. The appeal of the SNP for the electorate of Scotland was not any burning desire for complete independence, which most Scots rejected, but rather from a feeling that here was a party that really would put Scotland on an equal basis with England and Wales. At this period the SNP was 'seen as a pressure group for Scottish interests' (Bogdanor, 1999, p. 124).

The Welsh Council of Labour had promoted the idea of a Welsh Assembly as early as the mid-1960s. In 1965 the suggestion was made that local government should be reformed in Wales so as to establish a two-tier system of local administration in which district councils would form the lower tier and a single all-Wales council would form the only body in the upper tier. This would not have been a devolved administration with the functions of central government but merely a grandiose sort of county council employing delegated legislation but it would still have played a useful role in decentralising government. The idea was lost to a more orthodox two-tier system of local government but, as from 1968, the question of Welsh devolution was firmly fixed on the agenda of the Wilson government.

In the second half of the 1960s, Harold Wilson recognised that the upsurge of Scottish and Welsh nationalism was posing a serious threat to Labour's electoral supremacy in both countries. And since the number of Labour seats was always disproportionate in terms of the national UK vote, this meant that a loss of support in Scotland and Wales could threaten Labour's position in Great Britain as a whole.

Wilson recognised that he had to do something to soothe nationalist feelings and, as was his practice in those years, he chose to do so by way of a royal commission. In 1968 he instituted a Royal Commission on the Constitution which was supposed to look at the entire field of possible constitutional reforms but which nevertheless concentrated its attentions on the issue of devolution for Scotland, Wales and the English regions. Originally the chairman of the commission was Geoffrey Crowther, a much-respected former editor of the *Economist*, but he died and his place was taken by a Scottish lawyer, Lord Kilbrandon. When the report of the commission was published in 1973 it was known as the Kilbrandon Report.

The outcome of the Kilbrandon Report was very confused. Two commissioners were so disillusioned by the commission's concentration on devolution to the exclusion of other constitutional matters, like the reform of Parliament and the committee system, that they signed a Memorandum of Dissent. The remainder of the commissioners agreed on three recommendations regarding devolution:

- the UK Parliament must remain sovereign and any suggestions of separatism or federalism were rejected;
- members of the devolved Assemblies must be directly elected, not nominated;
- elections to the devolved Assemblies should be by the single transferable vote (STV) form of proportional representation, not first past the post (FPTP).

Other than these agreed points the commission was seriously divided. All the Scottish, Welsh and Northern Ireland commissioners wanted devolution for Scotland and Wales but not for the regions of England. A number of English commissioners, however, wanted devolution for the English regions on a basis of parity with Scotland and Wales but without legislative powers. A very small group recommended that there should be devolution for Scotland but not for Wales and indeed the tone of the report taken as a whole suggested that the argument for Welsh devolution was not as strong as the Scottish case.

The report also stated that Scottish and Welsh devolution should not affect representation in the UK parliament but it is from this time that we can date what later became known as the West Lothian Question.

The report was delivered to Parliament in 1973, when Edward Heath's Conservative government was far more concerned with Britain's entry into the EC and the reform of local government in England, Scotland and Wales. As a result the report was shelved and would have been forgotten if it had not been for the February 1974 election in which the SNP won six seats and PC gained two. Suddenly the Labour party began to look vulnerable.

This was particularly true in Scotland where the nationalist parties had found a new cause in the early 1970s with the discovery and exploitation of oil in the North Sea. This worked for the SNP in two ways:

• Any demand for Scottish independence had been countered in the past by the argument that an independent Scotland was not economically viable. The wealth created by the oil industry turned this argument on its head.
• After the oil was brought ashore in Scotland from oilfields off the Scottish coasts and processed in Scottish refineries, it was piped south to England for the benefit of multinational companies and the UK exchequer. This caused resentment in itself but the resentment was made greater by the belief that the UK was giving less to Scotland in terms of government expenditure than it was gaining in tax revenue from the Scottish oil industry.

The SNP soon adopted the slogan 'It's Scotland's oil!', meaning that the party had a cause to fight for that was easily understood by the electorate. It is easy to overestimate the effect of the oil bonanza, however, and it should be remembered that the SNP revival was well under way before the first barrel of crude came ashore in Shetland. 'Oil reinforced electoral support for the SNP, it did not create it' (Bogdanor, 1999, p. 126).

Despite the worries obviously felt at party headquarters in London, Labour's Scottish Council voted to reject devolution by six votes to five in June 1974, claiming that devolution was 'irrelevant to the real needs of the people of Scotland' (quoted in Bogdanor, 1999, p. 141). London, however, was very insistent and pressure was applied to the extent that, just two days before the date of the second election of 1974 was announced, the Labour party agreed that a commitment to devolution should be written into the party manifesto.

On 17 September 1974, just three weeks before the election, the government issued a White Paper called *Democracy and Devolution: Proposals for Scotland and Wales*, a move that was widely seen as a cynical bid to save Labour seats from the nationalist threat. The White Paper contained six proposals:

• directly elected Assemblies for Scotland and Wales;
• the Scottish Assembly should have legislative powers, the Welsh Assembly only executive powers;
• the Assemblies to be elected by the first-past-the-post system;
• the devolved administrations should be financed by block grant, with no tax-raising powers;
• there should be no reduction in the number of Scottish or Welsh MPs at Westminster;
• the Secretaries of State would remain as positions with cabinet rank.

After the election a new, revised White Paper was issued in November 1974, entitled *Our Changing Democracy: Devolution to Scotland and Wales*. This restricted even further the powers that were to be granted to the devolved

Assembly so as not to undermine the supremacy of the UK Parliament. Under the proposed arrangements matters relating to the economy, industry, energy and agriculture were not to be devolved.

Although the form of devolution being offered to Wales was very different to that being offered to Scotland, the government decided for various reasons to deal with both Scottish and Welsh devolution in the same piece of legislation. This was done because there was a substantial number of Labour MPs who were bitterly opposed to Welsh devolution and the government felt that these MPs would be less likely to oppose the bill if they ran the risk of damaging the much-desired Scottish devolution by so doing.

The Scotland and Wales Bill secured its second reading on 13 December 1976 by 292 votes to 247, a comfortable majority of 45 which nevertheless included the votes of 47 pro-devolution Tories who were liable to return to their natural allegiance and vote 'no' at the committee stage. The Liberals also threatened to withdraw their support unless they were promised proportional representation, which was unacceptable to most Labour members. It was a rebel Welsh Labour MP, Leo Abse, who proposed an amendment to the bill requiring that devolution should be approved by a referendum of the electorate before it could have effect. In order to pacify Labour dissidents and build up some sort of coalition grouping, the government agreed that the proposed referendums would be held after the bill had received the royal assent, ensuring that it would never become law without the approval of the electorate. Moreover the referendums would be mandatory rather than advisory as the referendum on EC membership had been.

The rather shaky alliance moved on into the committee stage but there was so much dissension between the groups involved that the discussions showed every sign of running out of time. In order not to lose the bill through having it talked out, the government attempted to impose a guillotine on the discussions. The motion was defeated by 312 votes to 283, on 22 February 1977, and all progress on the Scotland and Wales Bill came to an end.

By now the Callaghan government was in a minority and the loss of the devolution bill meant that the nationalist parties withdrew their support. In March the Prime Minister secured his position by coming to an agreement with the Liberals, known as the Lib-Lab Pact. Part of the agreement with David Steel's party was that a new and improved devolution bill was to be presented to parliament. The Liberals argued hard for some of their ideas to be included in the bill and as a result there were to be separate bills for Scotland and Wales this time. But they failed to get agreement on two important points:

- The Assemblies were not to have any tax-raising powers but would be reliant on a block grant from London. This was paid according to a formula devised by the Chief Secretary to the Treasury in the Callaghan government, Joel Barnett. The Barnett formula was supposed to move towards equality of spending per head of population and originally stated that for every £85 by

which public expenditure on English services rose, Scotland would receive £10 and Wales would get £5.
• Assembly members would be elected by first-past-the-post and not proportional representation, a stipulation which angered the Liberals and caused many to question the value of the Pact.

The proposals were widely unpopular at Westminster but MPs voted for the bills rather than see the government defeated and forced to resign. There was also the factor that the original rejection of devolution had transformed the SNP into the most popular party in Scotland. 'Labour dissidents, worried by the rise of nationalist fervour and anxious to preserve their own seats after the next general election, suddenly warmed to the government's proposals' (Evans, 1999, p. 53). The bills for both Scotland and Wales received their second reading on 14 and 15 November 1977 and received the royal assent on 31 July 1978.

By the time the bills had cleared Parliament they had acquired a number of important amendments, and one of these had serious consequences for the forthcoming referendum. An anti-devolution Labour MP, George Cunningham, had proposed and gained an amendment which said that in considering the mandatory referendum a repeal motion would be laid before the House if fewer than 40 per cent of those Scots entitled to vote had said 'Yes'. This was done to ensure that a poor turnout in the referendum did not mean that devolution was granted on a minority vote. The result of the referendum held on 1 March 1979 was highly unsatisfactory for Scotland since, while a majority voted for devolution, a turnout of 62.9 per cent meant that the 'Yes' vote did not reach the 40 per cent threshold. Of those voting: 51.6 per cent voted 'Yes', representing 32.85 per cent of electorate; 48.5 per cent voted 'No', representing 30.78 per cent of the electorate.

The government tried to get parliament to vote down the repeal motion but failed. In the light of that failure the Conservatives laid down a motion of no confidence which was passed by just one vote on 28 March 1979. Callaghan resigned and called a general election that was duly won by the Conservatives under Mrs Thatcher. It was the new Tory government which repealed the Scotland Act in June 1979 with a division of 301 votes to 206. Of the 71 MPs for Scottish constituencies 43 voted against repeal, 19 voted for and 9 abstained.

For Wales, as was the case in Scotland, a quota of 40 per cent of the Welsh electorate was needed to vote 'Yes' for devolution to become law. As it happens, unlike Scotland, there was no need for a minimum vote to be imposed on the Welsh electorate. The 'No' vote was comprehensively successful by 956,330 votes (80 per cent) to 243,048 (20 per cent).

The Thatcher factor

On election in 1979 Mrs Thatcher made vague promises that devolution was not dead because of the referendum result and claimed herself to be closely in touch with Scottish thoughts. 'Tory values,' she said, 'are in tune with everything that is finest in the Scottish character' (Young, 1989, p. 528). Nevertheless there is no doubt that devolution was directly opposed to the set of beliefs which became known as Thatcherism:

- Margaret Thatcher wished to reduce the role of government and devolution would mean adding an extra layer of government.
- Margaret Thatcher worked hard to centralise government and was committed to sidelining local government and rendering it impotent. She was unlikely to wish to strengthen regional government.
- Margaret Thatcher was vehemently unionist and opposed to anything that might work towards the break-up of the United Kingdom.
- Margaret Thatcher's English middle-class accent, personality, attitudes and life style were antipathetic to the Scots and Welsh and contributed to their alienation.

One comment on the Thatcher years seems to summarise the situation: 'Margaret Thatcher weakened local government, abolished the Greater London Council, and favoured the south-east of England. Scotland and Wales in particular felt an acute sense of neglect' (Davies, 1999, p. 927).

During the years of Conservative government, support for the Tories in Scotland drained away. The popular belief was that Scotland was hit disproportionately by the economic slump in wages, employment and the decline of manufacturing industry. In fact, Scotland was not as badly hit as the West Midlands and Northern England but, fanned by enthusiastic supporters of constitutional reform, the flames of Scottish dissatisfaction with London rule grew ever higher. That alienation reached its peak when the government reformed the financing of local government and replaced the rates with the community charge or poll tax. It was not only that the poll tax was seen to be unfair and regressive which caused most unrest in Scotland but the fact that the government chose to impose that tax on Scotland in 1989, a full year ahead of its introduction into England and Wales, and to do so without even consulting the Scottish Office. An immediate effect was to spark off a campaign for non-payment, led by the SNP, with Scotland having the highest number of individuals refusing to pay the tax when levied. The irony of the situation was not lost on the Scots when the Tory government ignored Scottish protests over the tax and yet withdrew the tax as soon as English protests began. 'The fiasco of the poll tax seemed to prove to the Scots and Welsh that, in rejecting devolution, they have surrendered themselves to a government which cared little for their interests' (Bogdanor, 1999, p. 196).

The unpopularity of the government began to show in election results. In the 1979 general election the Conservatives won 22 out of the 71 Scottish seats, exactly half as many as Labour. In 1983, a year when Labour was virtually wiped out nationwide, with the Conservatives winning more than 60 per cent of parliamentary seats in the UK as a whole, the Tories slipped back to just 21 seats in Scotland. By 1987 the unpopularity of the Thatcher government was such that six out of every seven constituencies elected an anti-Conservative MP, reducing the government to just 10 seats. There was a slight improvement in 1992 when the Tories gained 11 seats but this is partially explained by the fact that the total number of Scottish seats rose to 72 for that election. With John Major every bit as much a unionist as Margaret Thatcher, Tory support continued to slip away and people began to talk of the 'nightmare scenario' when no Conservatives at all would be elected for Scotland: an event which duly came about in 1997.[2]

The most obvious effect of this dwindling support was on what became known as the 'Scottish mandate'. At times of Conservative governments this meant that it was questionable for Westminster governments to impose legislation on a country like Scotland where only a tiny minority of the electorate had voted for the party forming that government. Apart from the legitimacy of the Tory government in constitutional terms there were also serious problems posed for the practical reality of administrative devolution.

Within Parliament Scottish affairs were handled by the Scottish Office, to which eleven preferably Scottish MPs were appointed as ministers. In addition there were two standing committees to handle Scottish legislation and a Scottish Affairs select committee on which party membership was proportional to the composition of the Commons as a whole and did not reflect the party balance in Scotland. After Conservative representation in Scotland had dropped to ten in 1987 the Tories did not have sufficient Scottish seats to staff the select committee, once Scottish Office ministers had been appointed. The Scottish Affairs Committee was suspended between 1987 and 1992 and was only resumed after the 1992 election by being allowed a Labour chairman and having Conservative numbers made up by English MPs (Pilkington, 1997, p. 272).

Pre-devolution groups had started to mobilise support to overturn the referendum decision almost immediately afterward; these disparate groups forming themselves into the all-party Campaign for a Scottish Assembly on 1 March 1980. In 1983 the Labour party committed itself to supporting the idea of the Assembly and Donald Dewar became the acknowledged leader of the campaign for devolution in 1984. In 1987 the Labour manifesto in Scotland promised that there would be a Scottish Assembly with tax-raising powers created in the first parliamentary session. Labour lost the election but the disastrous slump in Conservative support in Scotland led Labour to claim that the Scottish mandate belonged to them.

Er gwaetha 'rhen Fagi a'i chriw – despite Maggie and her crew![3]

The comprehensive defeat of the devolution process in the 1979 referendum might well have been expected to bury the possibility of devolution for Wales for ever. For a time, indeed, that did seem to be the case. The Welsh started to discuss the matter more publicly and it became clear that there was one very deep division in Wales over the question of devolution and very little enthusiasm for the idea. The people of the north were concerned that a Welsh Assembly would be dominated by Cardiff politicians and the Labour party machine, while in the south there was a similar suspicion that the Assembly would fall into the hands of a Welsh-speaking clique from the north-west. In June 1979 the Wales Act was repealed by 191 votes to 8 and it looked very much as though devolution for Wales was ruled out for the foreseeable future.

Yet the character of the Conservative administrations of first Margaret Thatcher and then John Major meant that in Wales, every bit as much as in Scotland, the legitimacy of a London-based Tory government for Wales was called into question. The Conservative government that had won 11 Welsh seats in 1979 and 14 in Labour's nightmare election year of 1983, had fallen back to just 8 Welsh seats in 1987, 6 in 1992, and was headed for the complete wipe-out of 1997 when the Conservatives won no seats in either Scotland or Wales.

A perception that the Welsh economy suffered unduly in comparison to that of England was a major factor in the Tories' electoral fortunes. The 1980s began with massive closures in the Welsh steel industry, which led in their turn to a severe decline in heavy industry throughout South Wales. In 1984–85 the miners' strike led inevitably to so many pit closures in the South Wales coalfield that the industry and the employment it gave virtually disappeared. The dispiriting effect of this economic factor permanently damaged the Conservatives' status in the principality but there were four additional factors that put the seal on the Tory decline and strengthened the case for devolution in Wales.

1 Under the Conservatives Wales became a quango-dominated society. Since the Tories seemed unable to elect MPs for Welsh constituencies they nevertheless retained control over most aspects of Welsh life, the Welsh Secretary having the right to make appointments to a whole range of quasi-governmental organisations. It was estimated that by 1989 the Secretary of State for Wales had 1,429 part-time salaried appointments to quangos in his gift (Evans, 1999, p. 63). The amount of public money administered by Welsh quangos ran into billions of pounds and was certainly more than the amount of money spent by democratically-elected local authorities. One of the main arguments advanced in 1997 for the setting up of a Welsh Assembly was the need for some body to assume responsibility for the large numbers of quangos which otherwise were not accountable to any democratic body.

2 No more than about 20 per cent of the Welsh people ever voted for the Conservative party and yet for the greatest part of the twentieth century

Wales was governed by a Conservative government and a Conservative Welsh Office. In no sense whatsoever could the Conservative government be said to have a mandate to govern Wales. The situation grew even worse in 1995 when local elections reduced the number of Tory councillors in the whole of Wales to a mere 41.

3 Between 1987 and 1997 the Secretaries of State for Wales were all English and were generally disliked and distrusted. It is said, possibly apocryphally, that civil servants in the Welsh Office opened bottles of champagne and danced in the streets of Cardiff at the news of John Redwood's departure. His successor, William Hague, at least made an effort by marrying a Welshwoman but opposition Labour Welsh MPs boycotted Welsh Question Time in parliament in protest at his appointment.

4 Welsh Labour, Liberal Democrat and Nationalist politicians all took heart from Jacques Delors' appointment as President of the European Commission and his advocacy of a 'Europe of the Regions'. This conjured up the possibility of Welsh representatives negotiating directly with Brussels without having to use the British government as intermediary.

Preparing the ground

In 1988 the newly created Constitutional Steering Committee made a Claim of Right in Scotland and this was followed in 1989 by the formation of a Scottish Constitutional Convention to consider how devolution could be achieved. The Conservatives from a unionist standpoint and the SNP as separatists both refused to participate in the Convention but the extent of the support given to the Convention was impressive. Those taking part included:

- 57 MPs (49 Labour and 8 Liberal Democrat) and 7 out of the 8 MEPs);
- 12 regional and island councils, together with the Orkney and Shetland Movement;
- 47 out of the 53 Scottish district councils;
- the Co-operative, Communist and Scottish Green parties;
- the Scottish TUC;
- the Scottish churches;
- National federation for the self-employed and small businesses;
- groups representing blacks, Asians, women and Gaelic-speakers.

The logistics and secretariat for the Convention was provided by the Convention of Scottish Local Authorities (Evans, 1999, pp. 58–9).

Despite their general election defeat in the UK as a whole in 1992, the continuing strong position in Scotland kept Labour in support of devolution. Indeed, as Neil Kinnock was replaced as leader of the party, first by John Smith in 1992, and then by Tony Blair in 1994, support for devolution grew even stronger. The party began to work even more closely with the Convention and it was recognised that any proposals made by the Convention were likely to be adopted as party policy if Labour were to win the next general election. There was also growing support for the SNP who overtook the Conservatives to become the second largest party in Scotland in 1992. In the European elections of May 1994 the SNP won two Euro-seats with 32.6 per cent of the vote.

By mid-term, following the election of 1992, the issue of devolution came to occupy an increasing role in the thoughts of all the political parties who set about clarifying what stance they would adopt if they were successful in the forthcoming general election. Generally speaking, there seemed to be three possible solutions for the future governance of Scotland:

1 The status quo could be maintained, but with increased and improved administrative devolution. This was the position adopted by the Conservative Party.
2 There could be executive and legislative devolution, as advocated by the Labour and Liberal Democrat parties.
3 There could be full sovereign independence for Scotland within Europe, as desired by the SNP.

The Scottish local election results of 1995, which saw the Conservative Party virtually eliminated north of the border and the SNP capturing three councils with 181 councillors, awoke renewed interest in the plans being made by the various parties for the future governance of Scotland and the Scottish Constitutional Convention decided that the time had come to announce their proposals. But other parties and groupings had their own agendas and within the space of just one week three alternative proposals for the future of Scotland were announced.

On 28 November 1995 the then Scottish Secretary, Michael Forsyth, made a series of declarations to outline government proposals for changes in how Scotland should be governed, concentrating on strengthening the existing Grand Committee of 72 Scottish MPs who would be given the right to scrutinise Scottish legislation by having the second and third readings heard in committee rather than the full Commons, while the Prime Minister, Chancellor and other ministers would be asked to debate legislation with the Grand Committee. There would be a strengthening of local government in Scotland but the proposals all related to administrative rather then legislative devolution.

Two days after these declarations, aptly enough on St Andrew's Day, the Convention held a special meeting and press conference in Edinburgh. This meeting marked the publication of their findings, which proposed that there should be a Scottish Parliament of 129 members, 73 of them elected according to the first-past-the-post system in Westminster-like constituencies, but with 56 top-up members elected proportionately for Euro-constituencies. The Scottish parliament would have powers over all decisions previously taken by the Scottish Office and would have tax-raising powers to pay for services and legislation peculiar to Scotland.

While the Convention was meeting, the SNP was also in Edinburgh to outline the Nationalists' proposals for an independent Scotland: the main one being that there should be a single chamber parliament of 200 members. Of these, 144 would be elected for constituencies by the existing first-past-the-post system, augmented by 56 members chosen by a list system of proportional representation. A Chancellor would be elected to preside over parliaments, there would be no place for peers except as elected members and there would be a written constitution and a Bill of Rights (Pilkington, 1997, pp. 273–5).

Just over a year after the publication of these three proposals Scotland found itself faced with a general election in which the issue of devolution might well play a leading role, as one commentator said: 'Labour's commitment to a Scottish parliament and Conservative attachment to the status quo ensured that Scotland's governance was going to be a crucial issue in the campaign' (Sell, 1998, p. 204). For the Labour and Liberal Democrat parties there was no problem as the Convention's recommendations were adopted without question as party policy and featured largely unaltered in the parties' election manifestos. Unlike the situation in 1979 the appearance of devolution in the party manifesto meant that when Labour won its landslide victory it could rightfully claim to have received a mandate from the public.

The Scottish Nationalists fought the general election on the issue of separation but, once Labour was elected with a full mandate for devolution the SNP chose to accept Labour's plans as the best offer they were going to get, at least for the time being. In the referendum on devolution that Blair had insisted upon, the SNP swung alongside Labour and the Lib Dems in campaigning for a 'Yes-Yes' vote. The Conservatives on the other hand remained devoted to the union and as such formed the most vigorous voice in the 'No-No' referendum campaign, insisting that their proposals for the committee system were all that Scotland required, even though the tide of events meant they were no longer relevant.

During the late 1980s the issue of devolution for Scotland had became ever more important for the Labour party and, although there was a greater reluctance to consider devolution for Wales after the failure of such moves in 1979, it was obviously difficult to argue over the democratic deficit in Scotland without considering the matching deficit in Wales. In 1989 the Welsh Labour party issued a policy paper entitled *The Future of Local Government in Wales*, in which it was suggested that any reform should include: 'an elected body for Wales to deal with Welsh Office functions and with functions carried out on an all-Wales basis by nominated bodies' (quoted in Evans, 1999, p. 64). A commission to maintain an overview of the policy was set up in 1992, producing an interim report in 1993 called *The Welsh Assembly, the Way Forward* and culminating in 1995 with the policy document *Shaping the Vision* which was accepted by the party conference and endorsed by Tony Blair as being legislation that would be introduced during the first year of a Labour government.

What Wales lacked was an all-party constitutional talking-shop like the

Scottish Consitutional Convention. An independent pressure group, the Parliament for Wales Campaign, attempted to set up a group similar to the SCC but the move failed because Welsh Labour refused to take part and the Labour party alone set up a Constitutional Policy Commission in 1994. While there was by no means the same support for devolution in Wales as there was in Scotland, and the experience of failure in 1979 was daunting to say the least, there was still sufficient support for the setting up of a Welsh Assembly to be included in the Labour manifesto for the 1997 general election.

On 27 June 1996, George Robertson, as shadow Secretary of State for Scotland and Ron Davies, as shadow Secretary of State for Wales, jointly announced that legislation for devolution was promised for the first year of the new parliament and that any such legislation would be preceded by referendums seeking the endorsement of the electorate.

Notes

1 Figures for the by-elections given in Cook and Ramsden, 1997, pp. 183–90.
2 The figures quoted are from Mark Evans's chapter in *Developments in Politics, Volume 10*, Causeway, Ormskirk, 1999, p. 57.
3 The part played by Margaret Thatcher in the demonology of Welsh nationalism is shown in a song celebrating the survival of the Welsh language despite the efforts of the English, written by Dafydd Iwan in 1983, and called *Yma O Hyd* (We're still here), in which a couplet from the last verse runs:

Er gwaetha 'rhen Fagi a'i chriw,	(Despite Maggie and her crew,
Byddwn yma hyd ddiwedd amser.	we will be here to the end of time.)

5

Northern Ireland –
Stormont, the first devolution,
and the aftermath

It is one of the ironies of history that the one part of the United Kingdom to have had any real experience of legislative and executive devolution before 1999, was the one that very definitely did not want anything to do with devolution: and that one part was the province of Northern Ireland as it existed after 1922. Elsewhere in Britain devolution was sought or granted as a product of nationalism but in Northern Ireland the population was fervently unionist and anti-nationalist. We therefore have the anomaly that Ulster was given its own parliament because it wished to remain subject to the Westminster Parliament. In his memoirs the former Liberal Prime Minister, Herbert Asquith, said that Northern Ireland was 'to be given a parliament it did not want while the rest of Ireland was to be given a parliament it would not accept'.[1]

Events leading to partition

The third Home Rule Bill had been passed in 1912 but its implementation was so delayed that it was overtaken by events in the form of the First World War, causing the Act to be suspended for the duration of hostilities. During the war attitudes changed considerably. The executions and brutal repression that followed the Easter Rising of 1916 and the way in which conscription was enforced in Ireland combined to alienate large sections of the Irish population. The old moderate Nationalist party founded by Charles Parnell was in decline. In the 1918 elections Sinn Fein swept the board, winning 72 of the 103 Irish seats. Having won those seats, however, Sinn Fein members refused to take their place at Westminster. On 21 January 1919 those Sinn Fein MPs who were not in prison formed themselves into Dáil Éireann and proclaimed the Republic. The Dáil was immediately declared illegal by the British government and forcibly closed by the army in September.

When the Home Rule Bill of 1912 was re-submitted in December 1919 it was amended by Lloyd George's government to accept partition and included plans for two devolved parliaments in Dublin and Belfast, elected by proportional representation, both continuing to send MPs to an imperial parliament in Westminster which would retain excepted and reserved powers. There was also to be a Council of Ireland which would deal with all-Ireland concerns and work for unity. Ulster Unionists accepted the provisions of the act in March 1920, in the same month as the Home Rule Bill was passed by the Westminster parliament.

The plan was rejected by the Dáil, the members of which demanded an all-Ireland, independent republic. Open warfare followed between the IRA on one side and the British army, the Royal Irish Constabulary and the specials known as Black and Tans on the other. An escalating succession of murders and atrocities were carried out by both sides and martial law was imposed in Counties Cork, Kerry, Limerick and Tipperary. In May 1921 the first elections for the devolved parliaments were held, Sinn Fein winning 124 seats out of 128 in the south and Unionists capturing 40 seats in the north, as against 12 seats for a mixture of Nationalist and Sinn Fein candidates. Éamon de Valera and Sir James Craig were nominated as prime ministers in south and north respectively.

Northern Ireland went ahead according to the settlement, with George V opening the Northern Ireland Parliament on 22 June 1921. In the south a ceasefire was called in July and Lloyd George and de Valera entered into talks, which broke down almost immediately, with de Valera refusing dominion status. An Irish conference was reconvened in October, with Arthur Griffith and Michael Collins representing Ireland. The Anglo-Irish Treaty that emerged from these talks was signed on 6 December. Under the terms of the new treaty:

- 26 counties of southern Ireland would become the Irish Free State, with full dominion status within the British Empire.
- Six of the nine counties of Ulster were to have the option of withdrawing from the Free State to become the devolved government of Northern Ireland, continuing to send MPs to the imperial parliament in Westminster.

The Dáil reluctantly accepted partition on 7 January 1922 by 64 votes to 57. De Valera refused the presidency of the Free State, the office passing to Arthur Griffith. The Treaty was signed in London on 17 February 1922, with the agreement coming into effect on 6 December 1922. A large section of Sinn Fein refused to accept partition and a bitter and savage civil war broke out between the official Free State government under Collins and Griffith, and the IRA, who supported de Valera's view. The conflict which followed proved the truth of Michael Collins's prophecy that, by signing the Treaty he had signed his own death warrant.

Events in the south did not affect the Protestant north which exercised its right to opt out of a united Ireland and continue with its own Parliament.

The nature of partition

At the root of the need for partition was sectarian ideology and the irremedial division of Irish society into two communities. Although many leading Irish nationalists, from Wolfe Tone through the leaders of Young Ireland to Charles Parnell, were all Protestant, the overwhelming majority of nationalist sympathisers were Catholic. The politics and religion of Ireland had been inextricably linked since the seventeenth century, with attitudes entrenched by memories of the Rebellion of 1641, when so many Protestants were massacred by Catholics, and of Cromwell's expedition, when the Catholic populations of Drogheda and Wexford were also slaughtered. By the end of the nineteenth century attitudes were so entrenched that the terms 'Catholic' and 'nationalist' were interchangeable, as were 'Protestant' and 'unionist'.

Although there were both Catholics and Protestants throughout Ireland the two communities were polarised to a large extent, with most Protestants existing in the north-east corner of the island around Belfast, where the Scottish plantations had been located. Not entirely coincidentally the north-east was also the industrial and wealth-creating heart of Ireland. This created one interesting by-product of the sectarian division. In southern Ireland the men and women of the Protestant ascendancy were thinly-spread members of the upper middle class and minor gentry. Around the shipyards of Belfast and the industrial centres of the north there was a substantial Protestant working class. They were, and remain, the footsoldiers of Orange Unionism in the north, since the Orange Order was founded as a 'means of mobilising lower-class Protestants for the defence of the institutions of the state, the established Church of Ireland and landed property' (Aughey and Morrow, 1996, p. 3).

It is therefore obvious that there is a substantial section of Northern Irish society that has always refused to contemplate incorporation within a Catholic-dominated home rule Ireland. Protestant feeling whipped up by men like the Craig brothers and Edward Carson culminated in outright defiance at the time of the 1912 Home Rule Bill. Arms were smuggled into the country and used to set up the paramilitary Ulster Volunteer Force, while hundreds of men were willing to sign the Ulster Covenant. They made it clear that if a home rule government were set up in Dublin, Ulster would leave that parliament and fight if necessary for the right to rule themselves. As they said, they would: 'vote against Home Rule for Ireland to the end of time, but they would only *fight* for the exclusion of Ulster' (Bogdanor, 1999, p. 59). If the Protestants did prove to be willing to fight for exclusion, there was very little the British government could or would do about it. Certainly they could not suppress such a movement since the so-called Curragh Mutiny of 1914 showed that there was a substantial part of the British army that was prepared to desert rather than to take up arms against Ulstermen, while the leaders of that army proved unwilling to treat the mutineers with the severity usually meted out to those guilty of mutiny.

The possibility of partition had first been proposed by Lord Macaulay when he criticised Daniel O'Connell by pointing out that Ireland was not all the same and that there should be separate treatment for 'Protestant Ulster and Catholic Munster'. The problem with partition, however, related to where the dividing line was to be drawn. The Protestant presence was only significant in the northern province of Ulster but even there the religious divide was not neat. Of the nine counties of Ulster only four had a clear Protestant majority – Antrim, Armagh, Down and Londonderry. Almost half the population was Protestant in Fermanagh and Tyrone but the proportion was little more than 20 per cent in Cavan, Donegal and Monaghan.

The 1912 bill, as amended in the Lords, allowed for the exclusion of all nine counties of Ulster but the matter had not been resolved when the act was suspended in 1914. In 1918 the dilemma facing Lloyd George was that he had a Home Rule Bill on the statute book for which he was unable to gain acceptance from the Ulstermen. He was also hamstrung by a government commitment that no agreement on Ireland as a whole would be reached without agreement from the Protestants of the north.

According to unionist thinking, partition did not mean devolution. As they saw it, the south would accept a home rule government in Dublin from which Ulster would be excluded, allowing the north to remain under direct rule from Westminster. It was the committee drafting the post-1919 agreement which finally decided that Northern Ireland would have to have its own devolved assembly. It was felt that the Catholic-nationalist community had as their priority the need to escape from British rule. Yet, if Ulster continued to be ruled directly from London that would leave the sizeable Catholic population of Ulster still in British hands. A devolved government in Ulster would at least be Irish, albeit Protestant.

It was thought that partition would only be temporary. The government believed that with time the differences between the communities would be ironed out, the Catholics would be reconciled to a less coercive British rule and people from both sides of the divide would see the practical and economic benefits of working together. At some point the mechanism of the Council of Ireland, on which both Belfast and Dublin were represented, would be used to reach agreement on ending partition. In producing its legislation the government stated quite openly that its ultimate aim was: 'a united Ireland with a separate parliament of its own' (Bogdanor, 1999, p. 63).

Over the question as to how many counties should be excluded, the government had wanted to include all the nine traditional counties of Ulster on the grounds that this would give the Protestants such a small majority that it would only require a reasonably short time for demographic changes to alter the balance. The Protestant leaders on the other hand were sufficiently proficient in mathematics as to know that Cavan, Donegal and Monaghan had only 70,000 Protestant inhabitants as against 250,000 Catholics and they realised the threat this posed to the size of the overall Protestant majority in a nine-county

Ulster. The unionists therefore forced the government to accept a six-county solution. A move to allow each individual county self-determination was prevented on the grounds that if it had been allowed Fermanagh and Tyrone might well have abandoned exclusion and rejoined the twenty-six counties making up the Free State.

Stormont and the Northern Ireland government

The government of the six counties was established by the Government of Ireland Act of 1920, which was designed to maintain the link established in the Act of Union of 1801 and was part of the home rule settlement. The devolved government of Northern Ireland and the partition of Ireland that created it was defined in the Irish Free State Act of 1922, and ultimately underpinned by the Ireland Act of 1949.

In 1932 the parliament of the north was finally established at Stormont Castle, a grandiose building on the outskirts of Belfast, set in a park with an impressively long approach driveway. The whole structure of government in Northern Ireland was simply referred to, by enemies and supporters alike, as Stormont, a term that was also used for the ideological ethos which underlay the government of Northern Ireland. 'The word [Stormont] became a synonym for intransigent unionism' (Cannon, 1997, p. 893). This bicameral institution was modelled closely on the Parliament at Westminster, albeit so much smaller, having a directly elected House of Commons of 52 members from which a Speaker, prime minister and cabinet were drawn; the 52 members being made up of 48 territorial members and four representing the Queen's University of Belfast. The second chamber was known as the Senate and consisted of two ex officio members and 24 members elected by the Commons. The elected senators held office for eight years with half the elected members retiring every four years: the Senate being unaffected by any dissolution of Parliament. The Commons had a maximum life of five years, although it could be dissolved before that at the wish of the prime minister. For Stormont the Crown in Parliament was represented by the Lord Lieutenant of Ireland, while the home rule settlement still prevailed, and by a Governor after 1922.

The purpose of the Parliament, according to the declaration establishing its existence, was to 'make laws for the peace, order and good government of Northern Ireland'. The procedure was the same as that of the Westminster Parliament, with bills passing through both houses before receiving the Royal Assent from the Governor. Financial legislation had to begin in the Commons and could not be amended by the Senate. If the two houses disagreed over any matter the Governor could convene a joint session of both houses. If a bill received a majority vote from a joint session it was judged to have passed both houses.[2]

Stormont was made subordinate to the imperial Parliament in Westminster, which retained certain powers for itself, the most important of which related to matters affecting the Crown, the armed forces, foreign relations and external trade: these being known as **excepted** matters. When the agreement setting up the Northern Ireland Parliament was made in 1920 it was still expected that the north and south would be reunited in a few years' time. Therefore there were certain powers, known as **reserved** matters, that were retained by Westminster for the moment, although the ultimate intention was the transfer of these powers to an all-Ireland Parliament. The reserved powers consisted of such things as the issue of postage stamps, savings banks, the registration of deeds and land purchase. The reunion of the two Parliaments never happened, however, and the reserved powers were retained with the exception of the registration of deeds and land which was transferred to Stormont.

In more recent times, what were then called 'excepted' powers have become known as 'reserved' powers and what were then known as 'transferred' powers are known as 'devolved' powers. In 1920 so many powers were transferred or devolved to Stormont that there seemed to be little need for there to be so many MPs representing the province at Westminster and Northern Ireland representation was consequently cut to 13, instead of the 17 that the population of the province would seem to demand.[3]

Ambitious politicians in Northern Ireland knew that their best hope for ministerial office lay in service at Stormont. The more able therefore did not bother to contest the Westminster seats and the representatives serving in the imperial parliament always had far less prestige at home than those at Stormont. At Westminster the 12 Unionist MPs regularly returned all took the Conservative whip and, until the 1960s, were treated as an integral part of the Conservative party. It was very seldom that the Ulster members held the balance of power at Westminster as Parnell's Nationalists had held the balance in the 1880s, except in the period 1951–55 when the Conservative majority was so small that the government relied on the votes of the Unionists to maintain itself in power; although Labour made no complaint about this at the time. In 1965 Harold Wilson felt it necessary to warn the Unionists that they should not vote against the government on the issue of steel nationalisation because in Northern Ireland regulation of the steel industry was a devolved area of interest. But on the whole there was never the possibility of Irish members holding the government to ransom by the threat of disrupting parliament.

There were two important questions about the form of devolved government established at Stormont, both of which remain important, since they need to be asked of any devolved legislature and administration:

1 How independent was the devolved parliament in Belfast, in relation to the imperial parliament in London, and how far did it retain sovereignty in Northern Ireland?
2 How would the devolved government be financed and would it have primary tax-raising powers itself?

If parliamentary sovereignty means that Parliament is the sole body able to legislate by passing laws without referring them to any higher authority, then Stormont was not sovereign. Northern Ireland legislation was open to appeals made to the courts, the House of Lords and the judicial committee of the Privy Council. There was a clear implication for democracy here in that the unelected law courts retained the power to overturn legislation passed by a democratically elected Parliament. Furthermore the UK government could ask the monarch to instruct the Governor of Northern Ireland not to give assent to a bill of which London disapproved. Moreover, Westminster still retained the right to pass legislation that would be binding on Northern Ireland – even though the matter in question dealt with devolved powers and should be outside the remit of London.

Although the Westminster Parliament had the power to intervene in Northern Irish affairs it was nevertheless very non-interventionist and this can be seen to have an important outcome for Northern Ireland in two specific instances:

- Although not laid down in parliamentary procedures, the convention grew that Westminster should not legislate on devolved matters. In 1923 the Speaker of the Westminster House of Commons ruled definitively that questions to ministers about Irish devolved issues should be asked at Stormont and not at Westminster. As late as 1967 it was established that there were certain questions in respect of Northern Ireland politics and civil rights that London should not consider under any circumstances. The areas mentioned related to discrimination in housing, education and local government.
- Section 5 of the 1920 Act outlawed any form of religious intolerance and discrimination and the London government was supposed to ensure that this was upheld. As it happens, the London government totally ignored the fact that Stormont was quite blatantly intolerant and discriminatory. Sir James Craig (later Viscount Craigavon), the first Northern Ireland prime minister, stated that his intention was to build 'a Protestant parliament in a Protestant state' (Jones, 1989, p. 277) and that is just what he did.[4] The majority of members at Stormont were members of the Unionist party, as were 15 out of the 20 High Court judges in the Northern Ireland courts and the entire command structure of the Royal Ulster Constabulary. Property qualifications restricted the right to vote and serve on juries, the franchise in local elections only being given to ratepayers. At the same time, the ownership of property and business premises gave the right for the owners of property to have a vote for each of the properties and businesses that they owned, giving some individuals up to six votes in local government elections. As should be obvious, all property qualifications discriminated against the less prosperous 33 per cent of the population who were Catholic and who tended not to own property.

The economy and fiscal policy

We have seen in Chapter 3 that a major problem faced by those framing home rule legislation concerned the budget and the division of expenditure between the Imperial Contribution that went to London and the amount of money set aside for the day-to-day expense of running Ireland. This problem became even more serious in coping with the budget for Northern Ireland.

The 1920 Act insisted that the Imperial Contribution would have first charge on Irish revenue and nominated, as taxes reserved for the Imperial Contribution, income tax, customs dues, excise duty and profits tax. Devolved taxation that would go to Stormont after the Contribution had been met was limited to:

- motor vehicle licences;
- entertainment duties;
- stamp duty.

In all, the reserved taxes added up to no more than 20 per cent of the taxation income for Northern Ireland.

From the very start Northern Ireland was unable to fund the level of public services required by the UK government out of Irish revenue alone. Quite apart from the growing number of welfare services such as pensions and unemployment pay there was the need for a far greater expenditure on police and security in the province in the light of the nationalist agitation which later became IRA terrorism. The suggestion was made that there should be a lower level of public service provision in Northern Ireland. Yet the people were paying the same level of taxation as the rest of the United Kingdom and expected the same level of service as a result. There was also a need to preserve a high level of public provision because it was a way of reminding the Catholic population of Ulster as to how much better off they were than their co-religionists in the impoverished south.

In 1925 the Northern Ireland Arbitration Committee which had been set up under Lord Colwyn to examine the Northern Ireland budget, recommended that the current procedure should be turned on its head. From then on the Imperial Contribution would cease to be a first charge on expenditure and would become a residual charge on what was left when necessary Irish expenditure had been met. It was also proposed that specific needs could be met by agreed subsidies paid directly into the Northern Ireland exchequer by the UK government. Such agreements began with the Unemployment Insurance Agreement of 1926.

Ensuring that Stormont could afford to pay the dole to the unemployed came not a moment too soon because the depression that began in 1929 hit Northern Ireland disproportionately hard. By 1931 the demands on expenditure in the province were such that nearly as much money was received under the Unemployment Insurance Agreement as was paid out in the Imperial Contribution. In 1932 the procedures put in place by the Colwyn Committee were scrapped and long and hard negotiations began in order to find a new formula. In 1936 the UK government conceded the principle of parity in the provision of public services between Great Britain and Northern Ireland under which any deficit in the Northern Ireland budget would be made good by the Treasury in order that services could be provided at the same level as applied in Great Britain. The principle was outlined in a speech by the chancellor, Sir John Simon, in which he agreed that the UK government would '. . . make good any deficit in such a way as to ensure that Northern Ireland should be in a financial situation to continue to enjoy the same social services and have the same standards as Britain'.[5] In 1942 the promise was repeated by the then Chancellor, Sir Kingsley Wood, who guaranteed, in the light of the impending Beveridge Report, that the UK government would make up any leeway in service provision for Northern Ireland. Over the years, and especially after the 1945 Labour government instituted the Welfare State, the list of services for which additional UK funding was required grew ever longer and came to include housing, schools, hospitals, national insurance, family allowances, pensions, regional employment, the health service and supplementary benefit.

The emphasis of the Northern Ireland budget shifted from being revenue-based to being expenditure-based. After 1946 the amount of money to be given to Northern Ireland was decided in talks between the British Treasury and the Stormont Minister of Finance. Unlike the money that was given to local government in Great Britain there were no block grants available to Stormont since the UK was determined that Northern Ireland should not have more money than it needed: parity meant 'not more than' just as much as it meant 'not less than'. All moneys were therefore given for specific purposes, which had the effect of depriving Stormont of the full powers that should belong to a parliament according to the theory of parliamentary sovereignty. Stormont was totally dependent on UK budgetary decisions over which it had no say, thereby depriving the people of Ulster of one of their democratic rights. It also meant that the Northern Ireland government could not make any plans for the long term because Stormont had no knowledge of the amount of tax revenue that would be made available in future budgets.

By the time Stormont was suspended in 1972 the fiscal situation had become one where 90 per cent of Northern Ireland expenditure was determined by Stormont while 15 per cent of its revenue was provided by Westminster. This meant that Belfast had no fiscal autonomy, given that only spending powers came within Stormont's competence, while taxing powers were retained in London.

Division of responsibilities

The division of responsibilities between London and Belfast and the question of how to determine the difference between devolved and reserved powers was complicated by the fact that the Northern Ireland settlement was drawn up before anyone suspected the extent of the social legislation that would be passed after 1945. A good example is to be seen in the funding and management of the National Health Service in the province. Health was one of the main areas where responsibilities were devolved to Stormont but where policy decisions were made at Westminster. National standards were laid down for the province in UK legislation but the Northern Ireland constitution demanded that identical legislation had to be passed by Stormont if it were to have effect. This duplication of legislation, which also applied in other areas, was the cause of a considerable waste of time and effort.

On the other hand there were great benefits to be gained from devolution in the fields of industry and agriculture. This showed itself particularly in two fields:

- The extent of government aid to industry in Northern Ireland was second to none and, as a result, a significant number of firms was induced to set up operations in Northern Ireland.
- In order to ensure that Northern Ireland agricultural produce could compete with the rest of Britain, despite the cost of shipping that produce across the Irish Sea, quality control agencies were set up that created a particularly high standard for anything produced in the province. Many years later, the legacy of that quality control proved to be justified when Northern Ireland was the one part of the UK said to be free of the BSE problem.

When the Royal Commission on the Constitution, created by the Wilson government in 1968, and led by Lord Kilbrandon, came to consider Northern Ireland they were very enthusiastic over the devolution of legislative, administrative and executive powers in fields such as those of industry and agriculture. The success of devolution according to the Kilbrandon Report was due to the easier access to central government provided by the proximity of decision-takers to the public. It was, thought Kilbrandon, a good argument in favour of regional devolution. It has to be said, however, that part of the benefit to the province came from Stormont's unique status at the time and there is no guarantee that Ulster's performance would have been the same if devolved assemblies for Scotland and Wales had also been in contention as competitors. Northern Irish MPs at Westminster were always fiercely opposed to any proposals that were put forward for Scottish and Welsh devolution; not wanting to see too many snouts in the trough.

A somewhat less pleasing aspect of the Stormont version of devolution became apparent now that the Northern Ireland government had taken over responsibility for services that were within the remit of local government in Great Britain. Important areas that were dealt with by Stormont included the police, fire service, housing and education. It was argued that local government in Northern Ireland was dominated by sectarianism and that services such as the distribution of housing or the appointment of teachers to schools could be affected by discrimination on sectarian grounds. It is possible that the situation might have been worse if these services had been in the hands of local councils but their control by Stormont did leave them open to abuse by the Protestant agenda of Stormont's Unionist government.

One thing that has to be remembered is that the Westminster Parliament did not spend much time in dealing with Northern Irish matters. Bogdanor quotes figures which show that, during the entire thirty-year period that Stormont was in existence between 1922 and 1972, Westminster devoted a mere *two hours a year* to discussion of Northern Ireland issues (Bogdanor, 1999, p. 79).

A Protestant parliament in a Protestant state

It was Sir James Craig as first prime minister of Northern Ireland who defined the nature of Stormont by stating that he wished to create a 'Protestant parliament in a Protestant state'. The partition of Ireland and the Stormont Parliament were the product of unionist intransigence in opposing home rule and it is only natural that the Unionist party should then dominate that parliament, and have the aim of maintaining that domination. Dominating Ulster and the future of the province was a Protestant triumvirate made up of the Unionist party, the Orange Order and what had been the Royal Irish Constabulary (RIC) but which became the Royal Ulster Constabulary (the RUC).

In 1922 the Protestant establishment used the excuse of threats from the Free State in the south to strengthen the means by which they controlled the province. In that year the Civil Authorities (Special Powers) Act gave widespread powers of detention and internment to the authorities: powers that were renewed annually but which became permanent in 1933. Under the provisions of the Act the RUC was formed as a force 3,000 strong, one third of which was supposed to be Catholic. But, although some Catholics transferred to the RUC from the RIC, the Catholic quota was never filled, dwindling from 21 per cent of the strength in 1921 to less than 8 per cent by the 1970s. Also founded in 1922 was the Ulster Special Constabulary, a paramilitary part-time police force in the mould of the infamous Black and Tans and largely recruited from the ranks of the Ulster Volunteer Force. Known as the B Specials they were notorious for their discriminatory use of violence in support of Protestantism.

In Northern Ireland every election, starting with the first in 1921, returned a Protestant majority and the institutions of the state ensured that the Catholic minority would neither gain power nor achieve parity of representation. The pluralist parliamentary system as exemplified by Westminster envisaged an alternation of parties in government but at Stormont there was never the prospect of anything other than a permanent Unionist party majority and Stormont as a result exhibited all the characteristics of a one-party state, with a variety of mechanisms in place to ensure the continuation of that one-party hegemony.

The 1920 Act established that voting in Northern Ireland should be by the single transferable vote (STV) form of proportional representation (PR) so as to ensure cross-community representation. However, in the 1921 local government elections, PR produced nationalist majorities in 21 local government districts in the counties of Fermanagh and Tyrone. In both these counties, where the Nationalists had gained control, the councils proceeded to vote that they should decline to recognise Stormont, declare their independence of Ulster and rejoin the Irish Free State. The Craig government thereupon replaced the errant councillors with commissioners who would run the councils until the next election could be held. For that election, and for all local elections after 1922, the STV voting system was abolished and simple majority voting reintroduced. The British government required the Lord Lieutenant to withhold his consent to this abolition and the bill remained unapproved for two months but the Craig government threatened to resign if the act were not approved and, faced with the prospect of having to take Ulster into direct rule with a constitutional crisis on their hands, the British government backed down and the bill received the Governor's assent.

The reintroduction of first-past-the-post (FPTP) voting led to gerrymandering of local authority ward boundaries on a massive scale so as to ensure Protestant majorities. The favoured situation was where the Catholic population was concentrated centrally in a fairly small geographical area like the Bogside district of Derry, surrounded by more diffuse Protestant areas. The electoral map would divide up the wards like slicing a cake, each slice biting into the Catholic area but with the largest part of the slice located in the Protestant outer sector. By devices such as this the unionists always gained a majority of council seats even in areas like Fermanagh, Tyrone and Derry City where Catholics formed a majority of the population. There was also the point that, although the franchise in all elections had been extended to the entire male adult population in Great Britain, in Northern Ireland only ratepayers could vote in local elections and then they had a vote for each property on which they paid rates. This was, of course, discriminatory since very few Catholics owned rather than rented any property and therefore not many Catholics were ratepayers.

In the 1925 election an anti-Unionist mixture of Nationalists and Sinn Fein won twelve seats as they had done in 1921 but the Unionists lost eight seats to a mixture of independent Unionists and candidates of the Northern Ireland Labour Party, which had been formed in 1924 as a non-sectarian alternative to the Unionists. In the face of this threat to the Protestant ascendancy Craig proposed the abolition of STV for Stormont elections as well as local elections and this was done in 1929. While there was PR the Protestant working class felt that they could safely vote Labour but the reintroduction of FPTP reawakened fears that a vote for anyone other than the Unionists would let in the Catholic Nationalists. And out of that fear of the Catholics the working-class Protestants remained loyal to Unionism, a loyalty that was reinforced by the large working-class membership of the Orange Lodges.

The abolition of PR effectively put the seal on the one-party state. Between 1926 and 1969 37.5 per cent of seats at Stormont returned a Unionist member unopposed simply because a Unionist victory in those seats was inevitable. 'Terence O'Neill, for example, entered Stormont in 1946 when he won an unopposed by-election and did not fight his first opponent until 1969' (Aughey and Morrow, 1996, p. 68). In the so-called 'union flag' election of 1949, held after the Republic of Ireland had been established and the Irish government had inaugurated an all-party anti-partition campaign, the Northern Ireland Labour Party was attacked in the north for its encroachment on the working-class Protestant vote: unemployed workers being told that, 'you might vote for Labour to get a job but it would mean rule by Dublin and the Pope'. Such a warning was virtually redundant since the FPTP voting system had effectively neutralised Northern Ireland Labour whose 29 per cent of votes in the 1938 election gained them a mere three seats at Stormont.

Northern Ireland politics were notoriously corrupt: the motto of Ulster being said to be, 'Vote early and vote often.' All parties kept a constant watch on the 'Death' columns in the local papers so as to get their hands on the dead voter's voting card. Every election saw a proportion of 'dead men voting' and there is a story, possibly apocryphal, which states that there are electoral areas where more people voted than actually lived there. And where corrupt practices did not have effect there was always intimidation. As John Cole, the former BBC correspondent and an Ulsterman himself, said of reporting in the province: 'One of the least reported aspects of the Ulster crisis was the conspiracy of fear ... When Gerry Adams defeated Gerry Fitt in West Belfast it was said that SDLP supporters feared IRA violence against them' (Cole, 1995, p. 135).

The end of Stormont – 1968–72

The Protestant ascendancy in Ireland before partition, and Northern Ireland thereafter, was maintained by an Anglo-Irish, Church of Ireland hierarchy, with a largely Presbyterian working-class rank and file organised within the lodges of the Orange Order. The working-class Catholic population of Northern Ireland remained permanently oppressed and dispossessed since the influence wielded by the Orange Order ensured that Protestants had preferential treatment in employment and housing. In the 1950s, however, the growing prosperity of what was known as 'the affluent society' touched the province and created an emergent middle class, both Protestant and Catholic, which had entirely different expectations from those of earlier generations.

The working-class Catholic community had grudgingly come to accept the status quo and to acknowledge that the general prosperity, living standards and welfare provision of the north was far better than what was offered in the Republic to the south. An IRA campaign in the late 1950s failed completely and there were those who believed that confrontation had had its day and the end of partition was in sight as extremism on both sides faded away. The growing Catholic middle classes, however, although optimistic, resented their exclusion from the political process, by which they essentially became second-class citizens. They were joined in their concern by a middle class within the Protestant community that was more liberal in its outlook than the hardline members of the Orange Order.

It was a liberal Unionist, Terence O'Neill, who replaced Lord Brookeborough as Prime Minister in 1963 and he began to make modest reforms, admittedly under some pressure from London. He met with opposition from hardline members of his own party, who regarded any concessions to the Catholic community as a betrayal, but he was also attacked from the opposing point of view by a movement campaigning for civil rights. Thanks to events unfolding in the United States, a great deal of international interest and involvement had been stirred up by Martin Luther King's campaign to gain civil rights for the black community. In the light of the international support given to the American civil rights movement the reaction of Northern Irish Catholics was to point out to the world that they suffered from discrimination every bit as badly as did the blacks of America.

The Northern Ireland Civil Rights Association (NICRA) was founded in County Derry in 1966 and immediately declared that their principal aim was to gain the elementary right of 'one man one vote' in local elections, extending the franchise to the whole adult population and getting rid of the business vote which meant that some people had the right to up to six votes! NICRA was essentially non-violent and moderate in its actions and parts of the membership were not happy with the campaign's peaceful nature, particularly after a march in Derry during 1968 had been broken up amid accusations of police over-reaction and brutality. One faction of the movement, led by students from Queen's University and a number of Young Socialists, broke away from NICRA and formed a group known as People's Democracy. This group drew up a list of six demands:

- one man, one vote;
- a fairer drawing of ward boundaries;
- houses distributed according to the needs of the people;
- jobs to be awarded on merit;
- free speech;
- abolition of the Special Powers Act.

Although the leaders of NICRA and founders of the Social Democratic and Labour Party (SDLP) like Gerry Fitt and John Hume were advocates of peaceful protest there were those who wanted direct action and did not mind if the protest became rather less than peaceful. This was especially true of the republican element in the movement.

There was a Protestant backlash against the protest movement, led from within the government by the Minister for Home Affairs, William Craig, who directed somewhat heavy-handed police action against the protesters. The Revd Ian Paisley also began to operate at this time as a militant Unionist, leading counter-demonstrations that often ended in violence. O'Neill granted a number of reforms in November 1968 that were well-received by NICRA but which antagonised members of his own party: Ian Paisley, for example, who founded the Protestant Unionist party, which would later become the Democratic Unionist Party (DUP) and William Craig who organised his supporters into the Vanguard Unionist Progressive party.[6] A fragmentation of the Unionists had begun that would result in the 1973 election being contested by no fewer than thirteen separate parties each of whom had the word 'unionist' contained in their title.

In February 1969 O'Neill called a general election which he duly won but with the Unionist vote seriously split: O'Neill's Official Unionists won 33 seats but 11 went to anti-O'Neill candidates. In April O'Neill was forced to resign and in the subsequent by-election his seat at Stormont was won by Ian Paisley. On the other side of the sectarian divide the success of the agitation for civil rights had the result of finally eclipsing the declining Nationalist party. A prominent leader of NICRA, John Hume, defeated the Nationalist leader Eddie McAteer. Hume and other independents elected in 1969 formed the Social and Democratic Labour party in the following year, the party rapidly becoming the party for those Catholic or Nationalist supporters who were seeking a peaceful settlement.

Events in Northern Ireland reached their climax in 1969, the flashpoint coming during the summer's marching season. Despite the government imposing a ban on political marches such as those organised by NICRA they permitted the traditional marches of the Orange Order to go ahead, stating that they were religious rather than political. But religion and politics are inseparable in Northern Ireland. In August came the Prentice Boys' March in Derry where the procession's traditional route lies along the city walls in full view of Catholic Bogside beyond the walls, in a provocative display of Protestant triumphalism. Serious rioting in the Bogside followed, suppressed rather more brutally than usual by the RUC. The rioting spread across the province and in Belfast a Protestant mob from the Shankill descended on the Catholic Clonard area, burning and wrecking homes in the process. The most serious aspect of the Belfast trouble was that the Protestant mob was spearheaded by off-duty B Specials.

In London the Wilson government was horrified and they put pressure on Prime Minister James Chichester-Clark to make him initiate a further round of reforms, including the disbandment of the B Specials and a return to proportional representation in local elections. In return for these reforms Chichester-Clark appealed for help in controlling the situation, asking for and getting the posting of British soldiers to Northern Ireland. As is well known, there is a certain irony in the fact that the army was initially received with open arms by Catholics who saw the army as their protection from the B Specials.

The army presence was exploited by both sides. The Northern Ireland government insisted that the army should play a key role in supporting the RUC in its operations but, since those operations were all taken against the Catholic community the army was soon perceived as being partisan, losing their original support and alienating the catholics. At the same time, the somewhat obsolescent Official IRA, in decline and becoming increasingly Marxist, spawned a new, active faction calling itself the Provisional IRA, known as 'the Provos', with a political wing in 'Provisional Sinn Fein'. The Provos now declared that since the army had failed, they themselves would act as defenders of the Catholic, nationalist community. In the months that followed the Provos were involved in a number of confrontations with the RUC and army, leading to an escalation of violence.

In February 1971 the first British soldier was killed by provisional IRA and Chichester-Clark demanded reinforcements. London was reluctant to be drawn into what was coming to seem like a war and, after a long dispute, Chichester-Clark resigned in March and was replaced by Brian Faulkner. Within months Faulkner invoked the existing emergency powers act to reintroduce internment without trial, an alienating measure sometimes referred to as 'the recruiting officer of the IRA' (Coxall and Robins, 1995, p. 433). Alienation set in when the army was called on to support the RUC in making arrests: most of those arrested proving to be innocent while many of the guilty escaped.

On 30 January 1972 (Bloody Sunday) paratroopers opened fire on a civil rights march in Derry, killing thirteen people in circumstances that are still in dispute. It was the final straw inasmuch as it showed that the divided responsibility for security between Stormont and London was not working. Stormont was thoroughly discredited and the British Prime Minister, Ted Heath, wanted to be rid of it. On 22 March 1972 Stormont was prorogued and within a week direct rule came into effect with the installation of William Whitelaw as Secretary of State for Northern Ireland.

The search for a political solution

In Northern Ireland the situation after 1972 was totally different from that obtaining in mainland Great Britain, partly because of the continuing state of emergency and terrorist activity and partly because the province was seeking to regain a devolution they had had and lost rather than gain devolution for the first time. The whole process was also complicated because the search for a political solution to the troubles of Northern Ireland was inextricably mixed up with the search for a military solution. Throughout all the negotiations that followed the suppression of Stormont, all sides claimed that they wanted peace for the province when in fact what each side wanted was not peace by negotiation but peace by victory for one side and surrender on the other.

That confusion between political and military solutions led to the great paradox in the Ulster situation: the only way to peace was through a political settlement but it was impossible to achieve a political settlement without first achieving a peaceful solution.

At the beginning the principal concern was to get rid of direct rule, which was an emergency measure forced upon the British government but which was unsatisfactory as a long-term solution. The problem with direct rule was that it was too similar to Britain's rule of dependent territories and could be misrepresented by the nationalist community as modern colonialism. As to what could replace direct rule, there were two possible alternatives: either the province could revert to a form of devolved government or it could be fully integrated with Great Britain, with a status like Wales or an English region.

The problem inherent in any proposals for integration was that the politics of Northern Ireland were not those of Great Britain. Even the political party system was different and state institutions like education, the law, railways, public utilities and the Civil Service of Northern Ireland were quite separate and incapable of integration. Integration had few supporters apart from a handful of unionists.

The only possible answer was therefore an agreed renewal of devolved government. But the two main stumbling blocks to this solution were that the nationalist community did not want any devolution that might restore rule by the unionist parties, while the loyalist community refused any form of power-sharing devolution which might permit the Dublin government some say in Northern Irish affairs (Cunningham, 1992, p. 30).

In 1973 the Northern Ireland Constitution Act represented an attempt to restore devolution promoted by William Whitelaw, the first Secretary of State for Northern Ireland. A 78-seat, multi-party assembly was elected by the STV system of proportional representation in June 1973 and a power-sharing executive composed of the Official Unionists, the Alliance Party and the SDLP took office on 1 January 1974. Allied to the new settlement were talks called by William Whitelaw at Sunningdale in Berkshire, in which representatives of the IRA took part and which proposed a Council of Ireland made up of seven representatives from Dublin and seven from Belfast.

The Sunningdale Agreement with its recognition of the role of Dublin in the government of Northern Ireland provoked opposition from the less moderate parties such as Ian Paisley's Democratic Unionist Party and such a storm of protest in Northern Ireland that eleven of the twelve MPs elected for Northern Ireland in the February 1974 general election were candidates opposed to the Sunningdale Agreement. The executive was undermined by this and, although members struggled on for a few months, it was finally brought down in May 1974 by a general strike called by the Protestant Ulster Workers' Council. Brian Faulkner resigned from the executive and as leader of the Unionists. The Northern Ireland Act of 1974 which followed dissolved the Assembly and reimposed direct rule.

In May 1975 Labour's Northern Ireland Secretary, Merlyn Rees, called a constitutional convention, but it was only a discussion group and in March

1976 it collapsed without achieving anything. The security situation was, however, getting better under the Callaghan government and there were hopes that the IRA was getting weary with the continuing struggle and would seek a peaceful solution. That changed in 1979, however, with the election of Margaret Thatcher, who promised to be more interventionist in her Northern Ireland policy. Constant confrontation created a resurgence of support for the IRA, particularly in 1981, after the death in the Maze prison of the IRA hunger striker, Bobby Sands, who had been elected to Westminster in a parliamentary by-election only a short time previously.

Margaret Thatcher's Northern Ireland Secretary, James Prior, began a process of what he called 'rolling devolution' in 1982. A Northern Ireland Assembly of 78 members was elected in October of that year with the promise that devolution would be granted according to any proposal put forward that had the support of 70 per cent of Assembly members. The process was hampered from the start by the refusal of Unionist parties to share power with the republicans. As a result it was boycotted by Sinn Fein and the SDLP, the latter party entering into talks with Dublin in the separate so-called New Ireland Forum. The unionist parties continued in the Assembly for nearly four years as a form of scrutinising committee looking at Northern Ireland legislation coming from London but a unionist boycott of the Assembly in 1985 led to the venture being abandoned in June 1986.

The agreement of 1985 between the London and Dublin governments, signed by Margaret Thatcher and Dr Garrett Fitzgerald and known as the Anglo-Irish or Hillsborough Agreement, was a major advance because Dublin openly recognised for the first time that there could only be change in Northern Ireland with the consent of the majority.[7] The agreement provided for regular meetings between British and Irish ministers and a permanent staff of British and Irish civil servants was based at Stormont to help negotiate agreement on cross-border disputes. The agreement was totally opposed by unionist parties who refused to allow that Dublin had any say in Northern Ireland, and ignored by Sinn Fein who claimed that the point about majority consent was irrelevant because a majority in Northern Ireland is a minority when the whole of Ireland is considered. Support was restricted to the political parties of Britain and the Republic of Ireland together with the SDLP.

A serious peace process began in the second half of 1994 with an IRA cease-fire, followed by similar announcements from the loyalist paramilitaries. However, the British government and unionist parties refused to take part in talks with parties such as Sinn Fein, as long as paramilitaries kept their weapons and could threaten to restart the violence if talks failed. Sinn Fein, for the IRA, stated that they were willing to enter talks as equal partners, but to give up their weapons would be like admitting defeat. They would do nothing that might suggest surrender. In late November 1995, only days before President Clinton was due to arrive in Northern Ireland on a peacemaking visit, a deal was fixed. A twin-track approach would be adopted by which the arms issue should be separated from the question of talks. Negotiations for talks would continue on one track while the arms question would be examined separately by an international and independent commission under a former US Senator, George Mitchell.

The IRA ceasefire ended in February 1996 with a bomb set off at Canary Wharf in London, Sinn Fein blaming the British government for bad faith and delaying tactics. Other bombs followed in Germany and Manchester and it began to look as though the peace process was irremediably breaking down. During the Protestant marching season in the summer of 1996 there were confrontations and renewed violence between the two communities.

Soon after his election in 1997, Tony Blair, with his Northern Ireland Secretary, Mo Mowlam, made serious efforts to get the peace process back on track, taking a middle track that ran the risk of offending both extremes. For a time during the 1997 marching season it looked as though the whole process could break down yet again in communal violence. On 15 July the entire province was horrified when 'loyalist' gunmen dragged Catholic Bernadette Martin from her Protestant boyfriend's home and shot her dead. Three days later Gerry Adams and Martin McGuinness for Sinn Fein urged the IRA to call a ceasefire and, on 19 July, that ceasefire was restored. In September, the government accepted that the IRA ceasefire had lasted long enough for Sinn Fein to be admitted to the peace talks, as a result of which Sinn Fein agreed to the Mitchell Principles, foreswore violence and accepted that weapons would have to be surrendered at some future date.

On Good Friday 1998 the renewed peace talks bore fruit when agreement was reached that there was to be an elected Northern Ireland Assembly of 108 members, elected by STV in six-member constituencies; the legislative powers of the Assembly being weighted to prevent domination by unionists. An Executive or 'cabinet' of 12 members was to be appointed, including first minister, deputy first minister and ministers for finance, health, education, agriculture etc. The Assembly was also to set up and supervise a North–South body to deal with cross-border issues. Efforts were to be made to settle outstanding issues such as the decommissioning of arms and the accelerated release of paramilitary prisoners.

Notes

1   This is quoted in Bogdanor (page 66) but was originally said in H. H. Asquith, *Memories and Reflections 1852–1927*, Cassell, 1928.
2   Information on the structure and function of the Stormont parliament is provided in a doctoral thesis on *The Senate in Northern Ireland 1921–62*, written by a student called McGill.
3   The 13 became 12 in 1948 when university seats were abolished, including that of Queen's University, Belfast. When Stormont was suppressed in 1972 and direct rule was introduced, the number of Northern Ireland MPs once more became 17.

4 Craigavon made this statement in 1933 when he was responding to a declaration by de Valera that 'Ireland is a Catholic state'.
5 A statement made to the House of Commons, 12 May 1938.
6 The Vanguard party was fairly short-lived and ceased to exist after 1976 but of course the DUP went on to achieve and still maintain a prominent position in the province.
7 The recognition of the North's right to self-determination was in direct contradiction of the Republic's written constitution which committed the Irish government to the abolition of partition.

Part III

The devolution settlement

6

Scotland –
success of a sort

In June 1996, eleven months before he won the general election, Tony Blair acknowledged the difficulties he would face in steering such a complex piece of legislation as devolution for Scotland through parliament and laid down certain guide rules in advance. Despite critics from his own and other parties, who said that there was no need for there to be a referendum when the commitment to devolution was so clearly written into the party manifesto, Blair announced that there would indeed be a referendum. The need to gain public approval for his actions was, he said, a necessary by-product of returning the government of Scotland to the Scottish people themselves. He went even further: conscious of the problems posed by the 1979 referendum and determined that mistakes made then should not be repeated on this occasion, Blair detailed three ways in which this referendum would differ from the first:

- The referendum would take place before legislation was placed before parliament and not afterwards as was previously the case.
- No minimum level of support was required. Instead of a threshold of 40 per cent, as in 1979, a simple majority of those voting would suffice to decide the outcome.
- Two questions would be asked in the referendum: '*I agree that there should be a Scottish Parliament*' and '*I agree that a Scottish Parliament should have tax-varying powers*'.

Unlike all those previous prime ministers who had introduced home rule or devolution measures, from Gladstone onwards, Tony Blair was not under either of the pressures to which his predecessors had been subjected. With an overall majority of 177, Labour: (a) did not need to feel threatened by the possibility of a surge in nationalist popularity undermining that majority, (b) did not require any voting deal with other parties in the Commons to ensure the passage of government legislation, as had been the case when nationalist support had sustained the minority Callaghan government in 1979.

Given the strength of Labour's position the government moved remarkably quickly once the Blair administration took power on 2 May 1997. Before the end of July a White Paper, *Scotland's Parliament*, had been published, setting out the proposed legislation. At the same time the Referendums (Scotland and Wales) Act passed successfully through both Houses of Parliament and received the Royal Assent. The Scottish referendum itself took place on Thursday 11 September, with two questions on two separate papers, as decided earlier.

The campaign to get agreement to both questions was known as the 'Yes-yes' campaign and was very strong, especially when the SNP joined in along-side Labour and the Liberal Democrats. Some concern was expressed that the government had substantially funded the 'Yes-yes' campaign while the opposition had had to rely on its own resources. It was felt that opposition groups had indeed been disadvantaged by this and legislation has since been passed to ensure that public funds will be provided to both sides in any future referendum.

The only hope of the 'Just say no' campaign lay with the fact that opinion polls showed that less than half the Scottish people were in favour of the parliament being granted tax-raising powers. The Conservatives, who were virtually alone in the 'Just say no' campaign, tried to exploit people's fears with talk of the parliament's proposed 'tartan tax', but their efforts failed. The public were rather less keen on the tax-varying powers than they were on the simple issue of the parliament but there was still a 2:1 vote in favour of tax-varying. The percentage vote was 44.7 per cent of the Scottish electorate in favour of the parliament and 38.1 per cent in favour of tax-varying powers. This means, of course, that had the 40 per cent threshold been applied, as it was in 1979, there would still have been a vote in favour of the parliament but the question of tax-ation would have been lost. A closer look, however, will show that in the whole of Scotland only two local authority areas voted against the tax-varying powers, Orkney was one and Dumfries and Galloway the other.[1]

Turnout in Scotland as a whole was 60.4 per cent, as against 62.9 per cent in 1979. Of those who voted, 74.3 per cent said 'Yes' to the basic question, while 60.2 per cent approved of the tax-varying powers. The result was satis-factory enough for Tony Blair to proclaim on the 13th: 'Well done. This is a good day for Scotland, and a good day for Britain and the United Kingdom . . . the era of big, centralised government is over!' (quoted in Evans, 1999, p. 68).

The Scotland Act 1998

The Scotland Bill to set up the Parliament and Scottish executive was intro-duced to the Westminster parliament on 18 December 1997, at the very start of the 1997–98 session, and had its second reading on 13 January 1998. It had a relatively easy passage through the Commons with most clauses getting through the committee stage unaltered. This was probably because it was judged that the referendum decision had given public approval to the measures involved without needing to concern the electorate's representatives. The Lords, with their unionist sympathies, might have treated the bill more severely but for the Salisbury Convention, which precludes the Lords from querying a bill passed by the Commons if the measure in question was mandated by the public by inclusion in the party manifesto – all the more so when the bill had been approved by the electorate in a referendum. The Act received the Royal Assent in November 1998 with elections to the new parliament scheduled for May 1999.

Provisions of the Scotland Act relating to the parliament's composition and powers:[2]

The Parliament will have 129 Members, 73 from constituencies elected on the first past the post system and 56 additional members selected on a proportional basis from party lists drawn up for each of the current 8 European Parliament constituencies. Each elector will be able to cast two votes: one for a constituency MSP (Member of the Scottish Parliament) and one for the party of their choice. The Parliament will be kept in order by a Presiding Officer who will be an MSP and will be elected by the Parliament.

The 73 constituencies for which MSPs were elected consisted of the 72 Westminster constituencies but with the Westminster constituency of the Orkneys having Shetland separated from Orkney so as to provide an extra constituency.

'The Scottish Parliament will be able to make primary legislation (Acts of the Scottish Parliament). Its legislative competence will be limited in a number of ways. It will not be able to legislate about reserved matters. At Schedule 5 the Act specifies all matters which are to be reserved.' The main **reservations** are:

- the Constitution
- Defence
- Finance and the Economy
- Trade and Industry
- Transport not particular to Scotland (e.g. railways)
- Social security
- Medical ethics – abortion, genetics, surrogacy, medicines, misuse of drugs
- Broadcasting
- Foreign affairs
- the Civil Service
- National Security, immigration, nationality
- Electricity, coal, oil, gas, nuclear energy
- Employment
- Equal opportunities

Apart from these, the main **devolved matters** are:

- Health
- Local government
- Housing
- Planning, economic development, financial assistance to industry
- Transport within Scotland (roads, buses, ports and harbours)
- Criminal justice and prosecution system, the Courts
- Police and Fire Service
- Agriculture, food, forestry and fisheries
- Sport
- Statistics, public registers and records
- Education, training and lifelong learning
- Social work
- Tourism
- Environment, natural and built heritage
- the Arts

'The Westminster Parliament will continue to be the sovereign parliament of the United Kingdom and it will retain the power to legislate about any matter, including devolved matters, in Scotland. We expect a convention to be established that, because the Scotland Act will have given specific powers to the Scottish Parliament, the Westminster Parliament will not normally legislate with regard to devolved matters in Scotland without the consent of the Scottish Parliament.' It should be noted that it is only the reserved powers that are positively identified, the devolved matters being defined negatively as those areas that are not reserved. The list given above is indicative rather than prescriptive.

As to the powers and composition of the Scottish Executive, the provisions were:

'The Scottish Executive (whose members are collectively referred to as 'the Scottish Ministers") will be the Government in Scotland for all devolved matters. The members of the Scottish Executive will be:

- the First Minister;
- the Lord Advocate and the Solicitor General for Scotland (the Law Officers);
- other Ministers appointed by the First Minister.

The First Minister will also be able to appoint junior ministers (who will not be members of the Executive) to assist the Scottish Ministers. It is expected that a Secretary of State for Scotland will continue to be appointed as a member of the UK Government after devolution, although that will be a matter for the Prime Minister. The Secretary of State will not be a member of the Scottish Executive.'

The First Minister and law officers all had specific duties assigned to them under the Act, the First Minister playing a prime ministerial role in the appointment of ministers while the Lord Advocate acts as senior law officer within the Scottish executive: the duties of these are known as 'retained functions'. But all the other ministers, once appointed, could be asked to fulfil any one of a variety of governmental functions at the discretion of the First Minister, just as UK ministers are appointed to departmental responsibilities by the prime minister.

Although there is a broad area where the ability to legislate is reserved to the Westminster parliament there is also the possibility of the executive devolution of many functions previously exercised by the Secretary of State for Scotland. An example of this would be, if the appointment of public officials based in Scotland were the responsibility of a UK minister, the UK minister may well consult Scottish ministers as to which appointee would best serve Scottish interests. An example of this could well be the appointment of someone to represent Scotland on the BBC Board of Governors.

The financial provisions of the Act are particularly important, given the nature of the second question in the referendum. The Act states very clearly: 'the Parliament's assigned budget (sometimes referred to as the 'block grant") will be determined, in much the same way as the Scottish Block is at present, using the so-called Barnett formula. In addition the Parliament will have the power to vary upwards or downwards the basic rate of income tax applicable in Scotland by up to three pence in the pound, with proceeds adding to or reducing, the Parliament's spending power.' The possibility of the Scottish parliament having a financial role does not end with its tax-varying powers since the way in which the parliament will control local government in Scotland gives parliament the further fiscal powers of being able to adjust the size of the Council Tax and fix the business rate.

The Parliament is elected for a fixed term of four years. It can only be dissolved earlier than that, and an extraordinary general election called, under two circumstances:

- if two-thirds of the Parliament vote that the Presiding Officer should ask the Queen to dissolve parliament;
- if the Parliament fails to elect a First Minister within 28 days of the election.

Both devices were introduced to prevent the First Minister and the majority party from exploiting the election date for electoral advantage, as is so often done by the prime minister in the UK. There is an additional safeguard in the rule that, if the Parliament is dissolved before it has completed three and a half years, any new Parliament that takes its place will be suspended four years after the election of its predecessor, even if that means that the new parliament has a life of no more than six months.

A Presiding Officer is elected to chair the proceedings of Parliament in much the same way as the Speaker acts at Westminster, although the Scottish post is rather more than simply that. The Presiding Officer has powers similar to the Speaker in the Swedish Parliament, with certain monarchical functions and a key role in the direct relationship between Parliament and monarch. When a bill has passed through Parliament the Presiding Officer must check very care-fully that the bill is not *ultra vires* by being outside the remit of the Parliament, having four weeks to carry out those checks by consulting the Scottish law offi-cers or sending the bill to the Judicial Committee of the Privy Council. At the end of those four weeks the Presiding Officer will pass on the bill for royal assent directly.

The role of the Secretary of State and the Civil Service in a devolved Scotland

There is of course a sense in which devolution has made the Secretary of State for Scotland redundant. The Scottish Office has been dispersed and its staff of 12,000 civil servants transferred to the Scottish parliament, the remaining government department changing its name from the 'Scottish Office' to the 'Scotland Office'. The Scottish Secretary is left with three special advisers and 140 civil servants to handle three areas where the Secretary still has a role:

1 There are some policy areas which affect Scotland and the rest of Great Britain in equal measure such as rail and air links, employment legislation and oil and gas extraction: control of these is retained by the Scottish Secretary.
2 There are certain reserved powers that the Secretary of State for Scotland must defend. The Secretary can issue an order to prohibit the presiding officer from submitting a Scottish bill for royal assent if the bill is incompat-ible with Britain's international, defence or security obligations. The hypoth-esis has been postulated that a Scottish Parliament and executive might be elected on a manifesto promise of unilateral nuclear disarmament but they would still be barred from taking any action against a nuclear submarine base in Scotland.
3 The Scottish Secretary can simply represent Scotland in cabinet. There is doubt, however, as to the extent to which the Secretary of State for Scotland can remain a cabinet position under these reduced circumstances. The posi-tion may become a non-cabinet ministerial position or a secretary of state could be appointed to look after all devolved administrations (Deacon, Griffith and Lynch, 2000, p. 43).

The civil servants providing the administration for the Scottish parliament are known as the Scottish Parliamentary Corporate Body (SPCB), which is part of the Civil Service although it has the power to appoint staff, hold property and enter into contracts in its own right. It is written into the Scotland Act that the Scottish Civil Service will be part of the Home Civil Service as 'all staff of the Scottish Administration should be regarded as civil servants in the UK Home Civil Service since . . . maintaining a unified Civil Service is considered essential for preserving the unity of the UK' (Pilkington, 1999a, p. 153).

Any Scottish legislation can be challenged in the courts but a question mark was raised as to where the final responsibility for any appeal would lie. If the UK were a federal state and had a written constitution there would be a supreme court to rule on matters in dispute between administrations. The House of Lords is supreme court for the UK as a whole but:

- the House of Lords has only a marginal role in the separate Scottish legal system;
- the House of Lords is part of the UK Parliament and would find it difficult to sustain a neutral position if there was conflict between the UK and Scottish legislatures.

The role of the constitutional court for Scotland is taken by the Judicial Committee of the Privy Council which already acts as a supreme court and court of appeal for a number of British dependencies, Crown territories and some Commonwealth countries.

The nature of the Scottish Parliament, executive and administration was therefore in place and legally defined by November 1998. In January 1998 the Consultative Steering Group had been set up under the Devolution minister in the Scottish Office, Henry McLeish, to decide how the parliament was going to work. The group published its report *Shaping Scotland's Parliament* in January 1999 and laid down the four principles which it believed should characterise the devolved parliament and administration:

- Power should be shared between the people of Scotland, the legislators (members of the Scottish Parliament) and the Scottish executive.
- The executive should be accountable to the Parliament and both Parliament and the executive should be accountable to the people of Scotland.
- The Parliament should be accessible, open and responsive, with procedures that permit participation in the consideration and scrutiny of policy and legislation.
- The Parliament should operate and make appointments in accordance with the principle of equal opportunities for all (Henderson and Sloat, 2000, pp. 321–2).

With the structure and constitution in place it only remained to elect those members of the Scottish Parliament (MSPs) who would make the whole thing work.

The elections of 6 May 1999

The elections for the Scottish Parliament held on 6 May 1999 differed in one important respect from the devolution proposed and rejected in 1979: on this occasion the elections were going to be held with some attention paid to proportionality. The devolution settlement had been worked out before Labour's 1997 victory by the Constitutional Convention and the role played by Liberal

Democrats in that convention, working alongside Labour, ensured that proportional representation (PR) was very strongly advocated.

Labour recognised that they would probably need the Liberal Democrats to resist the growing popularity of the Scottish National party and proportional representation was the price that Labour must be prepared to pay for Lib Dem support. Many Labour politicians disliked PR and would have liked to have stuck with the FPTP system that had given Labour its landslide victory in 1997. However, even supporters of FPTP knew that it could give a majority of seats on a minority vote and the possibility did exist that with FPTP the SNP could become the largest party in Scotland with a mere 35 per cent of the vote. What Labour feared was that the SNP might claim a mandate for Scottish independence when only a third of the electorate had voted for them. PR would mean that the SNP would have to obtain more than 50 per cent of the vote to be able to claim the mandate.

It was decided therefore that proportionality should play its part in the Scottish elections. But proportionality would not take the form of the single transferable vote (STV) that had been the preferred system of the Liberals since before the First World War and which has been used in Ireland, north and south, since 1920. The main argument advanced by Labour in rejecting STV was that the system required very large multi-member constituencies in which constituents cannot easily identify their elected member. Labour claimed that they valued the worth of constituency links for elected members and wished to retain it. Also influencing their decision was the fact that, with its multi-member constituencies, STV encourages voters to choose between members of the same party for the seats available and this would encourage splits and factions in the party such as left and right, Old Labour and New Labour and so on.

The result was an additional member system (AMS) roughly similar to that adopted in Germany. Under this system electors' votes count twice, the first time being for a named candidate in a regular constituency, voted for under the familiar FPTP system and the second being for the party and leading to additional members allocated by region from party lists. In Scotland this was translated into 73 constituency MSPs elected by FPTP in the existing Westminster constituencies, although the single constituency of Orkney was sub-divided into the two Holyrood constituencies of Orkney and Shetland. The 73 MSPs thus elected were topped up on a proportional basis by 56 party list candidates, seven chosen for each of the eight Euro-constituencies in Scotland, allocated by means of a formula known as the d'Hondt method.[3] It has to be said that this version of AMS is nowhere near fully proportional. Unlike the situation in Germany where the ratio between constituency and additional members is 50:50 and close to fully proportional, the ratio in Scotland is 57:43. This is more proportional than the 66:33 ratio adopted in Wales but it is further from the ideal than the German model.

The result of the election, as was to be expected of a proportional or near-proportional system, was that no party had an overall majority:

Party	Constituency seats	Regional seats	Total seats
Labour	53	3	56
SNP	7	28	35
Conservative	0	18	18
Liberal Democrat	12	5	17
Others	1	2	3

The problem with the electoral system chosen was that it risked creating a two-tier status for MSPs, with the list members seen as second-class representatives. The party lists from which the additional members were chosen were closed lists. This meant that the list of candidates was drawn up by the party machine and could not then be changed. Since members were judged elected according to the order in which they appeared on the list and the party determined that order, this meant that voters were deprived of any say in the choice of candidates: power being given to the party machine rather than the elector.

The use of a proportional system had important outcomes for the four main parties in the Scottish Parliament when the results of the 1999 Scottish elections under AMS are compared with the 1997 Westminster results using FPTP:

- Compared with the six MPs they had at Westminster and the seven MSPs elected for the constituencies, the SNP acquired a total of 35 MSPs, becoming the second largest party and the official opposition at Holyrood.
- Labour won a total of 56 MSPs, just as there are 56 Scottish Labour MPs at Westminster. They did so well by FPTP that only three regional seats were needed to top up their representation. As was expected, Labour failed to win an overall majority of the 129 seats.
- The Liberal Democrats were the second largest party under FPTP, winning 12 constituencies as against the 10 Scottish seats that they held at Westminster. However, those 12 seats were won with 14 per cent of the vote and only 5 regional seats were allocated to them, making a total of 17, or less than half the seats won by the SNP. Nevertheless, the coalition politics dictated by proportional representation mean that the Liberal Democrats have a share in power through association with Labour.
- The Conservatives won no constituencies, just as they had no Westminster MPs. The seats awarded them under the regional list system mean that they returned to Scottish politics with 18 MSPs, one more than the Liberal Democrats. This opens up another aspect of the two-tier status of MSPs since there will be a distinct difference in workload between the 56 Labour MSPs, 53 of whom have constituencies to look after, and the 18 Conservative MSPs, not one of whom has any.
- The 'others' who were elected included Tommy Sheriden, a former leader of Scottish Militant who was elected on the regional list for Glasgow as a member of the Scottish Socialist party. The Green party also won a regional vote in the Lothians, electing Robin Harper. The most notable victory,

however, was that of Dennis Canavan, a rebel Labour member who was not chosen as official Labour candidate for the Falkirk West constituency but who stood as an independent anyway, gaining 55 per cent of the vote and pushing Labour into a rather poor second place with 19 per cent. Even on the regional list Canavan, as an Independent, gained more votes than the Liberal Democrats and only just came behind the Conservatives.

Putting the structures in place

Negotiations between Donald Dewar, as leader of the Labour party in Scotland, and Jim Wallace, his Liberal Democrat opposite number, began as soon as the election results were known, although the fact that a coalition executive would be needed in Scotland had been recognised for some time. The Prime Minister, Tony Blair, in commenting on the Scottish election results, had acknowledged that the system of proportional representation was always likely to deny any party an overall majority but went on to say 'I have got no doubt at all that we will form a good, strong and stable government in Scotland.'[4]

The key issue in the negotiations between Dewar and Wallace concerned students' tuition fees, which had been imposed on all British students by the UK government but which the Lib Dems and others wanted to see abolished in Scotland. The Lib Dems made it clear that they would not settle for anything other than abolition, while Labour was unwilling to make the first act of a Scottish parliament the reversal of a policy introduced by a Labour government in London. The deadlock was broken by the setting up of a Scottish Committee of Inquiry into Student Finance to examine the matter. The prospect of a proper inquiry into the problem, together with a promise of PR in Scottish local government elections, was enough to satisfy the Lib Dems and to allow a deal to be struck between the two parties.

Wednesday 12 May 1999 saw the first meeting of a Scottish Parliament in 292 years. Its first task was to choose a Presiding Officer whose principal role would be to regulate proceedings and act as Speaker. On that first day David (Lord) Steel, former leader of the Liberal party, was chosen as the first Presiding Officer.

On Thursday 13 May the parliament elected its First Minister, the post in effect being that of a prime minister for Scotland. Unlike the UK system where a general election produces a clear majority party in the House of Commons, and where the leader of that party then becomes prime minister, the set-up in Scotland called for a different solution. A leadership election was held in which there were four candidates: Donald Dewar as Labour leader, Alex Salmond as SNP leader, David McLetchie, newly-chosen Tory leader in Scotland, and Dennis Canavan the independent. All 35 SNP MSPs voted for Salmond, 18 Conservatives voted for McLetchie, Canavan picked up 3 votes but 71 Labour and Lib Dem members voted together for Donald Dewar and he was duly declared to be first minister.

On Friday 14 May *A Partnership for Scotland*, under the joint signatures of Donald Dewar and Jim Wallace, laid out the details of the agreement between Labour and the Liberal Democrats to set up a joint administration. Dewar could then begin the process of forming the cabinet and team of ministers that would form the Scottish Executive.

The Scottish Executive consists of a cabinet with eleven members and a team of eleven junior ministers; the Liberal Democrats having two cabinet ministers and two junior ministers as part of the coalition agreement. That agreement was confirmed by Donald Dewar appointing Jim Wallace, the Lib Dem leader, to be deputy first minister. Wallace also acted as the justice minister, covering the same range of responsibilities in Scotland as was administered in the UK by the Home Secretary. Wallace had a junior minister, Angus Mackay, drawn from the Labour ranks to be deputy minister, with a special responsibility for land reform and drugs policy. Tom McCabe who became Minister for Parliament in the cabinet, a position rather like the leader of the house in the UK Parliament, also acted as Labour Whip, while his deputy, as junior minister, was Iain Smith, the Lib Dem Whip.

The ministers appointed were a mixture of the old and experienced together with the young and enterprising advocates of what has become known as the 'new politics'. Two important members of the cabinet, Henry McLeish and Sam Galbraith, had established a solid political reputation since they were formerly senior ministers within the Scottish Office. The law officers also had to be experienced politicians: Lord Hardie, who became Lord Advocate, had a cabinet seat as the senior law officer, while Colin Boyd became Solicitor General, acting as deputy to the Lord Advocate but responsible for prosecutions under Scottish criminal law. Some 30 per cent of MSPs were in their late forties or early fifties and had spent something like 25 years each in Scottish politics. However, Labour MSPs were rather less experienced than members of other parties: only 34 per cent of Labour MSPs were involved in local politics, while a mere 9 per cent had previously fought a Westminster election.

The inexperience of so many Labour MSPs mean that other ministers were not quite as representative of the old school of politics. For example, three cabinet ministers were women – Wendy Alexander, Sarah Boyack and Susan Deacon. Of the men a significant number were under forty years of age, a fact that indicates the number of young candidates who were elected to Holyrood. Of the first bunch of MSPs no fewer than 20 were less than 35 years old and 8 were in their twenties (Henderson and Sloat, 1999, p. 245). These facts were evidence of a trend that later become clearer, which is that the preferred career route for Scottish politicians is now seen as being through Holyrood rather than Westminster.

The responsibilities of cabinet ministers mirrored the changes that had been made to the government departments that had been transferred from the Scottish Office to the Scotland Office, subordinate to the Scottish Parliament. The Scottish Office had had five ministerial departments – education and industry,

agriculture and fisheries, health, home affairs and development and central services. The list was expanded, partly by dividing existing departments and partly
by creating new ones, to create a total of nine departments, although it must be
remembered that not all cabinet ministers were given a departmental portfolio:

- Justice
- Rural affairs
- Education
- Finance
- Health
- Development
- Enterprise and lifelong learning
- Corporate services
- Executive secretariat.

As well as these government departments, the Scottish executive also assumed
responsibility for a number of quangos and agencies such as Historic Scotland
and the Scottish Prison Service.

Changes to the executive

In mid-October 2000 the Scottish Parliament, the Labour party and indeed the
whole of Scotland were devastated by the death from a brain haemorrhage of
Donald Dewar, the man who had led Labour's devolution campaign for so many
years and the man who had done so much to establish the devolved parliament
as Scotland's initial First Minister. There was an immediate problem for the
Labour party in replacing Dewar, since he had been both leader of the Labour
party in Scotland and Scottish First Minister. As the largest party in the
Parliament and with support from its Lib Dem coalition allies, Labour would
expect the party leader to be chosen as First Minister. But the procedures and
complex electoral college created by the Labour party for electing its party
leader needed weeks to organise and the position laid down in the Scotland Act
was that a new First Minister had to be elected within 28 days of the death,
retirement or resignation of his predecessor.

The solution was to hold an emergency meeting of a Labour party electoral
college in Stirling on 21 October 2000 at which a temporary party leader was
elected in the person of Henry McLeish, who received 44 votes against 36 for
Jack McConnell. The constitutional position in the party required a formal
endorsement of McLeish's leadership from a meeting of the full electoral college
later in the year but it was unlikely that McConnell would stand again. His
standing had been no more than a token protest against a London nominee
getting the leader's position unopposed. It is interesting to note that, after
having been defeated so narrowly, McConnell became the obvious choice for
First Minister when McLeish resigned in November 2001. Having made their

protest the Labour MSPs were quite happy to vote for McLeish in the election for First Minister held on 26 October. In that election McLeish got more than twice as many votes as his nearest challenger, thanks to Lib Dem support:

Henry McLeish – Labour–Lib Dem coalition	68 votes
John Swinney – new SNP leader	33 votes
David McLetchie – Conservative	19 votes
Dennis Canavan – Independent	3 votes

It was seen as a watershed in the life of the Scottish Parliament. Shortly before Donald Dewar's death Alex Salmond had chosen to stand down as leader of the SNP and a moderate gradualist, John Swinney, had been elected leader in his place. Neither McLeish nor Swinney had the standing in Scotland of Dewar and Salmond but at least the former two were figures who had risen to prominence in the Holyrood Parliament, whereas the latter two had made their reputations at Westminster. Holyrood came of age with the new appointments.

Three days after he had been elected as First Minister, McLeish appointed his new cabinet. It was largely unaltered but, although few, some of the changes made were important. The Lord Advocate was Colin Boyd but he no longer counted as a cabinet member since he had no vote and merely attended as an adviser on legal matters. The unsuccessful leadership contender, Jack McConnell took over education from Sam Galbraith and added external affairs and relations with Europe, including the negotiations over regional funds that he had conducted as finance minister. Finance and a responsibility for local government went to Angus Mackay who had previously been a junior justice minister. Galbraith took over responsibility for the environment after the portfolio was split from transport. Wendy Alexander took over the enterprise and lifelong learning portfolio that had belonged to McLeish while her previous position as minister for communities was renamed as the minister for social justice and given to Wendy Alexander's previous deputy, Jackie Baillie. There were still four Liberal Democrats on the executive but Iain Smith lost the confidence of backbenchers and was replaced as deputy parliament minister by Tavish Scott.[5]

Legislation and policy-making

Even before the Queen opened the Parliament on 1 July 1999 the Scottish executive announced a very modest legislative programme of just eight bills. This was criticised as being too thin a programme and a revised programme was issued in September.[6]

The Scottish Parliament is involved in three different forms of legislation:

1 **Primary legislation**   Of the devolved bodies being considered in this book, the Scottish Parliament is the only body apart from Westminster to have the power to pass primary legislation. As is the case at Westminster the proposed legislation is debated at length both in committee and the parliament chamber. At the end of the process legislation is examined to ensure that it lies within the powers of the Parliament before it passes into law.

2 **Secondary legislation**   This concerns all the subordinate legislation that might well arise as a result of primary legislation passed either in Westminster or Holyrood. Most importantly it legitimises those statutory instruments issued by the Scottish executive.

3 **European legislation**   Community law takes the form of regulations and directives which are issued by the European Commission but which are scrutinised and implemented in each member country by the legislature of that country. In the UK prior to 1999 scrutiny of European legal instruments was carried out at Westminster but, after devolution, any European matter bearing upon Scotland must be scrutinised in Scotland. The Scottish Parliament has set up a European committee to carry out this task although its findings will be passed on to London since any response to Brussels must be made by the UK government. The Scottish executive has set up a Scottish Centre in Brussels to handle relations with the EU, while the Scottish Parliament is represented on the EU's Committee of the Regions which has an important role to play in EU legislation (Pilkington, 2001, pp. 71–2).

Scottish primary legislation is usually proposed by the executive although the mechanism does exist for private members' bills to be considered. The progress of a bill passing through the Parliament is very slow because the principles laid down by the Consultative Steering Group mean that the greatest possible opportunity is given for the participation of public and pressure groups in the process. Not only is there prolonged consultation in the form of pre-legislative scrutiny but the legislation itself is submitted to scrutiny by the whole Parliament in plenary session, by committee, and by the law officers who check the legal validity of the legislation, ensuring that it is *intra vires*.

The legislative process

1 A proposal is announced by the executive who may well issue a White Paper or other consultative document.

2 Pre-legislative consultation involves MSPs through committees, the public and pressure groups. The bill is drafted and the outcome of the consultation published.

3 The draft bill is scrutinised by the Presiding Officer and the Subordinate Legislation committee for its suitability for submission to Parliament.

4 The bill is introduced into Parliament together with a written memorandum from the executive setting out the main details of the proposed legislation.

5 The principle of the bill is debated in committee.
6 The measure is debated in a plenary session of the full Parliament and a vote is taken.
7 The details of the bill are discussed in committee in a process similar to the Westminster Committee stage, amendments are made and a final report on the measure written.
8 A final plenary session of the full Parliament debates the report stage of the bill.
9 There is a four-week period in which the measure is examined by the law officers to ensure that the legislation lies within the competence of the Scottish Parliament. The Secretary of State for Scotland also has the right to veto any legislation infringing the UK government's reserved powers or if it is incompatible with Britain's defence or foreign policy.
10 Having passed all these stages the bill is presented to the monarch by the Presiding Officer for royal assent.

Each MSP is allowed to introduce two private member's bills during the term of a parliament. For this purpose the MSP must secure the support of 10 per cent of MSPs for the proposal to be accepted; after which it goes through the same legislative process as an executive bill. Originally very few members chose to promote legislation but as the Parliament settled down into a routine, more and more MSPs chose to do so. By the end of the first year in July 2000, over fifteen such bills had been proposed, most notably the Protection of Wild Mammals Bill, co-sponsored by a Labour MSP, Mike Watson, and SNP member, Tricia Marwick, and intended to ban fox-hunting in Scotland. Even more significant was the success of Tommy Sheriden, sole representative of the Scottish Socialist party, who succeeded in promoting a bill to forbid the forced sale of debtors' property.

Legislation can also be initiated by committees. To do this the committee would submit a proposal to a plenary session of the Parliament. It may well be that the executive would approve the measure and take it over as an executive bill. If the Parliament liked the idea of the bill but it was not adopted by the executive the committee concerned could then draw up a draft bill; after which it would follow the same legislative route from point two onward. In the first eighteen months of the Parliament's life, however, no committee had felt it necessary to initiate legislation, leaving initiation very largely in the hands of the executive.

The first piece of legislation to be passed by the Scottish Parliament did not appear in the initial list of legislative proposals and it was not passed by any of the three processes described above. In August 1999 a mentally ill patient who was regarded as a danger to the public was released from Carstairs Hospital because the law did not permit his further detention. There was an outcry in the press and Jim Wallace, as justice minister, came under severe pressure to plug the loophole in the law. Wallace used a form of emergency legislative procedure which enabled a bill to be fast-tracked through parliament. The Mental Health (Public Safety and Appeals) (Scotland) Act 1999 was passed on 8 September 1999 and received the Royal Assent five days later.

Committees

It is said that the Scottish Parliament 'has been established as a committee-centred institution' (Deacon, Griffiths and Lynch, 2000, p. 48). Certainly the committee system devised for Holyrood is considerably stronger than that obtaining at Westminster. It is not just that Scottish committees combine the characteristics of both standing and select committees at Westminster but the committees have been given much wider powers from the start, including the ability to initiate legislation, even though this last has not as yet been used. The main powers granted to the committees are:

- scrutiny and amendment of legislation;
- scrutinising the work of the executive;
- initiating special inquiries as required by the Parliament;
- initiating legislation;
- scrutiny of financial proposals and the executive's budget;
- power to summon witnesses and documentation to provide necessary information.

Committees are divided into two types. The first are departmental and deal with the subject areas of the various departments of the executive, while the second type are business and procedural committees concerned with the functioning of Parliament in such areas as finance, standards and procedures. The membership of the committees, and the allocation of convenors to chair each committee, is decided proportionally by the d'Hondt method to reflect the numerical representation of the parties in Parliament. In the Parliament elected in May 1999 a committee of seven members like the Standards Committee has three Labour members, two from the SNP and one each from both the Conservatives and Liberal Democrats. Of sixteen convenors, eight were from Labour, four from the SNP, and two each from the Conservatives and Liberal Democrats. One committee out of seventeen does not fit this pattern and that is the Business Committee which can be compared to the meeting of party whips, Speaker and Leader of the House at Westminster which rules on parliamentary business and is known as 'the usual channels'. The Business Committee has one member each for the five parties represented in Parliament and has the Presiding Officer as its convenor.

Every MSP has to be a member of at least one committee and, with almost 170 committee places to fill, most of them will sit on two committees while, in the first batch of MSPs to be elected, there were six members who sat on three each. There are also a number of all-party groups in a parliament whose way of working has brought about a far less partisan approach than is to be found in other political bodies. Despite the requirement that a group must have members from all four main Scottish parties before it can be registered, no fewer than twenty such cross-party groups were registered in the first year of the Parliament.

Subject committees

There were eight subject committees covering executive departments, each with eleven members. The party affiliation of the convenor of each committee is given in parenthesis.

- Education, culture and sport[7] (Labour)
- Enterprise and lifelong learning (SNP)
- Health and community care (Lib Dem)
- Justice and home affairs (SNP)
- Local government (Labour)
- Rural affairs (Conservative)
- Social, housing and voluntary sector (Lab)
- Transport and environment (Labour)

Business and procedural committees

Apart from the unique case of the Business Committee, there are eight such committees, with membership ranging from seven to thirteen. In the following list parentheses contain the number of committee members and the party affiliation of the convenor.

- Audit (11, SNP)
- Equal opportunities (13, Labour)
- European (13, Labour)
- Finance (11, Labour)
- Procedures (7, Conservative)
  Public petitions (7, Labour)
- Standards (7, Lib Dem)
- Subordinate legislation (7, SNP)
- Business (5, Presiding Officer)

A number of these procedural committees were a result of the report, *Shaping Scotland's Parliament*, which was published in January 1999 and which laid down the principles which should characterise the devolved Parliament and administration. Those principles included the need to share power with the people, acknowledged the accountability of the executive to the people of Scotland and made the point that Parliament should be accessible, open and responsive to public participation. Out of these principles was born the public petitions committee, a unique feature of the Scottish system.

In the Westminster system a petition has to be presented to Parliament by way of an MP who may read out the subject of the petition to the Commons but do little more since the petition usually disappears into the care of civil servants and may never be seen again. In Scotland on the other hand, the receipt and processing of petitions is built into the institutional structure of the devolved Parliament in such a way as to address the grievances of the public in ways that are totally unknown either to the Westminster Parliament or to the other devolved assemblies (Lynch, 2001, p. 194):

- The system is open in that petitions can be submitted by e-mail and the entire business of the petitions committee can be found on the internet at: www.scottish.parliament.uk/parl_bus/petitions.html
- The committee is in permanent session and, once a petition has been accepted, its progress can be checked and followed – it does not just disappear.
- The petitioner, whether as an individual or group, is personally responsible for presenting the petition – it does not have to be submitted through the agency of an MSP. Petitioners can be asked to appear before the committee to explain the petition or answer questions. The committee is also ready to convene outside Edinburgh for easier contact with local bodies.
- All petitions are treated equally whether they are presented by an individual, a group or an organisation. Of the 242 petitions presented in the first year of devolution, 50.6 per cent came from individuals, 24.1 per cent from pressure groups, 15.8 per cent from local community groups and 4.2 per cent from the business community. Small and local pressure groups found the procedure a useful alternative to the lobbying done by the larger pressure groups.
- The committee is obliged to process all petitions received: it can only refuse those that that are illegal or illegible. The committee then has three alternative courses of action. It can:
  (a) decide to take no further action – but the petitioner must be fully informed, (b) forward the petition to a minister, local authority of quango for action, or (c) forward the petition to the relevant departmental committee for action.

Finance

The budgeting process in Scotland begins on 20 September each year, or on the first day after that when the Scottish Parliament is sitting. On that date all the Scottish ministers will submit detailed estimates of expected expenditure in the next financial year to the Finance Committee. The Finance Committee then consults with other committees and prepares a response to the ministers' proposals, possibly submitting their own alternative suggestions. Differences are ironed out in a plenary session of Parliament and a compromise budget put forward. This procedure is regarded by parliament as an experiment in open government.

Proposed expenditure is paid for out of the block grant provided by the UK government under the terms of the Barnett formula. This device was developed by Joel Barnett, the Chief Secretary to the Treasury in the Callaghan government of the 1970s, and was intended to prevent fighting for funds between the devolved and UK administrations. The Barnett formula was intended to be an objective yardstick by which the Scottish and Welsh finances could be made to converge with the finances of England.

As already explained in Chapter 5, the Barnett formula was supposed to move towards equality of spending per head of population and originally stated that for every £85 by which public expenditure on English services rose, Scotland would receive £10 and Wales would get £5. The formula is quite clearly defined for Scotland in relation to England and means that the Scottish finance minister:

- need not spend much time negotiating with Westminster,
- has a lump sum that is Scotland's to spend as Scotland wishes.

Through the 1980s and 1990s the Barnett formula protected Scotland against any decline in public expenditure because any cuts in public expenditure improve Scotland's position relative to England. When public spending rises, however, the 'Barnett Squeeze' factor comes into play, increasing convergence between Scotland and England. Since Scotland has always benefited from 'over-provision' in the past any move towards English levels means a drop in the amount spent on public services in Scotland. It has been estimated that, with the Barnett formula providing this 'squeeze' factor Scottish public services will receive almost £16 billion less by 2003–4 than if the growth rate had remained stable (Constitution Unit report, November 2000).

Within a short time of the Scottish Parliament being established it became clear that the means by which the parliament was financed needed reformation from the old and creaking Barnett formula. The difficulty in deciding on the best way to finance the devolved administration hinges upon whether public spending by the Scottish parliament is dictated by Scottish needs or resources: in other words, is the amount of money given to the devolved administration determined by what the administration estimates it will need to spend, or is the amount spent determined by what resources are available to the devolved body?

There are three possible ways in which the finance issue may be resolved, each of which has its advantages and disadvantages:

- Transferred taxes with a degree of equalisation to make the situation comparable with the UK as a whole. This would meet needs rather than depend on resources.
- Assigned taxes for the particular use of the devolved administration. This is

the procedure adopted by the German *länder* and similar arrangements apply in Belgium, Portugal and Spain.

- Devolution of tax-raising powers beyond the present simple 3p tax-varying powers. This exceeds the 1999 concept of devolution but, in first two years of the Scottish Parliament, there were signs that Scotland was developing its own particular education, health and social care services with their own needs that could possibly require different funding in the future.

Doing one's own thing

From the start, the Scottish Parliament and executive, together with Labour as the largest party, showed itself to be far less confrontational than Westminster and perfectly ready to pursue a Scottish rather than a British line on policy decisions, whether those decisions refer to the UK Parliament or the national party organisation. This difference in attitude was largely a result of the proportional electoral system denying any one party an overall majority in the parliament. The Scottish executive had to be formed as a coalition and there were bound to be occasions when the necessary compromise with another party like the Liberal Democrats was bound to conflict with a UK-wide policy decision made by a party with a massive overall majority. That members of the Scottish Parliament need to show themselves as working in the best interests of Scotland rather for England or Wales results in Holyrood taking a different line on certain issues from that dictated by Westminster.

Even before the formation of the first executive, Labour and Lib Dem MSPs found it difficult to formulate a coalition stance on two policy matters. The first such related to the issue of requiring students to pay tuition fees for their university or college education. If applied to Scotland such a policy would be seen to be unfair since degree courses in Scotland are normally four years in length rather than three, and this would mean that a Scottish university education would be £1000 more expensive than elsewhere. The imposition of students' fees was strongly resisted in Scotland and, by the time of the 1999 election every Scottish party except Labour was in favour of abolition. In negotiations over the formation of a coalition executive Jim Wallace for the Liberal Democrats held out for abolition of fees and would only sign an agreement with Labour after a committee of enquiry had been set up under Andrew Cubie. The committee reported just before Christmas 1999 and recommended that Scottish students attending Scottish universities would not have to pay any tuition fees but would make a retrospective payment after graduation.

It was less easy to agree to the other Liberal Democrat demand, which was for a system of proportional representation in Scottish local elections. On 27 June 2000 a committee chaired by Richard Kerley, that had been set up to investigate the issue, recommended the use of the single transferable vote system, as used for local elections in Ireland. The Labour party, which retains a stranglehold on most Scottish local government, largely through the use of first-past-the-post in local elections, is completely opposed to proportional representation and will say no more than that they hope to progress on this matter at some time before the next local elections in 2002. However, the situation in the Scottish Parliament has Labour (56 MSPs) totally opposed to PR and both the SNP (35 MSPs) and the Lib Dems (17 MSPs) very much in favour; leaving the decision balanced on a knife-edge and allowing the Conservatives a casting vote in the matter.

During the autumn of 1999 a dispute arose that led to the Parliament and executive taking up a position opposed to Scottish public opinion. The UK Parliament was proposing to abolish the so-called 'Section 28', the regulation which forbids the 'promotion of homosexuality'. Critics of the regulation claimed that legitimate advice given by teachers and others about the problems of sexual identity and homophobic bullying was in effect outlawed by the regulation and led to very necessary advice being categorised as illegal. The relevant minister in the Scottish executive, Wendy Alexander, proposed to abolish Section 28 in Scotland ahead of abolition in England and Wales. Initially no one saw any problem and abolition was proceeding smoothly enough until, in January 2000, opposition was voiced by an unlikely alliance of the *Daily Record* newspaper, Cardinal Winning, head of the Roman Catholic church in Scotland, and Brian Souter, the Thatcherite head of the Stagecoach bus and rail company. A 'keep Section 28' campaign followed in the press and a series of opinion polls suggested that the public was very strongly opposed to abolition. An opinion poll organised by Souter claimed that 86.5 per cent of those who had replied were in favour of retaining the regulation. Despite opposition the Bill continued through Parliament with the support of most MSPs and became law on 21 June 2000. The passing of the Bill coincided with a massive collapse of public support for the Parliament and executive and was held to be a typical example of the Scottish Parliament's lack of responsiveness to public opinion.

In November 2000 the Scottish Parliament was asked to look at a planning application that was already ten years old. A French quarrying company had wanted to extract stone from a quarry on the island of Harris in order to provide hard core for road-building in England and they had lodged a planning application for this extraction in 1991. The application was contested from the first by environmental and other groups but, while the decision was still in the hands of the Scottish Office it was thought that the development should go ahead, if only for the 200 jobs it was said to create. Then the application became the concern of the devolved parliament and the Scottish executive dismissed the application as a case of English needs being given priority over Scottish interests. It was pointed out that today there is little call for stone, thanks to technical advances in road construction, and that there was therefore no real future for the quarrying industry on Skye. This was one decision that turned around public opinion about the devolved administration.

Even more significant for the impact it had on Scottish opinion was the issue of care charges for the elderly. This had begun with a royal commission led by Sir Stewart Sutherland which recommended that charges for the personal care of the elderly should be abolished. At that time nursing care was free but services such as cleaning and cooking were subject to means-testing. Sutherland's proposal that all care should be free was rejected as being too expensive both north and south of the border. However, when Henry McLeish took over as first minister he announced that he was ready to implement the Sutherland proposals. Towards the end of 2000 McLeish seemed to backtrack on this, saying that charges would continue, although the means-testing procedure would be made fairer. This led to a rebellion by Lib Dem MSPs who threatened to vote with the SNP against their coalition partners. In the face of that threat the first minister made a statement on 29 January 2001 in which he said that 'we are embracing the principles of Sutherland in full'.

Later in 2001 it was announced that Scottish teachers would receive a salary increase of 23 per cent spread over three years, far beyond the pay settlement for English teachers. It was a move towards a two-tier Britain since it means that students, teachers and the elderly are all far better off in Scotland than they would be south of the border. These important changes in expenditure on education and social care have so far been contained within the block grant with which the Scottish Parliament is funded but, if the Parliament persists in voting through greater spending in Scotland on certain areas, there are obviously implications for the funding of government in Scotland that reawaken arguments over tax-raising powers.

Lobbygate and the SQA

In September 1999 the *Observer* newspaper printed an interview with two executives from the public relations company Beattie Media, one of whom was a former Labour party activist called Kevin Reid, son of Labour's Secretary of State for Scotland, John Reid. Among other things the two men were claiming as an important asset for Beattie Media the closeness of their contacts with members of the Holyrood executive. In particular they claimed to have a special relationship with Jack McConnell, the finance minister. McConnell had been involved in setting up Beattie Media and had an interest in the company. A former Beattie employee now worked in McConnell's private office and it was claimed that through her an appointment could be made for anyone to meet McConnell.

Donald Dewar instigated enquiries into the affair, as a result of which all ministers were cleared of any breach of the code of ministerial conduct. As far as the executive was concerned the matter was dead: Beattie Media had made claims that were exaggerated but ministers had done no wrong. It was thought worthwhile, however, for the question of lobbyists and their relationship with

MSPs to be referred to the parliament's Standards Committee, which was the correct body to deal with the matter. John Reid took the involvement of the committee as an insult to his son and, thanks to his reaction, what had been a fairly insignificant matter was blown up into a full-scale public row between himself and Dewar. The popular press seized on the argument and waged a campaign in which it was alleged that Holyrood was riddled with sleaze every bit as bad as Westminster in the last days of the Major government. Dewar insisted that 'there has been no breach of the ministerial code . . .' but the affair added to a general discontent with devolution in Scotland.[8]

For the best part of the year 2000 the Scottish Parliament and executive, together with the whole process of devolution, were deeply unpopular. It was a situation not helped by a hostile press, and in particular the *Scotsman* news-paper, as edited by Andrew Neil, and the Mirror Group's *Daily Record*, both of whom seized on every opportunity to denigrate anything to do with devolution. Events tending to discredit the devolution process seemed to follow one after another. Soon after the Lobbygate affair details were released concerning mis-management in the construction of the new parliament building. Originally intended to cost £40 million, its cost had risen within one year to an estimated £195 million.

In late summer came the scandal of the Scottish Qualifications Authority (SQA) when the publication of examination results went dreadfully wrong, with thousands of students being given the wrong grades, a major error that wreaked havoc for all students attempting to find university places. Although the education minister, Sam Galbraith, had some responsibility for SQA, the fiasco of August was not really his fault, but he was nevertheless discreetly moved sideways from education to the environment in Henry McLeish's new cabinet. Once the man at the top had been changed and the entire management of the SQA had been forced to resign, the issue faded somewhat. Nevertheless, it was one more negative factor which detracted from the parliament's reputa-tion and contributed to its unpopularity.

In September 2000 the parliament reached a new low in popularity. An opinion poll showed that 72 per cent of the Scottish people were either hostile and believed that the parliament was doing a bad job or they were indifferent and could not care less about it.[9]

By-elections

In February 2000, as the Scottish executive and parliament became steadily more unpopular, Ian Welsh, the Labour MSP for Ayr, resigned because he found the pressure of work too great. His going meant that the Holyrood parliament faced its first by-election within nine months of its inauguration and at the height of the its unpopularity: polling taking place on 16 March 2000.

Ayr constituency		Votes	%	% change since 1997
Scott	Con	12,580	39.4	+1.4
Mather	SNP	9,236	28.9	+9.4
Miller	Lab	7,054	22.1	−16.0
Stewart	SSP	1,345	4.2	
Ritchie	Lib Dem	800	2.5	−1.9
Corbet	Green	460	1.4	
4 Others		425	1.2	
Turnout			56.6	−9.9

It is worth noting that the electorate punished both the parties making up the executive coalition. It is not surprising that Labour should lose the seat since traditionally it was one of the Conservative party's safest seats in Scotland and was only gained by Labour in 1997. The significant point is not that Labour should lose to the Conservatives but that the party was beaten for second place by the SNP. The Liberal Democrats, for whom this was never a strong seat, fared even worse than their coalition partners, reduced to fifth place having been overtaken by the Scottish Socialist candidate.

A turning point in the perceptions of the electorate did come, ironically enough, with the death of Donald Dewar. After that the electorate began to see a more positive side to the Scottish Parliament. The abolition of care charges for the elderly was one positive benefit, as was the Parliament's willingness to take action in forcing the resignation of the entire Scottish Qualifications Authority. When Donald Dewar's Holyrood constituency of Anniesland voted to elect Dewar's successor on 23 November 2000 the change in attitude led to a much better result for Labour than had been seen in Ayr:

Anniesland constituency		Votes	%	% change since 1997
Butler	Lab	9,838	48.65	−10.16
Chalmers	SNP	4,462	22.07	+1.86
Pickering	Con	2,148	10.62	−0.03
Kane	SSP	1,429	7.07	+3.56
Fryer	Lib Dem	1,384	6.84	+0.51
Whitelaw	Green	662	3.27	
Ritchie	Soc Lab	298	1.47	+0.98
Turnout			38.29	−14.08

There was quite a drop in the Labour vote but that was only to be expected given the quite considerable personal vote that had previously gone to Donald Dewar. One significant point to arise from this and the previous by-election was confirmation that the SNP had replaced the Conservative party as the real opposition to Labour in Scotland.

Conclusion

Despite a decidedly shaky start it is clear that after two years the Scottish Parliament could be counted as a success. Issues such as students' tuition fees and care charges for the elderly show that the Holyrood Parliament has a different agenda to that of Westminster and one that is more receptive to Scottish needs and priorities. The press has become a little less hostile and opinion polls suggest that most Scots would be sorry to lose their parliament now.

The Scots, however, may be a little nervous about the way they are losing First Ministers. On 8 November 2001 Henry McLeish resigned as First Minister after little more than a year in office. McLeish was guilty of failing to declare to Parliament money he had received through subletting his Glenrothes constituency offices. The offence was committed before McLeish ensured the Scottish Parliament, he had apologised and promised to pay back the money and it had looked as though the matter was closed. But it was a public relations disaster and the press saw to it that McLeish was forced to resign. As had been the case with Labour in Wales, it was seen that a candidate who had been foisted on to the Scottish party by London had now been replaced by a more local choice.

There is now a movement to seek even more powers for the devolved administration:

- Many believe that there is no longer any need for a Scottish Secretary, the Grand Committee of the Scotland Office; and certainly there is no need for Scotland to have its own secretary of state of cabinet rank. Either the minister for Scotland could be a junior post within the Home Office or a cabinet minister could be appointed to co-ordinate relations between Holyrood, Cardiff Bay, Stormont and Westminster. Such a minister could also handle the concordats (non-statutory agreements) that need to be developed to regulate relations between the devolved administration and Whitehall, Westminster and Brussels.
- There needs to be a reconsideration of the division between reserved and devolved powers. Certain anomalies stand out, such as, for instance, why are all health issues devolved to Holyrood except for abortion? And why are all matters related to culture and the arts devolved except for broadcasting?
- Something needs to be done about the pressure of work at Holyrood. As the parliament has become more established so has the workload increased, not only through an extended legislative programme but because of an increased tendency for the Scots people to take their problems to Holyrood rather than Westminster. The demands being made on MSPs soon exceeded what had been envisaged when office expenses and the availability of secretarial services were first assessed. Within months of the parliament being elected the MSP for Ayr, Ian Welsh, had resigned because he could not cope

with the amount of work he was called upon to do. In March 2001 the cabinet minister Sam Galbraith returned to the backbenches, again because of pressure of work.

- The problem of over-representation needs to be tackled. The 'West Lothian Question' has been renamed the 'English Question' and will be dealt with in Chapter 9. But the fact remains that Scotland is over-represented *per capita* in comparison with England, a fact that has been true since 1707 but which has become even more important since Scotland has regained a parliament of its own. The Kilbrandon Report recognised this and recommended that Scottish representation at Westminster should be reduced to 57 MPs. Labour has proved reluctant to legislate for such a reduction in numbers but has instructed the Boundary Commission that in future reviews of constituency boundaries in Scotland the need to reduce the number of constituencies should be borne in mind. In the meantime the Scottish MPs have agreed to a form of self-regulation in that they will refrain from intervening or voting on matters that are specifically English or Welsh.
- Devolution to Scotland has had a mixed impact on the political parties but has generally started to produce cross-border national parties whose Scottish incarnations are very different from those adopted in London. Strangely enough, Labour has not fared very well, as many Scots voters who would vote for Labour in a Westminster election prefer to vote for the SNP or Scottish Socialists in a Holyrood election. On the other hand, there is no longer any real reason why anyone should vote for the SNP in a Westminster election. In fact, with the key bread and butter issues like education and housing, that are the everyday concerns of the people, being dealt with by Holyrood, it is hard to see why any Scot would need or choose to vote in a Westminster election. This decline in the fortunes of the SNP was borne out by the 2001 general election in which the party lost Galloway and Upper Nithsdale to the Conservatives and saw the nationalist majority in Perth reduced to forty-eight. Labour more than held its own, strengthening its position against the Tories, while their coalition partners, the Lib Dems, managed a 2 per cent swing in their favour. The SNP, nevertheless, remains the second largest party in Scotland and we must wait for the 2003 Scottish elections to judge whether party allegiances are different for Westminster and Holyrood.

One final irony thrown up by the devolution debate is a party political point. The Conservative party has neither Westminster MPs nor MEPs at Brussels for Scottish constituencies. But, thanks to proportional representation, the Conservatives have a significant presence at Holyrood, being the third largest party. And this means that the Conservatives are indebted for this political presence to devolution and proportional representation, both things that are totally opposed by the Conservatives!

Notes

1 Full details of voting percentages for each of the local government areas in Scotland are given in Appendix 1.
2 The details quoted are from a simplified version of the Scotland Act 1998. The full text of the Act is available from HMSO, either in the printed version or it can be downloaded from the internet at www.hmso.gov.uk/acts1998/19980046.htm
3 For details of the allocation of seats to regional MSPs by means of the d'Hondt method, see Appendix 2.
4 As reported in the *Guardian*, 7 May 1999.
5 For details of the cabinets of Donald Dewar and Hector McLeish, see Appendix 3.
6 *Making it Work together: A Programme for Government*, issued by the Scottish Executive, 9 September 1999.
7 It is interesting to note that when Donald Dewar originally made Sam Galbraith the education minister his responsibilities were given in the order: Culture and Sport. But when Henry McLeish became First Minister and moved Galbraith to be environment minister, he reversed his priorities and renamed the portfolio handed to Jack McConnell as Sport and Culture. As Gary Younge commented in the *Guardian* on 6 November 2000, 'less Puccini and Bach, more pies and Bovril'.
8 The fullest and best account of Lobbygate is to be found in the book by Philip Schlesinger, David Miller and William Dinan, *Open Scotland? Journalists, Spin Doctors and Lobbyists*, published by Polygon at Edinburgh, 2001.
9 Gary Younge in the *Guardian*, 6 November 2000.

7

Wales – Assembly,
or bubonic plague?

As was the case in Scotland, the nature of devolution for Wales and the process by which it would be achieved had been fixed long before the election of May 1997. The major difference between Scotland and Wales was that Wales did not have a cross-party, multi-organisational group like the Scottish Constitutional Convention. The Labour party accepted the idea of a Welsh Assembly after the 1987 election but any development of that idea was kept firmly in the hands of the party. Labour even refused to be associated in any way with pro-devolution pressure groups, especially if those groups were associated with Plaid Cymru. In 1994 the Welsh Labour party – Wales Labour, or *Plaid Lafur Cymru* – established a Constitutional Policy Commission to work out the form to be taken by the Assembly and how it would be run.

Over the next three years there were a number of communications from the commission, indicating the progress it was making. In 1996, for example, the Welsh Secretary, Ron Davies, announced two important decisions: firstly that elections for any Welsh Assembly would be by a form of proportional representation and, secondly, that such an assembly would have to be approved by a referendum of the Welsh people. As far as that referendum was concerned there were several factors that made it different from either the referendum that took place in 1979 or the referendum to be held in Scotland:

- Unlike 1979 there would be no threshold percentage of the vote which had to be reached; a simple majority would suffice.
- Since the Welsh Assembly would not have the ability to pass primary legislation there was therefore no need for a second question on tax-varying powers having to be included in the referendum.
- The Welsh referendum would be held a week later than that in Scotland. It was recognised that there was less popular support for devolution in Wales than there was in Scotland and it was hoped that, by following the Scottish referendum in which a 'Yes' vote was confidently expected, the Welsh electorate would be encouraged to vote the same way.

Within two months of winning the general election the Labour government was ready to announce its plans for Wales and the White Paper *A Voice for Wales* appeared in July 1997. In comparison with what had been announced for Scotland there was a very significant difference. According to the White Paper, Wales was to have an assembly rather than a parliament, which would be restricted to secondary legislation only. Wales would have executive devolution rather than the legislative devolution granted to Scotland but Labour believed that this important difference between the two countries was justified by Scotland's separate legal system. As Vernon Bogdanor said, Scottish devolution represented a semi-federal relationship, while Welsh devolution was more a form of regionalism: legislative devolution represents the transfer of powers while executive devolution concerns the division of powers (Bogdanor, 1999, p. 255).

One problem in defining the form of devolution for Wales lies in the fact that nothing in the British political system helps to define where the dividing line should be drawn between primary and secondary legislation. Under the Welsh model, primary legislation remains with the Westminster Parliament while the devolved assembly deals with the orders, rules and regulations by which the primary legislation is enacted. This function was previously the remit of the Secretary of State for Wales but all his executive powers have been devolved to the assembly.

While the Westminster Parliament retains the ability to pass primary legislation they will nevertheless have to enact a rather looser form of legislation as far as Wales is concerned so that the Assembly can freely amend the primary legislation before enacting any secondary legislation. The wording of the White Paper, *A Voice for Wales*, suggested that when the Westminster Parliament was framing a bill that would be applied to Wales then parliament should consider 'giving the Assembly responsibility for bringing the Bill's provisions into force in Wales' (Bogdanor, 1999, p. 259).

The White Paper made it clear that, despite the supremacy of the UK Parliament, it would be difficult for Westminster to impose its policies on Wales if the Assembly resisted them:

- the Assembly is much more influential than the Secretary of State for Wales;
- there is a far more detailed scrutiny of secondary legislation than is possible at Westminster;
- secondary legislation can be drawn up and amended by the Assembly;
- the Assembly will have control over the vast army of Welsh quangos.

The 'little yes' referendum

The referendum in Wales was held on 18 September 1997, exactly one week after the Scottish referendum. 'They expected a Yes result in Scotland and hoped that this would produce a momentum for a 'me too' attitude in Wales'

(Bradbury, 1998, p. 8). There was certainly a wide variety of supporters who would campaign for a 'yes' vote. To the forefront was Wales Labour, led by Ron Davies, the Secretary of State for Wales, and Peter Hain, his junior minister at the Welsh Office. Of the political parties there was support from the Liberal Democrats led by Richard Livesey and Plaid Cymru led by Dafydd Wigley, while a non-party pressure group called 'Yes for Wales' under the leadership of academics, Professor Kevin Morgan and Mari James gave strong support, as did the Cardiff newspaper, the *Western Mail*.

The pro-devolution movement suffered from certain disadvantages in publicising their activities and ideas. A quite considerable proportion of the Welsh population received their news and information by way of the English media. All along the border with England the people look east to English towns like Shrewsbury or Hereford, the most widely read newspaper in North Wales is the *Liverpool Daily Post* and the people in Cardiff and Glamorgan are most likely to watch West of England television. Apart from the information deficit that resulted from this there was a major distraction in the middle of the campaign caused by the death of Princess Diana.

The campaign for a 'no' vote was smaller than the pro-devolution lobby and was headed by Robert Hodge, son of millionaire businessman, Sir Julian Hodge. His main advantage was that the plans for Welsh devolution were very easily attacked. Without either legislative or tax-varying powers the proposed assembly could be seen as no more than a very expensive talking shop without the ability to achieve much and many people remained sceptical of its merits. As was said a little later by one activist, 'You ask people here what they would prefer to have, the National Assembly or bubonic plague, and most of them would opt for the latter'.[1] Although the only political party officially opposed to Welsh devolution was the Conservative party, many Labour party members, including half a dozen MPs, campaigned for a 'no' vote, against the party line. Divisions within Wales also acted against devolution since, as always, the Welsh-speaking north and west did not trust Cardiff, while the south was equally as wary of Welsh-speaking nationalism in rural Wales.

With opinion so divided and with both sides running lacklustre campaigns, the real winner was apathy. Only 50 per cent of the electorate voted in the referendum and those who did so voted for negative rather than positive reasons: they voted 'yes' to keep out the Conservatives or they voted 'yes' because that was Labour party policy and 'the Valleys always vote Labour'. Apathy produced such a lukewarm response either for or against devolution that is hard to discern any sort of positive response in the outcome of the referendum.

It was a contest so close that it was only decided when the very last electoral district declared a result. Throughout most of the count the contest had been seen to be very close but the 'no' vote seemed to have the edge on those voting 'yes'. By the time Carmarthen, as the last Welsh district to declare, was ready to announce the final figures, television pundits and politicians were busy discussing the victory for the 'no' vote and debating as to where the government went from there. And then Carmarthen voted 'yes' with a massive 65.28 per cent, the second largest favourable vote in the entire country. And that vote produced the slenderest of majorities for the 'yes' lobby. From over a million voters throughout Wales 50.3 per cent voted 'yes' giving a majority of 6,721, or 0.6 per cent of those voting. Coupled with a low turnout of just over 50 per cent, those who voted in favour represent not much more than 25 per cent of the population: hardly a strong mandate for constitutional reform. In Welsh the inconclusive positive vote became known as *yr ie bychan* – 'the little yes'.

In the way it voted, the country divided neatly into two halves, east and west. The largely English-speaking areas – along the Welsh Marches, in the north-east near Liverpool, in Pembrokeshire and around Cardiff – voted 'no', with Monmouthshire being the most strongly opposed on a 67.9 per cent adverse vote. The largely Welsh-speaking Plaid Cymru heartland of the north and west voted 'yes', with pro-devolution votes ranging from 50.9 per cent in Anglesey to 65.28 per cent in Carmarthen. Also voting 'yes' were the traditionally staunch Labour strongholds of the South Wales Valleys, districts located in the coalfields and the former iron and steel areas, with 'yes' votes ranging from 51.96 per cent in Swansea to 66.55 per cent in Neath/Port Talbot.[2] As has already been noted, the division of Wales into 'yes' and 'no' was made almost precisely along lines that were drawn up in the thirteenth century. The lands of the Marcher lords, together with Pembroke's 'Little England beyond Wales', voted 'no', while the lands conquered by Edward I were leading adherents of the 'yes' vote.

Supporters of the 'no' campaign claimed that the referendum was too close to justify going ahead with plans for devolution. But the government reaffirmed that there was no threshold vote to be passed on this occasion. A simple major-ity sufficed and the Welsh Office set up the National Assembly Advisory Group (NAAG) in October 1997. A Government of Wales Bill was introduced into par-liament on 26 November 1997, receiving the royal assent as the Government of Wales Act on 31 July 1998.

The Government of Wales Act

The Bill as submitted to the Westminster Parliament differed from the *A Voice for Wales* White Paper in just one respect. It was originally intended that the Assembly would be divided into a number of subject committees, each of which would choose its own chair as Assembly secretary: the Assembly secretaries together forming the Assembly executive. This pattern of committees having executive control has traditionally been the way local government has worked in England and Wales. However, at the same time as the government was setting up the Welsh Assembly they were proposing that local government should be reformed by replacing the outdated committee system with a more effective cabinet model. Since it would seem anomalous for the government to advocate a system for the Welsh Assembly that it was removing from local government, the Welsh Secretary, Ron Davies, proposed a number of amendments which instituted a cabinet model for Cardiff in which ministerial positions are chosen by the first secretary rather than subject committees.

Title and nature

The first section of the Act defined the title of the Assembly, in English and Welsh, as the National Assembly for Wales or *Cynulliad Cenedlaethol Cymru*. It is a single-chamber corporate body of sixty members, without a legally separate executive, which carries out certain functions on behalf of the Crown.

Elections

Assembly membership is by elections held in both Assembly constituencies and Assembly electoral regions. Assembly constituencies are the same as the existing Westminster Parliamentary constituencies in Wales and return one member each by the first-past-the-post system. The Assembly constituencies are divided between five Assembly electoral regions, each of them represented by a European parliamentary constituency. Each electoral region returns 4 members to the Assembly from regional lists under the Additional Member System. Overall, there are 60 Assembly members, with 40 constituency members and 20 regional members (see Appendix 5 for a breakdown of constituencies and regions). Registered electors have two votes: one for a member to represent the Assembly constituency, and the other for either a political party which has submitted a list of candidates (or for an individual who is standing as an independent candidate) for the Assembly electoral region.

General elections to the Assembly take place every four years on the first Thursday in May, beginning with the elections held on 6 May 1999. There are two circumstances under which that date might be changed:

- the date might be moved by up to one month in either direction in order to avoid clashing with a late Easter;
- local elections can be delayed by up to three months if they would otherwise coincide with the Welsh elections.

The Assembly is elected for a four-year fixed term. No mechanism exists for the dissolution of the Assembly in anything under four years.

Powers in relation to legislation

The Assembly has the power to consider any matter affecting Wales, whether or not it falls within the Assembly's executive functions. It can debate issues relating to Welsh matters and make recommendations to government ministers. The Assembly can promote or oppose a private bill in the West-minster Parliament, as long as a motion to do so attracts the support of at least two-thirds of Assembly members voting. Such a bill is subject to the procedures of the UK parliament since the Assembly does not have the power to pass private bills itself.

Civil service

The staff of the bureaucracy serving the Assembly, like the civil servants inher-ited from the Welsh Office, are and will remain, members of Her Majesty's Home Civil Service.

Officers and executive of the Assembly

The Assembly's first responsibility is to elect a Presiding Officer and a Deputy Presiding Officer – the equivalent of the Speaker and Deputy Speaker in the Commons.

The members must elect a First Secretary (or *Prif Ysgrifennydd y Cynulliad*), who is the Assembly's political leader and acts in much the same way as a Prime Minister, being elected by a majority vote of the whole Assembly. The First Sec-retary in turn appoints the necessary Assembly secretaries (*Ysgrifenyddion y Cynulliad*).

The Assembly establishes certain committees whose membership is selected to reflect the balance of parties in the Assembly, all committees having to consist entirely of Assembly members. The Assembly's executive committee, which effectively acts as the Assembly's 'cabinet' consists of the Assembly first secretary and the Assembly secretaries. The Assembly secretaries are allocated responsibilities by the First Secretary for each of the fields in which the Assembly has functions. However, there will always be certain secretaries without specific jobs or responsibilities who might be called 'secretaries without portfolio'.

Each secretary with responsibility for a particular field is accountable to the Assembly for that field while the first secretary is accountable for the executive committee. Standing Orders include provision for written and oral questions to the First Secretary and secretaries to allow individual Assembly members to hold them to account.

Regional committees

Regional committees advise the Assembly about matters concerning their respective regions. The Standing Orders will determine the boundaries of regional committees, but there is a statutory requirement for one such commit-tee covering North Wales. Each regional committee's membership is made up of all the Assembly members whose constituencies fall within its boundaries.

Role of the Secretary of State for Wales

Under Section 22 of the Government of Wales Act, a Transfer Order was issued by means of which virtually all the Secretary of State's functions were transferred to the Assembly. With the functions of the Welsh Office all transferred to the Assembly, there are just two ministers in the Westminster government who are responsible for Wales, the Welsh Secretary and a junior minister. They have offices in both London and Cardiff, while the junior minister heads a Welsh Office Bill Team which keeps a watching brief on the Welsh content of bills passing through parliament. The Secretary himself retains certain important functions:

- He represents the interests of Wales in cabinet. As Welsh Secretary, Paul Murphy revealed in 1999 that he and his junior minister sat on more than 20 cabinet committees to defend the Welsh interest (Hazell, 2000, p. 59).
- He supervises the passage of Welsh primary legislation through all the stages of the Westminster Parliament's legislative process. He must also answer any Welsh questions during ministerial question time.
- He is responsible for funding the Assembly in that he passes on the block grant to the Assembly after having deducted his own office's expenses, and for negotiating with the Treasury over other funding such as grants and subsidies from the European Union.
- He is required to consult the Assembly each year about the government's legislative programme for that year, principally as it is set out in the Queen's Speech. In theory he consults the Assembly about the entire legislative programme but in practice he is not likely to bother with bills relating solely to England and English concerns. As part of his duties the Secretary of State must attend the Assembly at least once per year.
- If he is not a member of the Assembly he may nevertheless attend any of its proceedings, but not any of its committees or sub-committees, nor may he vote. If, on the other hand, he is an Assembly member in his own right under the dual mandate, he will of course attend and vote in that capacity. The Assembly must make available to the Secretary of State all those documents which it routinely makes available to Assembly members, containing information about the Assembly's proceedings.

Finance

The Secretary of State will fund the Assembly out of money provided by parliament, which largely comes from funds voted to Wales annually in what is known as the block grant. The government expects the Secretary of State for Wales to pass on nearly all of these funds to the Assembly, although he will need to retain a small proportion of the funds available to cover the costs of his own office.

As was the case in Scotland, payments to the Welsh Assembly are determined by the 'Barnett formula', under which funds are allocated to Wales according to its population size relative to England. The value of this funding in 1999–2000 was approximately £7 billion per year. Other ministers and government departments may also make payments to the Assembly. For example, the Intervention Board makes payments to Wales on behalf of Europe in respect of the Common Agricultural Policy. Any such arrangements continue after devolution, and any such funds as grants and subsidies from Europe do not count against funds passed to the Assembly by the Secretary of State.

Powers of the Assembly

The Assembly has been granted a wide range of administrative and secondary legislative powers:

- To make rules and regulations for the administration of primary legislation enacted at Westminster: '. . . there are more than 300 Acts of Parliament under which the Welsh Assembly has the power to make rules and regulations' (Deacon, Griffiths and Lynch, 2000, p. 97).
- To enact secondary and delegated legislation through such devices as statutory instruments.
- To make appointments to a large number of quangos such as the various NHS Trusts in Wales.
- To allocate and spend funds assigned to Wales under the block grant.
- To acquire land and property and undertake work within the infrastructure such as the construction of new roads.

All decisions made by the Assembly can be challenged in the courts and, as with the Scottish Parliament, the final court of appeal is the judicial committee of the Privy Council. Also as in Scotland, governmental powers are divided into reserved powers, which are fully retained with the Westminster Parliament, and devolved powers that can be dealt with by the Welsh Assembly. It should be noted that in Scotland it was only the reserved powers that were positively identified, devolved matters being defined negatively as those areas that were not reserved. The position is very different for Wales, however, where, in Schedule 2 of the Government of Wales Act, the transferred functions were quite clearly specified:

- Agriculture and fisheries
- Culture
- Economic development
- Education and training
- Environment
- Health
- Highways
- Housing

- Industry
- Local government
- Social services
- Sport
- Tourism
- Town and country planning
- Transport
- Water
- The Welsh language

The First Secretary and cabinet (executive committee)

At the head of the Assembly, in what is essentially seen as a prime ministerial role, is the First Secretary. The First Secretary is not elected by the Assembly in the same way as the Scottish First Minister is elected by the Parliament. Instead, the leader of the majority party in the Assembly becomes First Secretary.

During the inaugural process when the Assembly was first constituted it was intended that the First Secretary should also be the Secretary of State for Wales, ensuring continuity of governmental involvement. The devolution referendums were overseen by Ron Davies as Welsh Secretary and leader of Wales Labour, putative First Secretary. After Davies's disgrace the dual role passed to Alun Michael and it was only after Michael's departure that the posts of First Secretary and Welsh Secretary became divided.

The First Secretary has several important roles to play:

- To lead the Assembly.
- To lead the executive through selecting Assembly secretaries to form the cabinet.
- To liaise with the Welsh Secretary to help draft Welsh legislation at Westminster.
- To act as party leader and ensure the implementation of the party manifesto.
- To represent the Assembly at Westminster, in Europe and overseas.
- To hold the equivalent of 'Prime Minister's question time' in the Assembly.
- To write and deliver an annual 'state of the nation' address.

According to the White Paper *A Voice for Wales*, and the original draft legislation for the Government of Wales Act, the Assembly was supposed to work with an executive committee modelled on the council leader's committee used in local government. It was changed by Ron Davies during the committee stage of the Government of Wales Act to a cabinet system, whereby the Assembly secretaries are chosen by the First Secretary rather than elected by the subject committees and where the Assembly will delegate its functions to the executive committee (Bogdanor, 1999, p. 211).

The executive committee or cabinet is restricted by standing orders to nine members including the First Secretary. The members are chosen by the First Secretary soon after a general election, or immediately after a change of First Secretary.[3] The most important ministerial post is the secretary for economic development who is responsible for employment policy and for promoting Wales as a location for industry and business. The importance of the position is reflected in the fact that the Assembly secretary for economic development is also deputy first minister and has been ever since Rhodri Morgan was given the position to compensate for having lost out to Alun Michael in the leadership contest. The second most important post is held by the Assembly business secretary who acts like the leader of the House of Commons in that he manages the business agenda of the Assembly. The post is doubled with that of chief whip for the majority party because the business secretary draws up the Assembly's agenda through a business committee formed by the whips of all those political parties represented in the Assembly.

The other six places on the cabinet are taken by Assembly secretaries having ministerial responsibilities for subject areas deemed to be devolved powers. The portfolios are at the dispensation of the First Secretary but the subjects are currently education and lifelong learning, environment, finance and local government, health and social services, rural affairs (largely agriculture and fisheries) and Welsh culture, language and sport (see Appendix 6).

The elections of 6 May 1999

The first elections to the Welsh Assembly took place on 6 May 1999, the same day as first elections to the Scottish Parliament, not to mention thousands of county council places in England. As in Scotland the electoral system chosen for Wales was the Additional Member System (AMS), in which forty Assembly members (AMs) are elected for constituencies by first-past-the-post. Four top-up members are then chosen for each of the five regions represented by Euro-constituencies, selection being by way of the d'Hondt method, under which the number of votes cast for each party list is divided by the number of constituency members already elected plus 1; the process being repeated until all the seats are filled. Being applied to a smaller total of seats and votes the system is not so proportional in Wales as it is in Scotland, although here too the Conservatives benefited from the proportional nature of the vote.

Party	Constituency seats	Regional seats	Total
Labour	27	1	28
Plaid Cymru	9	8	17
Conservative	1	8	9
Liberal Democrat	3	3	6
Turn out			40%

The results were a great shock to Labour whose 35 per cent share of the vote was their worst performance in Wales since 1918. On the basis of their opinion-poll rating and from long experience of the Welsh electorate, they had expected to sweep the board in elections that were the creation of a Labour government. Instead of which Labour, despite being the largest party in the Assembly still fell three seats short of an overall majority, thanks to a totally unexpected swing to Plaid Cymru in the Labour heartlands of the valleys. In a major electoral upset Labour lost the apparently rock-solid safe seats of Rhondda, Llanelli and Islwyn (Neil Kinnock's old constituency). Alun Michael, the highly unpopular Welsh Labour leader and First Secretary designate, only succeeded in taking his place in the Assembly by being placed on the party list for a top-up seat in the Mid and West Wales Euro-constituency.

Turnout was poor, running at 40 per cent overall but the size of the turnout seemed to be related to how the constituency voted in the referendum. The lowest turnout was 32 per cent in Alyn and Deeside, a strongly anti-devolution district in the referendum, while Caernarfon in the Plaid Cymru heartland of Gwynedd registered a turnout of 60 per cent. Labour party activists blamed both the poor turnout and Plaid Cymru's successes on a mixture of Labour complacency because of their large majority in the UK Parliament and dissatis-faction over the in-fighting within Wales Labour over the way in which Alun Michael had been imposed as leader by the national Labour party hierarchy in Millbank.

What was revealed in the performance of Wales Labour in Assembly elec-tions emphasised a factor that was equally true for Scotland in the Holyrood elections. Voters who remained perfectly loyal to Labour in Westminster elec-tions, and who expressed themselves as being quite satisfied with Labour's per-formance in government, nevertheless voted for Plaid Cymru in the Assembly elections. As was the case in Scotland, a vote for the nationalist party was not a protest vote against the Blair government but the result of a subtle distinction in the voters' minds between which was the best party to govern Britain as a whole and which was the party that would do most to represent Welsh inter-ests. 'Welsh voters had determined the Assembly elections as being a Welsh rather than a British concern' (Deacon, 2001, p. 190). Research showed that, while only 44 per cent of the Welsh people trusted Labour to look after Welsh interests, no less than 82 per cent believed that it was Plaid Cymru who would do most for Wales's best interests (*Guardian*, 20 October 2000).

Research in Scotland and Wales, which asked electors both how they had voted in the 1999 devolution elections and how they would vote in a Westminster by-election, revealed the extent to which people who were still willing to vote Labour for Westminster would choose to vote Plaid Cymru in the Cardiff elections. The result of the so-called 'devolution gap' was to suggest that Labour were 13 per cent worse off in the Welsh elections than they would have been in a Westminster election while Plaid Cymru did 17 per cent better.[5] This was partially borne out by the results of the 2001 Westminster general election where Labour was down on its 1997 result but only by 6 per cent rather than the 13 per cent drop in the Assembly elections. Similarly, Plaid Cymru increased its share of the vote, but by 4 per cent rather than 17 per cent. Plaid Cymru lost Ynys Môn to Labour but countered by winning Carmarthen East and Dinefwr from Labour. Plaid Cymru failed, however, to repeat its Assembly success in winning seats in Labour's valley heartlands and the Westminster constituency of Rhondda remained firmly Labour, if with a reduced majority.

Returning to 1999, the first task of the Assembly after the election was to select a Presiding Officer and this was done on 12 May, the choice falling on Dafydd Elis Thomas, who had been MP for Meirionydd Nant Conwy and president of Plaid Cymru, until he was made a life peer in 1992 as Lord Elis-Thomas of Nant Conwy.

The fact that Labour did not have an overall majority in the Assembly election was assumed at first to mean that Labour would try to form a coalition executive as they had done in Scotland. The idea was, however, rejected by Labour. Wales Labour was far more hostile to the Liberal Democrats than was the Labour party in either England or Scotland, while Plaid Cymru and the Conservatives were obviously out of the question as coalition partners. Alun Michael calculated that the three opposition parties would never be able to agree to the extent that they could combine together to vote against Labour. He announced that he would proceed with a minority administration which would work openly to provide an 'inclusive' approach through reaching a consensus with the other political parties. This original vision of consensus politics was one of the first casualties of the enforced resignation of Alun Michael.

The Alun Michael story

The first year of the Welsh Assembly was dominated by the ill-feeling generated in Wales by the way in which London and the national Labour party were seen to have imposed Alun Michael on the Assembly against the wishes of both the Assembly members themselves and of the Labour party in Wales. As John Osmond, director of the Institute of Welsh Affairs, has said, the replacement of Alun Michael by Rhodri Morgan can be seen as 'a defining moment in Welsh politics . . . an exercise in democracy . . . a shift in the underlying political culture of Wales' (Hazell (ed.), 2000, p. 41).

The saga surrounding Michael began in September 1998 when the Welsh Secretary, Ron Davies, was elected leader designate of the Wales Labour group in the Assembly after having beaten his rival, Rhodri Morgan, in a particularly bitter contest. Rhodri Morgan accepted the defeat, even though he was the favourite of the grass-roots membership. Ron Davies got on with the job of being both party leader and Secretary of State for Wales. In October, Davies had to deal with some of the worst floods Wales had known for 30 years, including serious damage in his own constituency of Caerphilly. On 26

October an obviously weary Davies drove back to London after meetings at the Welsh Office in Cardiff and, still feeling tired, went for a walk to clear his head on Clapham Common, not far from his home in Battersea. On 27 October Davies told the Prime Minister that, while on the Common, he met a man who later robbed him of his wallet, portable phone and car. Davies then tendered his resignation as Welsh Secretary so as not to embarrass the government because of his 'error of judgment'.

Davies was replaced as Welsh Secretary by Alun Michael, a friend of Tony Blair who had not hitherto played much part in Welsh politics and who had not planned to stand for the Assembly. On 29 October Ron Davies was forced to resign his position as prospective leader of the Assembly because of revelations of Davies's sexuality arising from the Clapham Common incident. Downing Street and the party hierarchy in Millbank determined that Michael should become the new leader of Wales Labour and reopened the party lists for Assembly candidates so that Michael might be elected by being 'parachuted' into a safe top up seat.

In the leadership election it became clear that the party hierarchy were determined not only that Alun Michael should win the contest but that, more importantly, Rhodri Morgan should not win it. Tony Blair made it very clear that he supported Alun Michael by visiting Wales on three occasions to speak on his behalf. Instead of electing the leader by means of one member one vote (OMOV) as was the case in other Welsh parties, the Labour party set up an electoral college divided into three sections of which the first was made up of ordinary party members, the second of trade unions and affiliated bodies and the third of Labour MPs, MEPs and Cardiff candidates, each section having one third of the vote – a device later repeated in London when Labour wished to rule out Ken Livingstone as candidate for Mayor.

Although the grass-roots membership and politicians voted by OMOV, the trades union section used the block vote and of the fifteen trade unions represented on the electoral college only five held OMOV ballots to determine the union candidate. Therefore, while the grass-roots membership was in favour of Rhodri Morgan by a margin of almost three to one, the leadership of the party and the larger unions insisted that Alun Michael should be elected. In the final result Alun Michael won the leadership by 52.68 per cent of the vote against 47.32 per cent. Within that total, however, the only part of the electoral college to support Michael was represented by the union block vote. One signal of possible trouble ahead can be seen in the fact that 21 out of the 28 Labour Assembly members were supporters of Rhodri Morgan.

The decision in favour of Alun Michael was unpopular in Wales where the *Wales on Sunday* newspaper called Michael's win a 'Defeat for Democracy' (Deacon, Griffiths and Lynch, 2000, p. 127). This unpopularity was largely due to the perceived imposition of Michael by London against the wishes and advice of the Welsh people. Any doubts that might have been felt as to Michael's competence were shortly reinforced by some fairly bizarre actions on his part. When he appointed his first cabinet, Michael antagonised the entire farming community by choosing a vegetarian, Christine Gwyther, to be his agriculture secretary. At the same time he made Tom Middlehurst the Assembly secretary responsible for the Welsh language despite the fact that Middlehurst does not speak Welsh!

In October 1999 the three opposition parties combined to pass a motion of censure against Christine Gwyther, the agriculture secretary, by 30 votes to 27, for her failure to get European agreement to a support scheme for Welsh farmers that had been passed by the Assembly. Michael simply ignored the censure motion aimed at his cabinet member and attempted to carry on as though nothing had happened, even managing to survive a vote of no confidence proposed by the Conservative leader, Nick Bourne, who famously said, 'The minority administration acts and fails to react as if it were a majority administration.'[6]

In February 2000 Plaid Cymru proposed a vote of no confidence in Alun Michael over what they claimed was the First Secretary's failure to get money from the Treasury so as to match European funding for the poorest regions of Wales. Michael protested that Plaid Cymru had no right to dictate who led the Labour party in Wales and intended, it was believed, to fight the no confidence vote by standing for re-election as Labour leader and First Secretary. However, there were clear signs of divisions within the Labour group in the Assembly, only five of whom were Michael loyalists, against around thirteen who supported Rhodri Morgan. In a surprise move Alun Michael sensed the inevitable and resigned before the vote could take place. Although Michael was personally applauded by the Labour group he lost the ensuing no confidence vote by 31 votes to 27, with one Labour abstention. The cabinet then chose Rhodri Morgan to be First Secretary, ensuring that the man who had twice failed to gain the nomination, finally became leader of Wales Labour, despite Downing Street and Millbank.

The replacement of Alun Michael by Rhodri Morgan was just one of several important changes of personnel in the Assembly. In August 1999, soon after the Assembly opened, the leader of the Conservatives, Rod Richards, was forced to resign after being arrested and charged with causing grievous bodily harm to a woman in London. He was later acquitted, but by then he had been replaced by Nick Bourne as leader and expelled from the Conservative group in the Assembly for ignoring the party whip. Then, after the departure of Alun Michael the leader of Plaid Cymru, Dafydd Wigley, the man who had guided Plaid to success in both the European and Assembly elections, announced that he was proposing to retire on health grounds. Ieuan Wyn Jones, Plaid Cymru's business manager or chief whip in the Assembly and MP for Ynys Môn since 1987, was elected leader with 77 per cent of a vote by all party members. The new leader was very much a moderate who described Plaid Cymru's aspirations for Wales as 'full national status' rather then 'independence' and who embarked on an internal consultation as to the party's constitutional aims. The party was, however, harmed early in 2001 when a Plaid councillor in Gwynedd, Simon Glyn, denounced English people living in Wales as being a 'mortal threat'. Labour accused Plaid of racism and Ieuan Wyn Jones was savaged on BBC1's *Question Time* by Glynis Kinnock, causing Plaid Cymru's standing in the polls to be reduced. Wyn Jones would later lose his constituency to Labour in the 2001 general election amid accusations of 'arrogance and neglect'.[7]

The point of these changes was that, as was the case in Scotland, the leaders of both the Labour and nationalist parties had been replaced within eighteen months of the original elections. In Scotland the legacy of Donald Dewar was a desire to make devolution work in his memory. In Wales the arrival of Rhodri Morgan was seen as the right man finally being given the job, with a change to a more clearly Welsh agenda for the Assembly.

How the Assembly works

Plenary sessions of the Assembly are informal with members seated at desks in a semi-circle facing the Presiding Officer and referring to each other by name. When Ron Davies once referred to another member as an 'honourable gentle-man', Dafydd Elis Thomas famously replied 'there are no honourable gentle-men in this Assembly' (Deacon, 2001, p. 189). Debates are bilingual although an instantaneous Welsh to English translation service is available. Assembly members do not have to give way to one another on points of order or informa-tion as they must at Westminster: the result of which is the possibility of members being able to speak at length without interruption or contradiction, as happened in a debate about Europe in 1999: 'A speech by a Labour member which attacked the Conservatives and Plaid Cymru but gave them no time to reply resulted in both of these parties walking out of the chamber in protest' (Deacon, Griffiths and Lynch, 2000, p. 103). Voting is done by way of computer terminals, without members having to leave their desks.

Plenary and committee sessions are restricted to Tuesdays, Wednesdays and Thursdays, so that members can carry out constituency work on Mondays and Fridays rather than at weekends. Daily business also closes at 5.30 p.m. and this, together with the free weekends, is supposed to make the workings of the Assembly family friendly. The proceedings of the Assembly are printed verba-tim in *The Assembly Record*, which is modelled on *Hansard*, while Rhodri Morgan, when he became First Secretary, established the practice in the name of open government of publishing cabinet minutes on the internet, at www.wales.gov.uk. As well as debates, plenary sessions of the Assembly are called to hear and question the First Secretary and the various cabinet secretar-ies. The Assembly, however, was designed to be a committee-led body and Assembly committees are the means by which Assembly members can take an active and important role in the running of the Assembly.

There are six subject committees:

- Agriculture
- Economic development
- Education pre-16
- Education post-16
- Environment
- Health and social services

A cabinet secretary will always attend meetings of the committee relevant to the secretary's portfolio: only the First Secretary and the secretaries for business and finance being without a corresponding committee.

There are also five further committees that do not have subject responsibilities:

- Audit
- European affairs
- Legislation scrutiny
- Regional
- Standards of conduct

The chairs of these committees and the composition of membership are chosen so as to be proportional to political party strengths in the Assembly. This does not apply to the four regional committees, each of which contains all Assembly members for that region, regardless of party affiliation.

The work of the committees is guided and controlled by the chair and cabinet member working together. The roles of the committees can be said to be:

- discussing and helping to make policy;
- scrutiny and oversight of bodies funded by the assembly (such as certain quangos);
- discussing and amending secondary legislation;
- scrutiny of Westminster and European legislation affecting the committee;
- communicating their views and conclusions to the cabinet.

One example of the degree to which the committee system could be effective was seen at the time of the first Assembly budget in December 1999. The budget in Wales is fixed over the period between June and February with ten consultative stages. This used to be done behind closed doors and treated as a strictly internal matter by the Welsh Office. The process adopted by the Assembly was an exercise in open government. Edwina Hart, the finance secretary, noted that Assembly committees made 33 recommendations, 29 of which were accepted in the draft budget; the committees therefore having a considerable impact on budget allocation. One important aspect of that first budget was the cabinet's acceptance of a programme of free eye tests, granted as a thank you to Plaid Cymru for not voting down the budget.

The Assembly is served by civil servants who were previously allocated to the Welsh Office. They have three major functions:

- to support the cabinet in fixing policy;
- to act as a secretariat for the committees;
- to maintain links with Whitehall.

Because of the increased involvement of the civil service in making policy the permanent secretary at the Welsh Office in 1998, Rachel Lomax, established a small policy unit which was expanded in 2000 to form a cabinet executive.

Initial disappointments and subsequent changes

Early experience of the committee system seemed to show that it did not work since in the first year of the Assembly the plenary sessions proved to be far more effective scrutineers than the committees whose job it was. There were three main complaints:

- None of the committees succeeded in holding the executive to account.
- The committees did not engage in policy-making.
- The committees did very little in respect of secondary legislation.

One possible explanation of poor performance can be found in the timing of committee meetings. Normally meetings were fortnightly and for only two to three hours. The situation was aggravated by the Assembly's 'socially-friendly' short day. In an attempt to fit meetings into this pattern many pre-meeting consultations were beginning at around 7.00 a.m.

A more likely explanation for the early disappointment in the committee system is that the poor results were a product of Alun Michael's acting as though a minority administration were in a majority and the constitutional outcome of executive devolution which effectively means that the Assembly has no backbenchers as such. Two early lessons to be learned reflected this:

- The committees appeared to have more impact when the chair of a committee is from a party other than the majority governing group. For example, one of the most effective chairs from the start was the Plaid Cymru Assembly member, Cynog Dafis, chair of the post-16 education committee, who proved effective over the issue of performance-related pay by fighting a series of measures originating with both the Assembly cabinet and the Department for Education and Employment (DfEE).
- Committees performed far better over clear-cut issues like Objective one funding than they did over abstract discussions on matters like the state of agriculture in Wales.

In January 2000, as the movement to get rid of Alun Michael was gaining ground, Ron Davies spoke to the Institute of Welsh Affairs and listed what he saw as being the five main areas of concern over the performance of the Assembly up to that time.

- There is no mechanism for the collective discussion of issues.
- There is no effective decision-making process in the Assembly, which bows to the will of the executive.
- Power is concentrated into a very few hands, with the executive dominating and completely over-shadowing the committees.
- There is no effective forum for policy formation in Wales and the policies pursued by the Assembly are those developed by the UK government or the old Welsh Office.
- There is no formal agreement between the parties over the nature of the administration, which results in a minority administration living a hand-to-mouth existence one day at a time with new one-off agreements on each occasion.

These statements were largely true but many were answered by the stance taken by Rhodri Morgan after he replaced Alun Michael. Instead of the pretence of a minority attempting to govern as though they had a majority, Morgan recognised that he had to make agreements with other parties. Soon after he became First Minister, Morgan made an informal deal with Plaid Cymru's director of policy, Cynog Dafis, which allowed the Assembly to proceed much more confidently. Later, Morgan reached a semi-formal coalition agreement with the Liberal Democrats which promised to assure the position of the Labour executive until the next Assembly elections in 2003.

Rhodri Morgan also improved relations with Westminster in alliance with the Secretary of State, Paul Murphy. When Gordon Brown announced the Comprehensive Spending Review in the autumn of 2000, there was an extra £421 million for Wales, intended to match EU structural funding for West Wales and the Valleys. The award virtually ignored the Barnett formula since the EU funding is treated as extra money that does not even enter into the Barnett equation. Unfortunately this triumph was shortly afterwards overshadowed by the decision of the steel company Corus to shed 2,500 jobs in South Wales and Deeside. Both Morgan and Murphy were criticised for what it was claimed was inadequate support and a failure to get sufficient funds from Westminster to ameliorate the problem.

Legislation by the Assembly

There are two main forms taken by the secondary legislation enacted by the Assembly. The most obvious is the drafting and authorising of statutory instruments but the more common consists of policy circulars produced for the guidance of local government and quangos in applying primary legislation passed in Westminster.

As far as statutory instruments are concerned, there are three possible routes for legislative action:

- The full procedure begins with the draft measure being discussed at length and amended by the relevant subject committee. It is then examined even more closely by the legislation scrutiny committee. Finally it is taken to the floor of the Assembly where it is discussed in plenary session, with room for further amendment.
- There is a fast-track option in which the measure is not seen by the committees but goes straight to the legislation scrutiny committee and then on to the Assembly.
- Emergency procedures allow the executive to pass legislation without reference either to the Assembly or to its component committees.

In the early history of the Assembly most secondary legislation was the product of the emergency procedure. For example, in the first three months of 2000 the Assembly issued 43 general orders, of which 19 were treated as matters of urgency. Such a display of executive power was what caused the media to start talking of a 'democratic deficit' in respect of the Assembly.

Much of the work of the Assembly relates to circulars and directives issued to local government, where the Assembly has assumed all the powers and duties previously carried out by the Welsh Office. Relations between the Assembly and local authorities are conducted through a Partnership Council made up of representatives of the Assembly and members nominated by the Welsh Local Government Association (WLGA), who can only act in an advisory capacity. In relation to local government the Assembly:

- allocates funds from the block grant to the local authorities;
- oversees and resources various services, including social services, housing, education and planning;
- regulates the collection of revenue through the council tax and business rate;
- funds the police service in Wales.

In much the same way the Assembly has acquired responsibility for quangos. During the years of Conservative government, when the Conservatives steadily lost ground in Welsh local government elections, the Welsh Office took powers away from the local authorities and handed them over to quangos. Wales came to be known as 'quango-land' – a country where local councils were Labour-dominated but services were provided by quasi-autonomous bodies headed by Conservative nominees. One of the arguments for devolution was the suggestion that transferring the quangos to Assembly control was somehow a democratic move. However, there is no indication that the intervention of the Assembly has made the quangos any more accountable. And, while the stated intention before the event was for the number of quangos to be reduced, indications are that if anything the number has increased.

Operational review

In reviewing the early days of the Assembly, John Osmond of the Constitution Unit (Hazell ed.), 2000, p. 72) concluded that the first year of the Welsh assembly was the equivalent for Wales of Scotland's constitutional convention. In other words the Assembly learned from its mistakes in order to create and recreate itself in the light of day-to-day experience.

There were four main areas where the Assembly had become very involved and where it made a significant contribution:

1 The question of European Objective one funding was so important that it was a major factor in forcing the resignation of Alun Michael. The question seemed to have been settled by the Comprehensive Spending Review of 2000 but the problem will return since one of the main criteria against which the Assembly will be measured will be its success in winning funds for the poorer areas of Wales.
2 Free eye tests proved to be one area where 'backbench' pressure on the executive forced the cabinet reluctantly to make provision for Wales that was significantly different from that obtaining in England.
3 Disputes over performance-related pay for teachers led to a judicial review of the competence of the Assembly over matters that lie on the borderline between reserved and devolved powers. Teachers' pay is governed by two acts of parliament. The 1986 Education Act is judged to fall within the scope of devolved powers but the 1991 Teachers' Pay Act does not. In a ruling on the matter requested by the National Union of Teachers (NUT), Lord Justice Jackson found against the DfEE by stating that the Welsh Assembly need not impose similar conditions in Wales to those existing in England (Hazell, 2000, p. 73).
4 Agriculture was a constant cause of friction where Welsh practices differed from those in England. Disputes over calf-processing and genetically modified (GM) foods helped to unseat Alun Michael and cost Christine Gwyther her job. More unsettling were the implications for Welsh agriculture of the continuing BSE situation and the foot and mouth outbreak of early 2001, with mass cullings of sheep on Welsh hill farms in Snowdonia and the Brecon Beacons.

Factors such as these led to a strong suggestion that the executive devolution granted to Wales was not enough and that there was need for: (a) a clearer division between the Assembly's executive and legislative functions, and (b) the possibility of primary legislative powers.

Alun Michael originally acted as though the Assembly had replaced the Welsh Office, but that nothing else had changed and Wales was still completely subordinate to the UK parliament at Westminster. The events leading up to the enforced resignation of Alun Michael and the agreement between Rhodri Morgan and the Liberal Democrats in October 2000 were indicative of a new, more distinctly Welsh mood and a possible move towards a more parliamentary position.

In March 2000 the Presiding Officer, Lord Elis-Thomas suggested that he should chair the equivalent of a Speaker's Conference to examine the possibility of giving the Assembly more legislative powers. Rhodri Morgan, as First Minister, refused to allow such a constitutional conference to take place but he did announce the setting up of an operational review to consider all aspects of the Assembly and its committees. This body was formed of the Presiding Officer with the party leaders and the party business managers. Despite its wide remit it seems that the review concentrated on the relations between the Assembly and the Westminster Parliament. The strength of feeling as to this matter in the Assembly was shown in a vote on the Queen's Speech in December 2000 when a motion proposing a stronger Assembly was passed by 49 votes.

Elis-Thomas originally called for his proposed conference to report before the scheduled Assembly elections in 2003 so that any changes could be in place before the new Assembly was chosen. The timetable, however, was soon extended. An inter-party review of Assembly powers was set up as part of the October 2000 partnership agreement between Labour and the Lib Dems and that is only due to report after the 2003 elections. It appeared that the question would now be referred to an EU intergovernmental conference on regional, national and European tiers of government scheduled for 2004.

Conclusion – the Civil Service view

The civil servants acting as officials for the Welsh Assembly responded to the operational review with a series of critical statements as to what they found wrong with the Assembly and devolution process as it was then constituted.[8]

- The Assembly in plenary session wastes too much time with minor procedural matters and points of order.
- Plenary debates are too vague and lack focus. Nor is there adequate feedback to the officials who must record and act upon Assembly decisions.
- The number of oral questions allowed in each session is too great for them all to be dealt with in one session.
- There are too many repetitive questions and questions allowed that could easily be answered by the Library.
- It is not clear as to whether officials are responsible to Assembly secretaries or Assembly members. This needs to be clarified before any separation between executive and legislative functions can take place.
- Much time and unnecessary effort might be saved if a whole range of routine, non-controversial measures could be passed by subject committees rather than plenary sessions.

The overall message seems to be that devolution in Wales has had a very shaky start and has still not achieved the popular acceptance that the Scottish Parliament has gained, simply because a large proportion of the Welsh population does not believe that the Assembly is more than an expensive talking shop, providing jobs for the boys. Much of the credibility gap is due to the decision to give Wales only executive devolution. Things have improved since Rhodri Morgan took over from Alun Michael with a more distinctively Welsh agenda but full acceptance would seem to be dependent on whether and how soon Wales could have a parliament rather than an Assembly: complete with the powers of primary legislation.

Notes

1 Quoted by Jonathan Freedland in the *Guardian*, 21 February 2001.
2 Figures are taken from the *South Wales Echo*, as quoted in *Politics Review*, April 1998. For a detailed breakdown of the 'yes' and 'no' votes according to the electoral districts of Wales, see Appendix 4.
3 For a list of cabinet members appointed by Rhodri Morgan, see Appendix 6.
4 The explanation and formula used in Scotland and described at length in Appendix 2 is equally as applicable to Wales.
5 Research reported by the University College of London Constitution Unit, whose reports can be read on their website at www.ucl.ac.uk/constitutionunit.
6 Reported in the *Assembly Record*, 2 November 1999.
7 Said by Glynis Kinnock and quoted in the *Guardian*, 9 June 2001.
8 Reported in the Constitution Unit's Quarterly Review for Wales, February 2001.

8

Northern Ireland –
the on–off agreement

Once a settlement in Northern Ireland was agreed on Good Friday, 10 April 1998, things moved very swiftly. On 22 May referendums on the agreement were held simultaneously in Northern Ireland and the Republic. A month later, on 25 June, elections to the Assembly took place and on 1 July the Northern Ireland Assembly held its first meeting in order to choose its First Minister and Deputy First Minister. And that is the point at which the process moved into slow motion or stop–go mode. Exactly one year after that first meeting of the Assembly, on 1 July 1999, it was officially confirmed that Scotland and Wales had both achieved full devolution but that in Northern Ireland the process had become impossibly bogged down in a resumption of sectarian squabbles: about the decommissioning of weapons, the demilitarisation of the security services, the reform of the police service and whether the union flag or Irish tricolour should be flown from public buildings on national holidays. Devolution day, which should have been 1 July 1998, was held back until 2 December 1999, with 17 months' shadowy existence for the Assembly and executive-designate intervening.

Referendums on the Good Friday Agreement

Referendums were held throughout the whole of Ireland, both north and south, on 22 May 1998. The main point at issue was the acceptability of the Good Friday Agreement but other points were involved that required some degree of compromise. For example, there was the question as to whether the Republic was willing to surrender its territorial claim to the six counties of Northern Ireland, a claim that had formed an integral part of the Irish constitution since 1937. Dublin was also asked to agree to a commitment that partition could be ended and the two parts of Ireland reunited only with the full assent of a majority of the people of Northern Ireland.

Given the normal apathy of the electorate, the turnout in Northern Ireland was remarkably high: 81.1 per cent of the electorate choosing to express their views, rather more than was normal in a general election. Of these, 71.12 per cent voted to support the agreement and 28.88 per cent voted against it. South of the border turnout was rather lower, at 56.3 per cent, but the vote was overwhelmingly in favour of the agreement, including the constitutional implications for the Republic: 94.4 per cent of those who took part voted in favour of the agreement, only 5.6 per cent voting against. An exit poll conducted in Northern Ireland by the Irish radio and television organisation, RTE, found that 99 per cent of the Catholic community had voted in favour of the agreement while the Protestants divided 55 to 45 per cent in favour. The same poll also showed that, of those Protestants voting 'no', as many as 69 per cent said that those members elected should try to make the Assembly work, only 17 per cent wanting to see it fail (Hunt, 1999, pp. 113, 117).

These figures show the very sizeable proportion of the Catholic and nationalist community that was pro-agreement, the RTE poll showing that 93 per cent of Sinn Fein supporters accepted all aspects of the agreement. In any other supposedly democratic society the 71 to 29 divide would mean that the issue was decided and settled for ever. But not in Northern Ireland! Ian Paisley's Democratic Unionist Party (DUP) and the one party in favour of full integration with the United Kingdom – the UK Unionist Party (UKUP) – together formed a vocal and influential minority that was totally opposed to the agreement. Alongside them there was a sizeable group within the Ulster Unionist Party (UUP) opposed to the party leader, David Trimble, and the official pro-agreement stance of the party. For this vociferous minority the Good Friday Agreement was represented as being a compromise too far.

This hostility to the agreement shows the extent to which sectarianism contrives to block progress towards a full settlement in Northern Ireland. For thirty years the received wisdom about the Ulster conflict was that there could be no military solution and that the answer lay with a political compromise. Which is what the Good Friday Agreement represents and what three-quarters of the population apparently want according to the referendum. Unfortunately, just over a quarter of the people in Northern Ireland are totally intransigent in their attitudes and still hanker after a military solution; believing that agreement can only be justified if it is linked with the surrender and humiliation of the 'enemy'. For anti-agreement unionists the key point at issue was the decommissioning of IRA arms, with Paisley and many others from the unionist community refusing to have anything to do with Sinn Fein (SF) until such time as the IRA's weapons and bomb-making equipment were rendered useless. Even sitting in the same assembly chamber as members of Sinn Fein was considered to be unthinkable, let alone sharing power with them on the executive. On the other side of the sectarian divide the SDLP represents the pro-agreement majority but Sinn Fein is unwilling to agree to decommissioning since this would imply unconditional surrender by the IRA and the IRA is as temperamentally opposed to surrender as is the DUP. Sinn Fein countered the dispute over decommissioning by demanding the demilitarisation of the British presence, removing army observation posts and taking soldiers off the streets, not to mention the virtual disbandment of the RUC in a wide-ranging reform of the police service.

The structure of government in Northern Ireland

In April 1998, as the negotiators came close to finalising the Good Friday Agreement, the Northern Ireland Office issued a paper on the structure of government in Northern Ireland which basically restated the governing structures under direct rule, into which a devolved administration could be inserted in the event of a settlement. In particular it named the government departments which would be in charge of devolved matters. In the same period Mo Mowlam, as Secretary of State, drew up a draft set of standing orders for the new assembly, based on the standing orders drawn up for the ill-fated Assembly of 1973–74.

As it was constituted in 1998, the Northern Ireland office consisted of the secretary of state (Mo Mowlam) with four junior ministers,[1] who dealt with constitutional matters, security, police and the courts, as well as six social and economic departments:

• Agriculture
• Economic development
• Education
• Environment
• Finance and personnel
• Health and social services

Assisting the Northern Ireland Office were 5 Education and Library Boards, 4 Health and Social Services Boards and 26 District Councils, responsible for street cleaning, refuse disposal, consumer protection, environmental health and recreational facilities.

This was the structure in which the Northern Ireland office was due to be replaced by the Assembly and Assembly Executive under the terms of the Good Friday Agreement. The settlement reached under the agreement consisted of five basic points:

• **There was to be an elected Northern Ireland Assembly of 108 members,** elected by PR in 16 six-member constituencies. The Assembly would have legislative powers by weighted majority so as to prevent unionist domination.
• **There was to be a 'cabinet' or controlling executive of 12 members,** including a first minister, a deputy first minister and ministers for finance, health,

education, agriculture and so on, according to the previous Northern Ireland office ministerial structure.

- **The Assembly would set up and supervise a North–South Ministerial Council to deal with cross-border issues,** a council which would take the form of joint meetings of ministers from Dublin and Belfast who could formulate all-Ireland policies on issues like transport, inland waterways, ports and harbours, as well as police matters such as drug trafficking and food safety.
- **A twice-yearly Council of the Isles (also known as the British-Irish Council),** being a discussion group drawn from the Dublin, Belfast, Westminster, Edinburgh and Cardiff parliaments or assemblies, together with representatives from the legislative bodies of the Isle of Man and Channel Islands.
- **Efforts would be made to settle outstanding issues over paramilitary groups,** including the decommissioning of arms, the accelerated release of paramilitary prisoners and the flying of flags on public buildings.

It was this last point and the continued failure of the two communities to reach any sort of agreement on these contentious issues that delayed full devolution for so long. An assembly of sorts did exist after the elections of June 1998 but the executive, the cross-border discussions and the British-Irish Council were all held in abeyance until all those parties that had gained representation in the Assembly elections could agree on how power should be shared. According to the complex structure of the Good Friday Agreement the three strands of that Agreement – the Northern Ireland Assembly, the North–South Ministerial Council (NSMC) and the British-Irish Council – stood or fell together. If one strand failed to meet the criteria set by the Agreement then the other two strands also failed.

The election of 25 June 1998

The election of 25 June was fought across the province, with 300 candidates seeking to become Members of the Legislative Assembly (MLAs) across 108 seats in 18 Westminster constituencies, with a 70 per cent turnout. The election was held under the single transferable vote (STV) system of proportional representation, with the aim of electing six members for each of the 18 constituencies.[2] The chief merit of STV, which has made it the preferred system for non-Westminster elections in Northern Ireland since 1979, is that the multimember constituencies ensure that electors from either side of the sectarian divide will have a representative with whom they can identify. Of the eighteen constituencies in the Northern Ireland Assembly there is only one that does not have both unionist and nationalist Assembly members with whom the constituents can identify (the exception is the entirely nationalist West Belfast with 4 Sinn Fein and 2 SDLP MLAs).

Party	% of first preference votes	Seats won
UUP	21.3	28
SDLP	22.0	24
DUP	18.1	20
SF	17.6	18
Alliance	6.5	6
UKUP	4.5	5
PUP	2.5	2
NIWC	1.6	2
UUAP	1.3	3

Although they did not win most seats the SDLP certainly polled the highest number of votes, with 177,000 or 22 per cent of first preference votes. The party's position as natural champion of the nationalist community was, however, strongly challenged by the 17.6 per cent polled by Sinn Fein, the highest ever vote for the IRA-linked party, a fact which contributed to Sinn Fein overtaking the SDLP to become the most popular nationalist party in West Tyrone.

The success of the nationalist parties was gained as a result of splits and divisions in the unionist ranks. The UUP led by David Trimble won its lowest ever share of the vote at 21.3 per cent, as against the 32.7 per cent recorded as recently as the 1997 general election. What was to make it worse for Trimble was that UUP supporters were slowly moving from the pro-agreement camp to being anti-agreement. For the first time since its foundation a century previously the party lost the support of the Orange Order, since the order opposed the agreement. The anti-agreement DUP, led by both Ian Paisleys, father and son, became the third most popular party with an 18.1 per cent share of the vote. But an even more significant statistic was the fact that the DUP topped the poll in seven constituencies, while the UUP only managed to do so in three. The only unionist party to give 100 per cent support to the agreement was David Ervine's Progressive Unionist party (PUP) which was linked with the paramilitary Ulster Volunteer Force. All the other splinter unionist groups were opposed to the agreement. The largest of these was Robert McCartney's UKUP which wanted an even closer integration with the UK than is provided by direct rule. The UKUP gained 4.5 per cent of the vote and won 5 seats. Shortly afterwards, however, four of the UKUP MLAs quarrelled with McCartney and went off to form the Northern Ireland Unionist Party (NIUP), leaving the UKUP as a rather idiosyncratic party of one. In December 1999, Roger Hutchinson of the NIUP agreed to join a statutory committee of the Assembly and was thereupon expelled from the NIUP and forced to sit in the Assembly as an Independent. Three members who were elected as independents formed themselves into the United Unionist Assembly Party (UUAP).

There were only two non-sectarian parties who gained representation. The more senior of the two, the liberally-inclined Alliance party, won 6.5 per cent of the vote and six seats, although it was an Alliance member, Lord Alderdice, who was nominated as the Assembly first Presiding Officer, or Speaker. The more recently formed Northern Ireland Women's Coalition (NIWC) was only able to achieve 1.6 per cent of the vote and 2 seats. But one of these members, Ms Jane Morrice, was chosen to be one of the three deputy Speakers.[3]

The American Senator George Mitchell was heard to say that what surprised him most about Northern Irish politics was the fact that, unlike the rest of the world where it seems to be a law of nature that political parties should always move towards a consensus in the centre of the political spectrum, in Northern Ireland the political groupings move steadily away from the centre and towards the extremes (Hazell (ed.), 2000, p. 111). As a result, the DUP is gaining rapidly on the UUP in its share of support within the unionist community, while Sinn Fein is moving to overtake the SDLP in winning the nationalist vote, a fact that was emphasised by the results of the 2001 Westminster general election. It has certainly always been the case that the entirely rational and moderate parties of the centre like the Alliance have been consistently squeezed to the periphery.

The Assembly that wasn't

Within a week of the elections of 25 June 1998 the Assembly was called together for the first time on 1 July. The meeting took place in the Castle Buildings on the Stormont estate, although all subsequent meetings would be held in Parliament Buildings. Lord Alderdice, former leader of the Alliance party, was nominated as Initial Presiding Officer by Mo Mowlam and the Assembly proceeded to elect David Trimble of the UUP as First Minister designate and Seamus Mallon of the SDLP as Deputy First Minister. The Assembly also appointed the statutory committees required by the Northern Ireland Act, most importantly a committee on standing orders and a committee to advise the Presiding Officer.

Appointment of the First Minister and his deputy, together with the statutory committees, was by cross-community voting procedures developed especially for the Northern Ireland situation, and would be used for any other contentious issues such as settling the budgetary process and deciding upon a programme for government. In order for these cross-community procedures to take place all members of the Assembly had to declare at the time of their election whether they were unionist, nationalist or other, so that their votes could be correctly weighted in any future cross-community procedures. There were two forms of cross-community agreements:

- Parallel consent – involving a majority of those voting who had to include both unionists and nationalists.
- Weighted majority – requiring 60 per cent of those present to vote, which must include at least 40 per cent of unionists and 40 per cent of nationalists.

With the basic decisions and appointments made, the Assembly meeting of 1 July came to an end. The whole process then simply marked time since the first minister had announced that he and his deputy would not move on to appoint members to the executive committee or cabinet until the IRA began the decommissioning of arms.

Over the summer a succession of events encouraged those who were opposed to the Good Friday Agreement and threatened to destroy the peace process. As usual the month of July was dominated by the Orange Order's marching season and confrontation over the peace settlement was once again threatened by a stand-off on the Drumcree march in Portadown. At the height of the confrontation a petrol bomb thrown at a house in Ballymoney killed three Catholic boys. The volatile situation at Drumcree was defused by a statement from the deputy chaplain of the Orange Order, the Revd William Bingham, who famously stated that *a fifteen-minute walk along the Garvaghy Road is not worth the lives of three wee boys*. The rest of the marching season passed off peacably.

On 15 August the province was rocked by a car bomb in Omagh, County Tyrone, which proved to be the worst terrorist incident of the whole troubled period; killing 29 and wounding 200, some of them sufficiently badly as to leave them permanently maimed. The bomb was shown to be the work of the so-called 'Real IRA', a splinter group that disowned the Good Friday Agreement and sought to continue the armed struggle. The Real IRA was disowned by Sinn Fein but there were those from the unionist community in the province who felt that Sinn Fein's condemnation of the atrocity was less than wholehearted and who therefore believed that any co-operation with Sinn Fein before decommissioning took place was out of the question and would betray the innocent victims who had died.

On 18 December 1998 Trimble and Mallon agreed on details of the structure of the proposed executive when it could be formed. There would be a total of ten departments, the ministers of which would form the cabinet along with the first minister and his deputy. Agreement was also reached at this meeting on the six north–south implementation bodies and the six areas of north–south co-operation which would be chosen from a list including such issues as inland waterways, food safety, trade and business development, special EU programmes, language, agriculture and marine matters. The two men were agreed that the executive would have 'parity of ministerial esteem' by which membership would be divided between six unionist and six nationalist members.

These talks also fleshed out what had been unformed proposals of the agreement and which divided into three strands:

- First strand – assembly and executive.
- Second strand – North-South implementation bodies – ministerial meetings.
- Third strand – British-Irish Council and a British-Irish intergovernmental committee.

It was understood under the terms of the agreement that the three strands stood or fell together and, during the shadowy period when only strand one had a partial existence, the second and third strands lapsed and fell by the wayside. The period was not entirely without activity, however, and the Assembly met in plenary session on nineteen occasions over the next seventeen months, mostly involved in drawing up a set of standing orders based on those drawn up for the ill-fated power-sharing executive of 1973–74.

On 1 April 1999 the British Prime Minister, Tony Blair, and the Irish *Taoiseach*, Bertie Ahern, engaged in talks intended to bring the two sides together and which resulted in an agreed position by the British and Irish governments, *The Way Forward*. During June both leaders were involved in talks at Stormont over arms decommissioning. Tony Blair was confident enough to claim that he detected 'a seismic movement' in the Northern Irish position. But unfortunately his optimism was not reflected in the unionist rejection of *The Way Forward*. The proposed simultaneous devolution scheduled for 1 July had to be deferred in Northern Ireland, leaving just Wales and Scotland to go ahead together.

On 15 July 1999 the Secretary of State called on the Assembly to meet in order to nominate ministers to membership of the executive committee, a nomination carried out by the d'Hondt method. Prior to the meeting she made it clear that the executive would be nominated subject to standing order number 22, which stated that the executive could only exist if it contained three designated unionists and three designated nationalists. This proved to be an impossible condition to meet since the UUP had refused to recognise the meeting and remained in their party headquarters in Belfast throughout. The Presiding Officer attempted to proceed under the d'Hondt rules but both the DUP and UKUP refused to nominate, while the Alliance also refused to nominate since it claimed that the sectarian nature of standing order 22 was an insult to any non-sectarian parties such as themselves. Since the SDLP and Sinn Fein were the only two parties prepared to nominate, the standing rule in question could not be honoured and the Secretary of State had to revoke her notice calling the Assembly, forcing the Presiding Officer to adjourn until further notice. Seamus Mallon resigned from the position of deputy first minister in protest at the UUP's stance.

In August the British and Irish premiers once again asked George Mitchell to arbitrate between the two sides. Mitchell's review lasted eleven weeks, during which time Mo Mowlam was replaced by Peter Mandelson as Secretary of State. Opinion in Northern Ireland believed that Mo Mowlam favoured the nationalists at the expense of the unionists but that Mandelson was more sympathetic to the unionist position. That seemed to influence events when Senator Mitchell reported on 18 November.

Everything hinged on David Trimble and the UUP position and David Trimble chose to interpret a decision by the IRA to send a representative to see the Commission on Decommissioning under General John de Chastelain, as meaning that decommissioning would get under way before the end of January 2000. Trimble thereupon agreed to devolution going ahead and got the Ulster

Unionist Council to agree to this on the basis that he himself would be willing to tender his resignation as first minister and bring down the executive if sufficient progress with decommissioning had not been made by the end of January 2000.

The 72-day devolution

The Ulster Unionist Council agreed to what they understood had been recommended by George Mitchell on 27 November 1999 and this enabled Westminster to process the devolution settlement that had been in abeyance for a year and a half: the vote on 30 November being in favour by 318 votes to 10. The day on which devolution was officially granted was 2 December.

Once the step had been taken and devolution declared, all the rest fell into place and the process of establishing government structures was completed remarkably swiftly. On 29 November the new Secretary of State, Peter Mandelson, granted a standing order which permitted the Assembly to reject Seamus Mallon's resignation. Rather than go through the long drawn-out procedure of re-electing the deputy first minister, an act which might well have failed, Mandelson's order simply set the resignation aside, as something that had never happened. Both the first minister and his deputy were therefore present when the Assembly met that same day in order to nominate members to the executive by means of the d'Hondt method. There were four nominating parties: who voted in the stipulated order: UUP, SDLP, DUP, SF, based on the share of the vote in Assembly elections, and they had to select 10 cabinet members in the agreed proportions of three each to the UUP and SDLP and two each for the DUP and SF.

A controversial issue as far as nominations to the executive were concerned was the question as to which of the ten departments would be given to Sinn Fein ministers. The big fear of the unionist parties was that Sinn Fein would gain control of the department of culture and would thereby have jurisdiction over matters like flags, public festivals, music and marches – all of which have a strong symbolic significance for the sectarian communities. Ironically enough, the UUP was so busy defending culture from the SF threat that they took their eye off the ball and failed to notice that Sinn Fein had captured the two major spending departments of education and health.

Having chosen its executive committee, the Assembly went on to appoint the ten statutory departmental committees, each of which had eleven members, with party allegiances proportional to the representation of the parties in the Assembly. The chairs and deputy chairs of these committees were similarly proportionately divided between the parties.[4]

The ten departmental statutory committees were:

* Agriculture and rural development
* Culture, art and leisure

- Education
- Enterprise, trade and investment
- Environment
- Finance and personnel
- Health, social services and public safety
- Higher and further education, training and employment
- Regional development
- Social development.

Also set up at this time were the six standing committees:

- Audit committee
- Business committee
- Committee of the Centre
- Procedure committee
- Public Accounts
- Standards and privilege.

On 2 December 1999 the government of the Republic of Ireland changed the two clauses of the 1937 constitution which had claimed possession of the six counties and which sought complete sovereignty over the whole of Ireland. The principle of any future unification of Ireland only being effected with the consent of the majority of the population of Northern Ireland was accepted, removing fears in the unionist community that any cross-border cooperation would lead inevitably to control by Dublin. Removal of that fear meant that progress could be made in setting up the three cross-border institutions: the North–South Ministerial Council (NSMC), the British-Irish Council (BIC) and British-Irish Intergovernmental Conference (BIIGC).

The NSMC met for the first time in Armagh on 13 December 1999, and agreed on the six all-Ireland implementation bodies:

- inland waterways
- food safety
- trade and business development
- special EU programmes
- language
- aquaculture and marine matters.

Also agreed were the six areas for north–south cooperation:

- agriculture
- education
- environment
- health
- tourism
- transport.

The NSMC was scheduled to have plenary sessions at six-month intervals, these sessions being led by the first minister and his deputy for Northern Ireland, together with the *Taoiseach* for the Republic. As well as the plenary sessions there should also be regular sectoral meetings for the areas of cross-border co-operation. Representation at these meetings should be on an equal basis between the Republic and the Province but is more often made up of one minister from Dublin and two representatives from Stormont, one from each of the two Northern Irish communities. The NSMC is jointly funded by both governments and, being accountable both to the Assembly and the Dáil, is supported by a 24-strong secretariat recruited equally from career civil servants in both north and south. The NSMC is based in Armagh which, as St Patrick's city, the ecclesiastical capital of Ireland and seat of both Catholic and Anglican Archbishops of all Ireland, is seen as neutral territory.

The first meeting of the NSMC took place in Armagh on 13 December 1999 but, because of the period of suspension, the body did not meet again until 26 September 2000 when the location was Dublin Castle and the meeting was attended by twelve of the 15-strong Dublin cabinet and all the Northern Ireland executive, except for DUP representatives. On either side of the suspension there was a full programme of meetings for the sectoral departments and implementation bodies. Most of the implementation bodies have 12 members, with equal representation from north and south. However, the body dealing with the issue of language is different in that it has 24 members, divided into 16 members for Gaelic and 8 members for Ulster-Scots, the two parts meeting and working separately.

Four days after the first meeting of the NSMC came the first meeting of the British-Irish Council, also sometimes known as the Council of the Isles, in that it includes eight delegations, not only from the London and Dublin governments but also from the Scottish Parliament, the Welsh and Northern Ireland assemblies, the Isle of Man, Jersey and Guernsey. The council meets at the same three levels as the NSMC: there being plenary sessions twice a year, a regular programme of sectoral meetings and ad hoc meetings as required. A secretariat for the council is jointly provided by the British Cabinet Office and the Republic of Ireland's Department of Foreign Affairs. The first meeting of the BIC took place in London on 17 December 1999.

On the same day, 17 December, the first meeting took place of the BIIGC, also held in London. This body was inherited from the 1985 Anglo-Irish agreement and exists in order to hold bilateral meetings on areas of mutual concern. Led by Blair and Ahern the meeting consisted of representatives of the London and Dublin governments, together with David Trimble and Seamus Mallon.

The final stage in setting up the institutions of the devolved Assembly came on 24 January 2000 when the chairs and deputy chairs of the standing committees were chosen (see Appendix 9). At the same session three deputy speakers were elected by cross-community voting. These were Donovan McClelland of the SDLP, Sir John Gorman of the UUP and Jane Morrice of the NI Women's

Coalition. A DUP member, William Hay, was nominated but failed to get cross-community support.

From the start, the DUP members of the Assembly refused to participate to the full in power-sharing and neither of the two DUP ministers would attend meetings of the executive at which Sinn Fein (SF) would be present, although DUP members sat quite happily on both statutory and standing committees, despite those committees having SF members.

Unlike the situation in Wales and Scotland, committee meetings at Stormont were mostly held in private. During the initial period of devolution there was just one committee matter that became public property, this being a debate in the Health departmental committee as to whether maternity services for Belfast should remain at the City Hospital or be transferred to the Royal Victoria. The Sinn Fein minister of health, Bairbre de Brun, stirred up a great deal of hostility by ruling that the service was transferred to the Royal Victoria, which is in Ms de Brun's own West Belfast constituency. The ruling was also made despite a seven to four vote in favour of the City Hospital by the committee. When referred to a plenary session of the Assembly, the vote went on a simple majority to the City Hospital and the minister's decision was also overturned in the courts by a judicial decision.

For Bairbre de Brun this proved to be just one of a series of controversies that involved her throughout this first period. As an Irish speaker she insisted on speaking Gaelic at question time in the Assembly but, because answers were drawn out by having to be given in both English and Gaelic, there was a limit to how many questions she could take in the 30 minutes of question time. This annoyed the other members of the Assembly, from both communities and it was noticeable that all her speeches in Irish were ignored and heckled, other members drowning her out with their conversations, although members seemed prepared to listen in silence to UUP members speaking in Ulster-Scots. Also arising from the use of Gaelic were accusations of waste because Ms de Brun insisted that all the many forms and items of stationery in her department that were printed only in English had to be pulped and replaced by bilingual versions.

Ms de Brun was also well to the fore in the other controversies that arose from Sinn Fein's demands and counter-demands. Both Sinn Fein ministers, Martin McGuinness and Bairbre de Brun, refused to allow the flying of the union flag over their ministries on public holidays. And, since unionists rejected the republic's tricolour equally vehemently, Sinn Fein adopted the position of 'neither flag or both together'. The flying of the two flags side by side was rejected by all unionists as a symbol of joint rule with Dublin so therefore no flags at all were flown although the argument continued to rage, on and off. In much the same spirit Sinn Fein ministers and chairs refused to accept bodyguards from the RUC, as a police authority they did not accept.

Despite all the work done by the Assembly in December and January, the issue of decommissioning would not go away and, as it became clear that the UUP's 'understanding' that decommissioning would begin in January, was just not going to happen, progress in the Assembly began to slow down. A meeting of the Ulster Unionist Council (UUC) was scheduled for 12 February 2000, at which it was expected that David Trimble would make good his promise to resign if decommissioning had not started. If he did resign the executive would collapse, with no guarantee that it could later be put back into place. To avoid that collapse Peter Mandelson made a pre-emptive strike on 11 February by suspending the Assembly and reimposing direct rule. Suspension of the institutions of the Northern Ireland Assembly took effect as of midnight 12 February 1999.

Devolution resumed

With the Assembly suspended, the Prime Minister and *Taoiseach* redoubled their efforts to get the process back on the rails. Extensive talks were held with all parties but most pressure was put on to Sinn Fein, and through them on to the IRA, in order to get movement on the decommissioning of arms. As a result of these talks the two leaders issued a statement on 5 May which virtually stated that devolution could be reinstated in return for a commitment that could be rather less than the 'permanently unusable' position asked for previously. In reply an IRA statement of 6 May spoke merely about putting arms 'beyond use', although, as a 'confidence-building' measure the IRA pronounced itself willing to open certain arms dumps to the arms inspection team of former African National Congress leader, Cyril Ramaphosa, and former Finnish president, Martii Ahtisaari.

As early as March David Trimble had announced that he was ready to re-enter government with republicans, surviving a leadership challenge from the Revd Martin Smyth at the UUP AGM, although Trimble's support declined to 57 per cent. On 27 May, in the light of the IRA statement, Trimble once more asked the Ulster Unionist Council to support him in re-entering government. He got that support, although it was reduced yet again to 53 per cent and he had to agree to end the Sinn Fein flag protest and to halt reform of the police service by retaining the name 'RUC', which Chris Patten's report had said must go.

Two days later, on 29 May, devolved powers were returned to the Assembly. The DUP, however, continued to object to sharing power with Sinn Fein and said that, not only would they continue to boycott the executive committee but would make government difficult by rotating the members filling their two assigned ministerial positions. As a result of this decision the first such rotation took place on 27 July when Gregory Campbell replaced Peter Robinson as minister for regional development and Maurice Morrow replaced Nigel Dodds as minister of social development. In retaliation the first minister and his deputy personally took over responsibility for transport from the regional ministry, blocked the DUP ministers from attending the joint ministerial committee and stopped the distribution of executive papers to DUP ministers. This DUP action put an end to hopes that the long-awaited Programme for Government was about to appear. In its place the executive issued an 'Agenda for Government' as a short-term interim measure on 29 June, outlining the programme proposed for the Assembly between July 2000 and April 2001.

On 26 June the arms inspection team made their report, saying that they had been allowed to see a substantial proportion of the arms held by the IRA and they were satisfied that those arms could not be used without their prior knowledge. Nevertheless the DUP, representing the anti-agreement parties in the Assembly, chose to bring a motion on 4 July condemning Sinn Fein for its support of the IRA and seeking to exclude Sinn Fein ministers from executive office. The motion was bound to be rejected since it would never receive the cross-community support required but it did reveal yet further rifts in the unionist ranks.

The unionist bloc in the Assembly was 58 members strong, made up of 28 UUP, 20 DUP, 2 PUP, 1 UKUP, 3 NIUP, 3 UUAP and 1 independent. Originally the 28 Ulster Unionists were all pro-agreement and were joined by 2 members of David Ervine's Progressive Unionists. In the vote of 4 July, however, 4 UUP members voted for the motion, leaving David Trimble leading a minority of just 26 members in the Protestant bloc, as against 32 anti-agreement MLAs. There was widespread pessimism in the Irish press as to the unionist position: 'Broad unionist opinion has swung over two dispiriting years, from a positive to a negative view of the Good Friday deal.'[5]

The Assembly rose for the summer recess on 7 July and Northern Ireland was immediately plunged into troubles arising from the marching season and the release of paramilitary prisoners. According to the time-scale laid down in the Good Friday Agreement the government had been steadily releasing paramilitary prisoners belonging to both communities. On 28 July the last major group of prisoners from both sides of the divide was released. Yet, while the Protestant prisoners tended to disperse and disappear quietly, the IRA prisoners were greeted with nationalist flags, songs and celebratory speeches. It was a counter-productive move because the celebrations of the IRA's supporters were perceived as triumphalism by unionist onlookers. The merest hint that the republicans were claiming a victory was enough to drive many unionists into an anti-agreement stance.

On the so-called loyalist side there was factional infighting when the Ulster Defence Association (UDA) and its political wing, the Ulster Democratic party (UDP), embarked on a feud with the Ulster Volunteer Force (UVF). Random attacks and beatings gave way to organised violence when the two sides clashed openly at a UDA parade in Belfast on 19 August. Even before that, the *Belfast Telegraph* had reported a series of attacks in Belfast, Ballymena, Carrickfergus and Newtownabbey under the headline 'Sectarian attacks reach new levels of hatred'. In the course of the disturbances 200 families were driven from their homes and two men died in attacks by the UVF. Peter Mandelson, as Secretary of State, was forced to make it clear that these disturbances were largely attacks by one loyalist group upon another, that they were disorganised and that they therefore were no threat to the continuation of paramilitary ceasefires. Things were made worse by an Assembly member, Billy Hutchinson of the UVF-connected PUP, who condoned attacks on the UDA. Part of the problem was that, of the two loyalist paramilitary groups' political wings, the UDA's UDP never won a seat in the Assembly, whereas the UVF's PUP won two seats. Now, however, a rift developed between the moderate David Ervine, who supported the Good Friday Agreement, and the more extreme Billy Hutchinson, who moved to adopt an anti-agreement stance and a return to paramilitary confrontation. As the press in the Republic reported, 'There is a dangerous sense of drift, with the real possibility of the initiative passing back to the gunmen.'[6] On 22 August Mandelson acted decisively to defuse the situation by re-imprisoning Johnny 'Mad Dog' Adair, leader of the UDA in West Belfast and major orchestrator of the violence.

The weakness of the unionist position was further revealed on 21 September in the Westminster by-election for South Antrim. This was the second safest of all the UUP's seats and should not have presented a problem. But a strong DUP challenge by William McCrae was met by a UUP candidate, David Burnside, who was an admirer of Enoch Powell, an opponent of David Trimble within the party and very vigorously anti-agreement. In the event the DUP won the seat with a majority of 822. The UUP vote collapsed and a low turnout of just 43 per cent showed that the seat was lost as a result of abstentions by UUP supporters.

October 2000, however, saw rather more progress on a practical level as the final devolved institutions were put into place. On 9 October the Civic Forum, agreed as long ago as 16 February 1999, met for the first time in Belfast's Waterfront Hall. This was an advisory discussion group that was representative of the entire Northern Ireland community, which was scheduled to meet in six plenary sessions each year, with ad hoc groups meeting between times. The Civic Forum has a membership of 60 nominated representatives and a chair and is administered by the Office of the First Minister and Deputy First Minister (OFMDFM):

- Agriculture and fisheries   3
- Arts and sport   4
- Business   7
- Churches   5
- Community relations   2
- Culture   4
- Education   2
- Trade unions   7
- Victims   2
- Voluntary/community   18
- Plus three places nominated by the First Minister and three by the Deputy First Minister.

At the inaugural session a businessman, Chris Gibson, was nominated to be chair of the forum. The meeting appeared to go well but the institution was heavily criticised by those opposed to the agreement, on four grounds: excessive bureaucracy; excessive cost; the under-representation of victims; a failure to accept representatives of the Orange Order.

Later that same month the Assembly finally succeeded in producing the Programme for Government that had been promised from the start of devolution. The programme, launched on 24 October 2000, laid out a total of 230 actions to be taken by the Northern Ireland government in an agenda that stretched through until the proposed elections of 2003 (if the Assembly lasted that long). These actions were divided between five goals that the Assembly had set itself:

• growing as a community;
• working for healthier people;
• investing in education and skills;
• securing a competitive economy;
• developing north–south, east–west and international relations.

The first of those goals was judged to be the most important since it tackled the issue of sectarianism head on with actions such as:

• the promotion of equality and human rights;
• tackling poverty;
• renewal of disadvantaged neighbourhoods;
• enhancing local communities;
• tackling divisions in society.

This programme counts as a major triumph for the devolved Assembly and executive in that the whole thing was published with the apparent agreement of all, despite internal divisions and the difficulties created in reaching four-party agreement while the DUP continued to absent itself from meetings of the executive.

On a knife edge – the paradox of success and failure

The final success of the Northern Ireland Assembly in producing an agreed programme for government served to emphasise the paradoxical situation in Northern Ireland, whereby the Assembly, both in plenary session and in its committees, appeared to be coping extremely well with the business of government administration and legislation, while the party political structure lurched from crisis to crisis, continually threatening to collapse. The same period that saw the Programme for Government published, the Civic Forum launched and the north–south cross-border bodies functioning well, also saw the parties divide among themselves over the same three problems:

- the decommissioning of IRA weapons and demilitarisation by the British;
- the reform of policing in Northern Ireland;
- the flying of flags over public buildings.

David Trimble tried to force the pace on decommissioning by refusing permission for Sinn Fein members of the executive to participate in any north–south cross-border meetings. The two ministers involved, however, Bairbre de Brun and Martin McGuinness, continued to meet their counterparts from the Republic on an informal, unofficial basis. In a gesture of nationalist solidarity Seamus Mallon also attended Ms de Brun's October meeting with her opposite number from Dublin. But Trimble's stance on this matter added yet another point at issue between the two communities.

At the same time, there was little progress on decommissioning since the IRA insisted that the undertaking to put their arms 'beyond use' should be considered to be sufficient. It was pointed out that the issue was largely irrelevant since, even if the IRA disposed of their arms, experience has shown that the IRA has never had any difficulty in obtaining further supplies and so could re-arm very quickly. Also, all the fuss was about guns while the real threat has always come from the bombers and they can make explosives from ordinary farm fertiliser!

During a visit to Belfast in December 2000, in the last month of his presidency, President Clinton attempted to find his way into the history books by securing a final Northern Ireland agreement. He failed to make progress, however, and was heard to claim that settling the conflict in Northern Ireland was every bit as difficult as finding a solution to the Arab–Israeli problem in the Middle East.

If the decommissioning of IRA weapons was the *sine qua non* for unionists then the reform of the police service fulfilled the same function for nationalists. Chris Patten had led the enquiry into reform and had come up with a number of proposals, including the removal of the name 'Royal Ulster Constabulary'. The nationalist position was that the RUC was too deeply implicated in the repression of the minority community in Northern Ireland for it to be deemed acceptable to the nationalist community. Nor could it be trusted as a police force for the entire community unless there were a change in its ethos, typified by a name that emphasised its link with the British Protestant supremacy. As a result the SDLP as well as Sinn Fein felt unable to accept a police force that continued to call itself the RUC and, above all, both nationalist parties were ready to speak out and campaign against recruitment to the police from the Catholic community.

The unionist instinct over policing was, however, to defend the RUC with everything they possessed. The commonplace sentiment expressed by unionist grass-roots opinion was that the RUC had bravely defended them against the IRA for thirty years, at the cost of many dead and wounded. But now the RUC had been betrayed and was being disbanded, at a time when the gunmen, in the form of Sinn Fein, were rewarded by being accepted into government. When the Police Bill came forward in November 2000 it was no surprise that the measures were deemed to be unacceptable by both sides.

There are those who believe that Sinn Fein's stance on policing was positional in anticipation of a possible breakdown of the Good Friday Agreement. If the agreement should fail Sinn Fein wanted to be able to blame the British position on policing for its failure rather than the IRA's stance on the decommissioning of arms.

In an attempt to support David Trimble, who fought off a challenge to his leadership of the UUP from Jeffrey Donaldson by promising to halt the police reforms, retain the name of the RUC and ban Sinn Fein from north–south meetings until decommissioning takes place, the then Secretary of State, Peter Mandelson, ruled that the union flag should be flown from public buildings on all of the 17 public holidays each year. And by saying 'all public buildings' he meant even those which housed departments headed by Sinn Fein or SDLP ministers.

It was as a result of that decision on flags that Peter Mandelson's resignation from office on 24 January 2001 was cheered by the nationalist community. Compared to Mo Mowlam's term as Secretary of State which was felt to favour the nationalist parties, particularly the SDLP, the sympathies of Peter Mandelson were felt to be with the UUP. At the time of his resignation there were very few voices raised in Mandelson's defence but many of those were in Northern Ireland where the loyalist community saw him go with genuine regret. The unionists feared that they would acquire Mo Mowlam's former deputy, Paul Murphy, as the new secretary but he was too useful to Rhodri Morgan as Welsh secretary and Northern Ireland received instead the former Scottish secretary, John Reid.

The true paradox in Northern Ireland is that a government exists which is doing good work against a constant background of inter-party squabbles, a situation which arises from the unique nature of the devolved government. The Northern Ireland executive is the only known example in the world of an enforced coalition of four political parties, each of them bitterly opposed to the others. It ends with the anomaly of a party acting as though it were in government and opposition at one and the same time.

An example of this was shown on 8 February 2001 when the Northern Ireland executive announced the granting of free travel for pensioners. The policy, which was very popular with the electorate, was immediately claimed as a success for the DUP, simply because the minister responsible for transport and the introduction of the measure was Gregory Campbell of the DUP, even though Mr Campbell refused to sit on the executive alongside Sinn Fein members. This was an example of the way that both the DUP and Sinn Fein pick out which measures they are going to support and which they are going to oppose. The Northern Ireland Assembly and executive could lay claim to a fair degree of success because all parties have felt able to vote for the large, important issues like the Programme for Government or the budget and have largely fought bitterly over peripheral issues like the flying of flags.

There is another paradox associated with the Northern Ireland devolution and this echoes a factor that has already been mentioned in relation to Scotland and Wales. In those countries it has been remarked that electors will claim to be loyal Labour voters and will act accordingly in Westminster elections but will nevertheless vote SNP or Plaid Cymru in elections for the devolved parliament or assembly. This is because they recognise the worth of the traditional parties on the broad UK stage but would prefer the nationalist parties to deal with purely Scottish or Welsh devolved matters. In the same way the electors of Northern Ireland seem to want purely Northern Irish matters to be dealt with the more dynamic and therefore more extreme parties who are seen to be closest to the Northern Irish people. As devolution has developed, the mainstream parties of the UUP and SDLP have gone into decline while the DUP and Sinn Fein are the 'rising stars' of Ulster politics.

This was made very clear in the Westminster general election of 2001. In May, David Trimble had tried to safeguard the UUP position by once again pledging that he would resign as first minister if the IRA did not begin the decommissioning of arms. His strategy failed because the UUP lost three of its nine Westminster seats while the DUP won two. Trimble only just managed to hold on to his own seat with a much reduced majority. Overall the UUP gained 26.8 per cent of the Westminster vote, against the DUP's 22.5 per cent. At the same time, on the other side of the sectarian divide, Sinn Fein doubled the number of seats it held, from two to four, becoming the largest nationalist party by taking 21.7 per cent of the vote, against the SDLP's 21 per cent.[7]

This rise in the fortunes of the hardline parties of Sinn Fein and the DUP made the position of David Trimble and any moderates much more difficult to sustain. It was pointed out that 74 per cent of the Northern Ireland electorate voted for parties supporting the Good Friday Agreement (including the UUP as a whole and Sinn Fein), leaving a mere 26 per cent openly opposed. And yet it seemed as though the minority opinion dictated public positions. On 1 July, before travelling to France for the 85th anniversary of the Somme, David Trimble resigned as first minister over the issue of the IRA's failure to put its arms out of use. Sir Reg Empey was appointed to be caretaker first minister while attempts were made to resolve the matter. If not resolved in six weeks, the Assembly would have to elect a new first and deputy first minister on a cross-community basis. Since that cross-community support looked unlikely it seemed inevitable that the Secretary of State, John Reid, would suspend Stormont and reimpose direct rule.

In mid-July the British and Irish prime ministers called a special conference of all parties involved in the peace process at the neutral location of a hotel on the Shropshire–Staffordshire border. Some progress was made but the entrenched positions of the unionists and Sinn Fein on decommissioning of arms and police reform made both sides unwilling to give way. As a member of the SDLP said, 'The Ulster Unionists and Sinn Fein are engaging in a blame game. . .'.[8] The London and Dublin governments continued to negotiate after the Northern Ireland parties had quit the meeting and in the next week produced an agreed document on matters such as reform of the police service that it was hoped would overcome the doubts of both sides.

The agreed statement, however, satisfied the demands of the nationalist community far more than it met the requirements of the unionists since there was still no timetable for the decommissioning of IRA weapons. The overall position worsened with the spread of sectarian violence against Catholics in Ulster and a bombing campaign by the Real IRA on the streets of London. In the first week of August, at the same time as a massive car bomb exploded in Ealing, General de Chastelain's commission announced that they had agreed with the IRA the means by which weapons were to be put beyond use. For the unionists it was still not enough since no timetable for the process to begin was announced. The six weeks from David Trimble's resignation ended and, at midnight on 10 August John Reid suspended the devolved institutions, reimposing direct rule. Twenty-four hours later, at midnight on 11 August, the devolved institutions were restored. The short break was a constitutional device that won a further six weeks of negotiation before the suspension of devolution had to become permanent, but the artificiality of the device annoyed both sides of the sectarian divide, the IRA for their part withdrawing the announcement they had made on weapons only a few days previously.

The timing of the suspension meant that half the six weeks gained was lost because the leaders of all sides went off for a much-needed summer holiday. Therefore, when the deadline of 22 September was reached, nothing whatsoever had changed and John Reid was forced to suspend Stormont for a second twenty-four hour period, thereby gaining a further six weeks' grace.

On 18 October David Trimble required three unionist ministers to withdraw from the executive and the Agreement seemed to be about to collapse. On 22 October John Reid told Sinn Fein that the IRA had to do something to break the deadlock and that if they did they would not find the British government ungrateful.

The IRA faced a new climate of public opinion following the terrorist outrages of 11 September in New York and they had lost a lot of that American support which had been the mainstay of the fundraising. On 23 October the IRA announced that they had begun to decommission arms, a fact that was confirmed by General de Chastelain's commission. Amid general feelings that the crisis was over, the British army began demilitarisation through the destruction of army watchtowers in nationalist areas. Further progress was represented by the RUC being replaced by the Police Service of Northern Ireland on 3 November. Nothing is ever straightforward in Northern Ireland, however, and when David Trimble offered himself for re-election as First Minister two member of his own Unionist party voted against him. David Trimble received 71 per cent of the Assembly vote 100 per cent of the nationalist vote but,

because he did not receive the required number of unionist votes, the complicated cross-community voting rules established under the Agreement meant
that he could not be elected as First Minister. In a hurried compromise deal,
three members of the non-aligned Alliance party redesignated themselves as
unionists for twenty-four hours. These three extra votes proved to be enough for
the claim to be made that the election of David Trimble as First Minister and
Mark Durkan of the SDLP as Deputy First Minister had the support of both
communities.

Notes

1   The most senior junior minister under Mo Mowlam was Paul Murphy, who was later
    to employ his experience of devolution in Belfast when he was appointed Secretary
    of State for Wales after the departure of Alun Michael.
2   See Appendix 7 for a discussion of the STV system of voting.
3   A full breakdown of the party composition in the 18 constituencies can be found in
    Appendix 8.
4   A list of those members nominated to the first executive committee on 29 November
    1999, together with the party distribution of chairs and deputy chairs of the depart-
    mental statutory committees, is given in Appendix 9.
5   *Belfast Telegraph*, 22 September 2000.
6   *Irish Times*, 20 November 2000.
7   Figures quoted by Rosie Cowan in the *Guardian*, 13 June 2001.
8   Quoted in the *Guardian*, 12 July 2001.

9

The English Question

For how long will English constituencies and English Honourable Members tolerate not just 71 Scots, 36 Welsh and a number of Ulstermen but at least 119 Honourable Members from Scotland, Wales and Northern Ireland exercising an important, and probably often decisive, effect on English politics while they themselves have no say in the same matters in Scotland, Wales and Ireland?[1]

The question set out above was asked by Tam Dalyell, MP for the Scottish constituency of West Lothian, during the second reading of Labour's Scottish devolution legislation in 1977, and has since become famous as 'the West Lothian Question'. It recognises the point that any devolution of power from Westminster would lead to a disproportionate presence of MPs from the devolved regions in the Westminster Parliament.

Scotland has always had more representatives at Westminster than its size would seem to warrant. In the 1707 Act of Union, Scotland was granted 45 MPs and 16 representative peers in the parliament of Great Britain, the overrepresentation being said to compensate Scotland for the loss of an independent parliament and to prevent the Scottish voice being swamped beneath the English majority. By the time of the 1992 election, Scotland contained 9 per cent of the UK population but its 72 MPs represented 11 per cent of Commons membership. The same picture is reflected for Wales, where 5 per cent of the population is represented by 6 per cent of MPs (Adonis, 1993, p. 8).

This disproportionality leads directly to the West Lothian Question, or rather to two related questions:

- If Scotland has its own parliament and Wales its own assembly, each dealing with Scottish or Welsh legislation, does either country need so many Westminster MPs? Would it not be the case that Scottish and Welsh electors would be twice as well represented as the electors of England?
- Would it be right for English MPs to have no say on legislation that was specifically Scottish or Welsh, when Scottish and Welsh MPs would be able to

speak and vote on legislation that was specifically English in nature? This is, of course, the real West Lothian Question.

The obvious answer was that the number of Westminster constituencies would have to be reduced for any part of the United Kingdom which became subject to a devolved assembly. The reverse was shown in 1972 when Stormont was suppressed. Before that time, while the Stormont Parliament existed, Northern Ireland had 12 Westminster MPs; after the abolition of Stormont the number of Northern Irish constituencies was increased to 17 and later 18. It was agreed at the time of devolution, on the basis of recommendations originally made by the Kilbrandon Report in 1973 that the Boundary Commission would look at the matter, with the suggestion that the number of Scottish constituencies would be reduced to 57 and Welsh constituencies to 31, at the time of the next boundary revision.

There is one fly in this ointment and that is the heavy reliance of Labour on Scottish and Welsh seats for the party's representation in Parliament. The party easily predominates in both countries: half the votes cast in Wales are for Labour, while almost a fifth of all Labour MPs sit for Scottish constituencies. The dilemma for Labour has always been that they are a party committed to devolution for Scotland, and yet to reduce the number of Scottish constituencies in the wake of devolution could well lose the Labour party up to twenty seats, thereby threatening future Labour majorities in the Westminster Parliament.

It remains, however, a bone of contention for English MPs in that, even if Westminster MPs for Scotland, Wales and Northern Ireland undertake, as they have done, not to participate in any legislation that is specifically English in nature, some 130 MPs would have a considerably lighter work load than their 529 colleagues in English constituencies. Following devolution for Scotland and Wales the problem of what to do with the English residue grew to the extent that the West Lothian Question was renamed as the English Question. As Vernon Bogdanor said, '. . . devolution will accentuate an already existing constitutional imbalance in favour of Scotland and Wales' (Bogdanor, 1999, p. 285).

Thus far the English Question was chiefly expressed in terms of representation and the comparative over- and under-representation of the devolved bodies and England. As the devolution process got under way an extra dimension was added in that Scotland, Wales and Northern Ireland, who are all financed in accordance with the Barnett formula, are comparatively much more affluent than many English regions. Figures issued for the financial year 2000–1 showed that public spending in Scotland was 23 per cent above the English average, while the figures for Northern Ireland and Wales were 39 and 18 per cent above English spending respectively (Hetherington, April 2001). Even more significant than the national figures are comparisons with many of the English regions. However poor Scotland was when the Barnett formula was devised in the 1970s the fact is that Scotland is now far more affluent than many neighbouring parts of Britain. The Yorkshire and Humberside region, which has much the same level of population as Scotland, would require an extra £5.2 billion a year in order to match the level of public spending north of the border.

The various strands of the English Question combine to suggest that something may have to be done with the English rump within the UK parliament. In 1998 the House of Commons Procedure Committee began an enquiry into the *Procedural Consequences of Devolution*, which reported in July 1999. Two of the areas they investigated concerned the so-called English question:

- What legislation would continue to be debated at Westminster and what new procedures should there be for its scrutiny?
- What would be the role of the territorial select and grand committees?

The second of these was the most important because even before devolution Scotland and Wales, whose affairs were dealt with by the Scottish and Welsh Offices respectively, had had their own select, standing and grand committees to consider all legislation for those territories. The Procedure Committee decided that it would be unfair to retain the Scottish, Welsh and Northern Irish Grand Committees if there were not some similar arrangement for English MPs; although it was conceded that an English Grand Committee with over 500 members was totally impracticable. Instead, for a period a new forum for discussing territorial matters was created which, because it is housed in the Grand Committee Room off Westminster Hall, has acquired the title of 'Westminster Hall'.

As to the question of the role of the Westminster Parliament after devolution, there are several possible ways forward which might deal with this:

Westminster as an English parliament

This might be run on much the same lines as Holyrood, Cardiff Bay and Stormont serve Scotland, Wales and Northern Ireland. In other words it would be a federal solution in which the constituent nations of the UK each had their own assemblies. However, the federal concept of an English parliament has been considered and rejected. Of the 659 MPs at Westminster, 529 represent English constituencies, while the English form 85 per cent of the UK population. Which makes the representation for England totally out of balance with the other constituent nations. Moreover, the argument for devolution is about decentralisation and the northern, western and midland regions of England are as concerned to escape from London domination as are Scotland or Wales.

On the other hand it might be feasible for Westminster to act as the UK Parliament when the whole house is sitting but to adopt a different approach in the administration of the departmental select committees. These committees could be composed of English MPs only when the committees are those which scrutinise departments dealing exclusively with devolved matters such as education or agriculture. There is some evidence that this is happening de facto. At the start of 2001 a survey conducted by the UCL Constitution Unit showed that four select committees have an exclusively English membership: these were the committees dealing with the devolved matters of education, employment, health and home affairs. It was also noted that there are no ministers in these departments who are Irish, Welsh or Scottish rather than English (Hazell, 2001).

'English votes for English laws'

This is a possible solution favoured by the Conservative party and a few others. When he was leader of the party William Hague set up a working party chaired by Lord Philip Norton and known as the Commission to Strengthen Parliament. Reporting in July 2000 the commission proposed a change in legislative procedures for bills that are certified by the Speaker as relating to just one constituent part of the UK. Such bills would be referred to a Bill Grand Committee formed by all the MPs from that constituent part, who would see the bill through the legislative process. In their passage through parliament the committee stage of such bills would be taken in a special standing committee whose membership would also be restricted to MPs from that constituent nation or region, the numbers of committee members reflecting party strengths in the Commons.

Something similar was proposed in June 2000 when the Labour backbencher, Frank Field proposed a bill to bar Scottish and Northern Irish MPs from speaking or voting on any devolved matter. The same bill also would have prevented Scottish or Irish MPs from being given ministerial rank in departments dealing with reserved matters. The bill was rejected by 190 votes to 131, showing that there is no real support for this solution.

The Standing Committee on Regional Affairs

As is mentioned above and will be reported again below, another proposed solution put forward in 1999 by Margaret Becket as Leader of the House, was to create a Grand Committee for England along the lines of the Scottish Grand Committee. But the number of English MPs would make such a committee too large to be practicable and in its place it was proposed to resurrect a defunct committee for the English regions that was originally created in 1975 but which had sat for the last time in 1978, the concept being alien to the thinking of Margaret Thatcher and her successors. Margaret Becket tried to resurrect the committee on a number of occasions after 1999, but met with such resistance from the Conservatives that it was not until 10 May 2001 – on the last day parliament sat before dissolution and the general election – that the 15-member committee could be convened (for membership, see Appendix 10). Only one Conservative member, Anthony Steen, attended and he immediately announced that he intended to leave early (shortly afterwards to lose his seat in Totnes). The members remaining began discussions but soon showed that there were inter-nal divisions in England over the nature and extent of devolution required and the committee was roughly divided into those from south-east England who were largely happy with the status quo and those from the north and west who wanted urgent reforms of the Barnett formula for the financing of the regions, as well as discussion of elected assemblies for the English regions.

Since the Queen's Speech of December 2000 promised measures to extend devolution to the English regions it seemed as though the solution favoured by the Blair government, and the then deputy prime minister, John Prescott, in particular, was a degree of devolved government for England. Indeed the com-mittee meeting of 10 May was promised that the next Labour administration would begin the legislative process that would provide elected assemblies for the English regions, although any mention of such legislation had disappeared from the first Queen's Speech after the 2001 election.

Regional agencies and regional assemblies

During the early 1990s, as part of the Tory government's reorganisation of the Civil Service, offices known as government offices for the regions (GOs) were instituted to perform the same service for the English regions as the Northern Ireland, Scottish and Welsh Offices did for the national regions. The regional director in each office became responsible for the regional policies of three Departments of State – Environment, Transport and the Regions; Trade and Industry; Education and Employment – reporting to and remaining account-able to the relevant Secretary of State. The ten regional offices and the popula-tions served by each were: London (6.9 million), South-East (7.7 million), East (5.2 million), South-West (4.8 million), West Midlands (5.3 million), East Midlands (4.1 million), Yorkshire and Humberside (5.0 million), North-East (2.6 million), North-West (2.6 million) and Merseyside (1.5 million) (Bradbury, 1996, pp. 16–19).

Following the 1997 election these arrangements began to change and widen so as to allow the GOs to form the nuclei of possible English devolved regions alongside developments in Scotland and Wales. On 14 January 1999, Margaret Becket, as Leader of the House of Commons, announced that the government was thinking of reconstituting the Standing Committee for Regional Affairs. The intention would be for the committee to come into being in the summer of 1999, after the Scottish Parliament and the Welsh and Northern Irish assemblies had taken up their duties. It was not quite clearly stated what function the committee would serve but the suggestion was that it could act for England and the English regions like the Scottish Grand Committee has acted for Scotland in the past. Margaret Becket was keen to play down any suggestion that such a committee could evolve into an English devolved parliament but she did also make it clear that all options were open.

In late 1998, John Prescott, who was not only deputy prime minister but also the Secretary of State for the super-department that had responsibility for the regions, announced the setting up in April 1999 of eight Regional Development Agencies (RDAs) which would replace the existing government offices for the regions. The new agencies were much the same as their predecessors but the creation of an elected Mayor and strategic authority for London removed the capital from the list of regions, while Merseyside was absorbed into the north-west region based on Manchester. These RDAs have a role in developing regional strategies and selected members represent the English regions in the deliberations of the European Union's Committee of the Regions. They also have a say in regional policies on transport, land use and the environment, further and higher education, crime prevention and public health (Hetherington, 1998).

The eight regional development agencies concerned are quangos which may or may not have 'councils' of business people, trade unionists and local government councillors to look after them. They represent a form of administrative or executive devolution for:

- South-East
- South-West
- East
- East Midlands
- West Midlands
- Yorkshire and Humberside
- North-West
- North-East.

A ninth region is represented by the Greater London Authority, with its mayor and strategic authority. Within each of those regions the agencies are responsible for the supervision of industrial development, urban and rural regeneration and transport and strategic planning.

These developments were therefore putting into place the raw building materials out of which some kind of English devolution might be created, even though these regional developments are seen as being 'top-heavy and unaccountable' (Bogdanor, 2001).

The deputy prime minister, John Prescott, and his minister for the regions at the time, Richard Caborn, suggested giving coordinating powers to the council–forums that oversee the development agencies. By going one step further and electing the members of these groups there might well be the beginnings of regional assemblies for England. In late 2000 Richard Caborn told a Fabian Society meeting in York: 'I believe the radical programme of constitutional change we embarked on in 1997 is incomplete without an answer to the so-called English question. Regions need a clear voice to promote economic development and that in my view is best achieved through (elected) regional assemblies' (Hetherington, January 2001).

However, at the same time, moves were afoot in the Labour government to extend the reorganisation of local government to encompass elected mayors and strategic bodies for the provincial cities along the lines of the London settlement. In addition there was the suggestion that local government in England should be made up entirely of unitary authorities as is the case in Scotland and Wales and that the unitary councils should be run on the cabinet system.

Assemblies all round

Following Scottish and Welsh devolution the government hinted at a willingness to consider a move towards English devolution and thus complete the 120-year-old Gladstonian vision of devolution.[2] The first stage, as we have said, was the creation of the eight English regional development agencies, set up by John Prescott with the aim of improving provincial economies. But their budgets were modest, less than £1 billion for the lot of them, and it was hard to be too enthused at their prospects. However, the eight agencies were given a big financial boost in the spending review of July 2000, with the prospect of even more massive extra funds being provided later. In the pre-budget statement in the autumn of 2000, Gordon Brown promised the RDAs a £500 million budget increase to £1.7 billion by the financial year 2003–4. He also hinted at a reform of the Barnett formula which would mean a reallocation of the funds which currently go so disproportionately to Scotland, Wales and Northern Ireland and would give the regions far more flexibility.

Alongside this promise of funding came the formation of regional chambers, popularly known as 'assemblies', which were set up by John Prescott to shadow the RDAs. With a membership comprising councillors, business people, trade unionists and religious leaders, they were given the blessing of the deputy prime minister. Full-time secretariats were established to service the assemblies and regional plans were prepared. In some regions the assemblies agreed terms and signed up to a permanent relationship with the RDAs. Gordon Brown later spoke of John Prescott as 'deserving congratulations for delivering the RDAs and their assemblies' (Hetherington, January 2001).

Delegates to Labour's national policy forum, meeting in Exeter to agree the content of the party's manifesto for the 2001 election, agreed that the party had to recognise the legitimate aspirations of the English regions and belief was expressed in the idea that elected regional assemblies might well be next step in Labour's reform programme of revising the constitution and empowering the ordinary citizen.

Jack Straw, as Home Secretary, developed the criteria by which English devolution might be developed during Labour's second term in office. What he proposed was a three-point plan that had to be followed for the establishment of regional bodies:

1 Plans for devolution should be drawn up and regional chamber members petitioned for their support.
2 The plan would be forwarded to parliament by the regional chamber, indicating that the plan has the support of a majority of local government councils in the region. The relevant Secretary of State must submit the plans to opposition parties to secure their support.
3 Evidence, most probably by way of a referendum, has to be provided to show that the public want devolution and would approve of the proposals.

The main point of these safeguards is to ensure that the people of England are not swamped by unnecessary layers of government. For the same reason a fourth criterion was added to make the point that regional chambers would only be permitted in areas of unitary authorities, since any elected regional bodies would replace the old county councils.

John Prescott and his supporters believed that these developments meant that they were on their way to committing a future Labour government to the introduction of English devolution during Labour's second term. Any such move would be different from the arrangements for Scotland and Wales. The various regions would be allowed to choose for themselves whether they wished to move towards devolved government, and what form that devolution would take. The intention was for England to have asymmetrical devolution similar to that introduced in Spain, where Andalusia, the Basque country, Catalonia, the Canary Islands, Galicia, Navarre and Valencia were granted a greater degree of autonomy than the other devolved regions, which chose for themselves which devolved measures they wished to adopt. In other words devolution would be delivered piecemeal in England, as and when requested by the regions, and not necessarily with all having the same degree of autonomy.

It is not clear that there is any real support for devolution in anything but a handful of English regions. A poll in the *Economist* during 1999 found that the North-East was the only region outside London that agreed with the hypothesis that a regional assembly would look after the region's interests better than central government, while the British Social Attitudes survey for 2000 showed a mere 18 per cent of the population favouring regional devolution for England while 62 per cent wanted the status quo to continue (Hazell, 2001). There is nevertheless a certain degree of interest in a number of areas that have felt neglected in the past, including Merseyside and the North-West and Cornwall and the South-West, areas that feel they are losing out to Wales or Scotland when it comes to inward investment and funds from Europe. Of the regions, the North-East is the most enthusiastic for regional devolution since it is the area of England closest to Scotland and the voters and MPs of the region can look across their border to a land where 'there are no student tuition fees, the prospect of free nursing care for the elderly, higher wages for teachers and a hands-on industrial policy pumping tens of millions annually into hi-tech industry' (Hetherington, January 2001).

The governance of London

While the policy-makers still speculate about the possibilities of regional government in England there is in fact one region where a form of devolved government has already been established and that is in Greater London. As far as the arrangements for London are concerned it is not totally clear whether the reform represented by the Greater London Authority (GLA) with its mayor and strategic assembly is indeed devolved government or simply a new form of local government. The Local Government Act of 2000 allows local authorities to hold referendums on the possibility of creating directly elected mayors with attendant assemblies for any city in England and Wales. But whether such a move would come under the heading of regional devolution or reformed local government is not entirely clear (Hazell (ed.), 2000, p. 241).

The road leading to the establishment of the GLA began when the Greater London Council (GLC) was abolished by the Thatcher government in 1986. When that happened it meant that London became the only major city in the developed world not to have some form of city-wide government. In its place the departure of the GLC left total chaos. Services that had been run and provided by the GLC passed into the hands of tens, if not hundreds, of different bodies. Some services reverted to the various London boroughs, others to government agencies and specially created quangos, while still others were contracted out to private companies. On the other hand some aspects of London government had always been in the hands of national government, as for example the Metropolitan Police which had been under the direction of the home secretary since the days of Robert Peel.

It was clear that something had to be done to clear up this confusion. When the Major government introduced their government offices in 1994, one of the nine instituted was the government office for London (GOL). Members of the Major administration, most notably Michael Heseltine, also became enthused with the idea of a directly elected mayor for London, on the grounds that most major cities such as Paris and New York were run by powerful elected mayors and their administrations.

The idea was taken up by the Labour party and a proposal that there should be an elected mayor for London was included in Labour's 1997 election manifesto. Acting quickly on that manifesto promise the Blair government issued a green paper, *New Leadership for London*, in July 1997. The green paper led in turn to the decision to consult the London electorate and, in the aftermath of the Scottish and Welsh referendums, the Greater London Authority (Referendum) Bill was introduced to Parliament in October 1997. The GLA proposed by the Labour government consisted of a directly elected mayor and assembly but there were amendments proposed by the Conservatives that would have led to a directly elected mayor and an indirectly elected assembly of borough council leaders; while the Liberal Democrats put down an amendment that would have had a directly elected assembly but no mayor (Hazell (ed.),

2000, p. 246). Both amendments were defeated and the referendum framed by the government was set for 7 May 1998, on the same day as London borough elections.

The result of the referendum appeared to be a resounding endorsement of the government's proposals, 72 per cent voting in favour and only 28 per cent against. However, it has to be said that turnout was a mere 34.6 per cent of the electorate and this meant that, in effect, only 23 per cent of Londoners had voted for the GLA.

Nevertheless, the government went ahead, publishing a white paper, *A Mayor and Assembly for London*, in March 1998. This became the Greater London Authority Act of 1999, receiving the royal assent on 11 November 1999, and came into force in a series of measures introduced between December 1999 and July 2000. The Act as passed was a massive 476 pages long – even longer than either the Scottish or Welsh devolution bills.

The Greater London Authority

The GLA as constituted in the Act consists of:

- **The Mayor**, directly elected by supplementary ballot.[3] His duties are to:
    - propose policy;
    - prepare a budget;
    - make appointments to the GLA agencies;
    - speak for London;
    - appoint his own cabinet.
- **The Assembly**, 25 members elected by the additional member system:
    - 14 members are constituency members, elected by simple majority;
    - 11 members as top-up members, chosen from London-wide party lists.
- **GLA Agencies**, known as the 'functional bodies', staffed by assembly members:
    - Transport for London (TfL);
    - London Development Agency (LDA);
    - Metropolitan Police Authority (MPA);
    - London Fire and Emergency Planning Authority (LFEPA).

Within this framework the mayor has executive powers and is expected to draw up strategies for a number of public issues, most notably transport, waste disposal, economic development and regeneration, air quality and pollution, and culture. In preparing these strategies the mayor is expected to consult the Assembly, whose duty it is to scrutinise the work of the mayor. He is also free to consult the boroughs, the GLA functional bodies or any other individual or corporate adviser who is thought to be appropriate. He can delegate his powers to a deputy mayor who is chosen by the assembly members from among themselves, or he can delegate to GLA officers, the functional bodies or the London boroughs.

The mayor is held accountable by a number of devices, including the monthly report he must make to the Assembly and a monthly question time session in the Assembly. Once a year the mayor must present a progress report to the Assembly which is then published as a 'State of London' address and debated by the Assembly. Twice a year, in association with the Assembly the mayor will speak directly to Londoners in 'People's Question Time'. The mayor also has the task of drawing up a budget that is presented to the Assembly before the end of February each year. The Assembly can approve a budget by a simple majority but an amendment requires a two-thirds majority.

The Assembly elects a chair and deputy chair who have the ability to take over many mayoral functions in his absence. The Assembly can also form its own politically-balanced committees who act in a way very similar to that adopted by parliamentary select committees, with the power to call witnesses and take evidence to help its enquiries.

Electing the mayor and Assembly

The selection of candidates for mayor proved to be more difficult and controversial than had been expected. In March 1999 Jeffrey Archer announced that he was a possible Conservative candidate, challenged shortly afterwards by Steven Norris. In October Jeffrey Archer was chosen as candidate by a very large majority, his candidature endorsed enthusiastically by William Hague and the party leadership. In the following month, however, Archer was charged with having perjured himself in the libel case of 1987 and was forced to retire from the mayoral contest. Against the wishes of many in the party Steven Norris was chosen as Conservative candidate.

In the meantime the struggle had begun for the man who believed that the post of mayor was his by rights and had been ever since he was rejected as leader of the GLC by Margaret Thatcher. Ken Livingstone had announced his bid for the Labour party candidature in March 1999, as had Trevor Phillips. But Livingstone was disliked and distrusted by the Labour party hierarchy and a 'Stop Livingstone' campaign began almost immediately. In July Glenda Jackson resigned from the government to seek the Labour party nomination, and other Labour party hopefuls seeking the nomination included Nick Raynsford, then minister for London. In October, however, Tony Blair's own choice, Frank Dobson, made his move and resigned as Health Secretary to seek the mayoral nomination. In the light of Downing Street's endorsement of Dobson both Trevor Phillips and Nick Raynsford withdrew from the contest.

The Labour party introduced a new electoral process to select its candidate, a political manoeuvre that mirrored exactly the process introduced in Wales to ensure the election of Alun Michael rather than Rhodri Morgan. There was to be an electoral college with three sections: rank and file members of London constituency Labour parties; membership of affiliated trade unions in London; London-based Labour MPs, MEPs and GLA candidates.

On 20 February 2000 Frank Dobson received 51.5 per cent of the vote against Ken Livingstone's 48.5 per cent, Glenda Jackson having been eliminated in the first round of voting. Frank Dobson was immediately adopted as Labour's official candidate but, despite an undertaking to abide by the decision, Ken Livingstone registered a protest. The union section of the electoral college had divided into those unions who had consulted their membership before voting and those who had not.[4] Those who consulted their membership ended by supporting Livingstone, those who had not consulted voted for Dobson: it was the same sort of manipulation of the union vote that had been used in Wales to secure the selection of first Ron Davies and then Alun Michael rather than Rhodri Morgan. Ken Livingstone claimed that if the unions had followed the wishes of their members he would have won and, after two weeks' hesitation, he announced on 6 March that he regarded the vote as 'tainted', saying that this allowed him to disregard his earlier undertaking and to stand as an independent candidate.

In the election of 5 May there was a total of eleven candidates although only four of these could be considered to have a reasonable chance of winning: those being Livingstone, Norris, Dobson and the Liberal Democrat candidate, Susan Kramer. On the first ballot Ken Livingstone came first with 39 per cent of the vote, Steven Norris came second with 27 per cent and Frank Dobson was third with 13 per cent, only a short distance ahead of Susan Kramer who gained just under 12 per cent. Counting second preferences added another 12.6 per cent to Livingstone's total, making him the clear winner ahead of Steven Norris who gained another 13 per cent. Frank Dobson got 16 per cent of second preference votes, but this was overshadowed by the 28.5 per cent second preferences given to Susan Kramer. Second preference votes also allowed a fifth candidate to make a showing, with Darren Johnson for the Green party claiming 13.6 per cent of second preferences.

Ken Livingstone was therefore elected mayor but, with a turnout of only 34.7 per cent, it is difficult for him to claim a strong mandate. What is clear is that the London electorate were determined to punish Tony Blair and the official Labour party position for the way in which Ken Livingstone was excluded and Frank Dobson was forced onto the ballot paper. The same revolt among Labour supporters can be seen in the assembly election results, where Labour did comparatively badly in the constituency section, winning only 7 of the 14 constituency seats, as did the Conservatives. In the Assembly elections Labour had a total of 9 seats, the Conservatives 8, the Liberal Democrats 4 and the Green party 3 (for list of members, see Appendix 11), the latter two parties having only list members. As in the other devolved assemblies third and fourth parties did very well from the additional member voting system.

The Livingstone administration

Ken Livingstone's main effort upon being elected mayor was to fulfil the promise that his administration would be inclusive. Despite his quarrel with the Labour hierarchy he appointed a Labour member of the Assembly (AM), Nicky Gavron, to be his deputy mayor. He then went on to appoint his cabinet, although stressing that the GLA cabinet would not be like the Westminster cabinet, in that it would be purely advisory and not decision-making. Gavron became a member of the cabinet, as did two other Labour AMs, Toby Harris and Val Shawcross, but the cabinet also included a Lib Dem AM, Graham Tope, and Darren Johnson who had been the Green party candidate for mayor. Cabinet nominees who were not assembly members included such familiar Labour names as Glenda Jackson and Diane Abbott; the latter personifying another aspect of Livingstone's inclusivity in that the cabinet and functional bodies appointed by the mayor included a high proportion of women and representatives of ethnic minorities.

The three functional bodies were set up in June 2000 and cast their membership nets wide:

- The Fire and Emergency Planning Authority was the only body to be almost entirely political in nature, constituting seventeen members as it did, nine of them being assembly members and eight being nominees representing the London boroughs.
- The London Development Agency, with fourteen members, had only two AMs on its strength, the others being representatives of business and the City.
- Transport for London also had fourteen members but they were the most diverse of the three. Ken Livingstone himself was chair but he also included his Lib Dem and Tory rivals for the mayoralty, Susan Kramer and Steve Norris. Other members included representatives of the unions, the academic world and transport specialists such as the chief executive of BAA and the chair of the Docklands Light Railway. Bob Kiley, the American who had revitalised the city transport systems of New York and Boston was later appointed Transport Commissioner.

The Assembly itself was inaugurated on 3 July 2000, choosing the journalist Trevor Phillips to take the chair, with the Lib Dem Lady Hamwee as deputy chair. The Assembly has no legislative powers but it has a powerful remit for scrutiny of the mayor's activities, as was stressed by Trevor Phillips in his inaugural address where he warned Livingstone against using the mayor's office for ideological purposes. To aid the scrutineering process the Assembly created nine committees:

- Transport policy, chaired by Lynne Featherstone (Lib Dem)
- Transport operations, chaired by John Biggs (Labour)

- Environment, chaired by Samantha Heath (Labour)
- Economic development, chaired by Eric Ollerenshaw (Conservative)
- Planning, chaired by Tony Arbour (Conservative)
- Appointments, chaired by Len Duvall (Labour)
- Budget, chaired by Sally Hamwee (Lib Dem)
- Audit, chaired by Valerie Shawcross (Labour)
- Standards, chaired by Jenny Jones (Green)

As can be seen, the committees, which work somewhat similarly to select committees in parliament, have chairs allocated according to the distribution of parties in the Assembly. The Assembly also maintained the right to form ad hoc committees to examine unexpected issues of short-term significance. Two such working parties were formed in the summer of 2000, one dealing with the issue of young professionals like teachers and nurses whose salaries are too low to be able to afford to buy housing in the capital. The other emergency committee dealt with the issue of freight trains carrying nuclear or radioactive waste through the capital.

The mayor's first year

In the first year of the GLA Ken Livingstone followed the example of Tony Blair, doing very little that might upset the middle ground in politics, content to exhibit administrative competence rather than any innovative measures that might alienate the voters. In one area at least he soothed the fears of the doubters and that was by proving himself capable of working with the police, supporting them in their methods of controlling the riots of May Day 2001 with a policy of 'zero tolerance'. By using his ability to raise council tax for specific purposes he was able to increase the size of the Metropolitan police by 1,050 officers, as well as increasing starting pay to cover the problem of housing costs in London.

Most of the concerns of the GLA, as well as most of the controversy, have centred on the question of transport. From before he was elected mayor Livingstone was hostile to the government's favoured public–private partnership (PPP) plans for funding the modernisation, development and daily running of London Underground. He claimed that the involvement of private operators would lead to problems similar to the difficulties of rail privatisation, particularly in its safety implications. In order to reform and modernise the Underground, Livingstone appointed as his transport commissioner, the American Bob Kiley, who had made his name by turning round the failing New York subway and had performed a similar service for the urban transport systems of Boston, Massachusetts. By the time of the 2001 election Kiley had achieved so much support in London that Tony Blair was forced to appoint him to be head of London Transport.

The issue of PPP funding for the rapidly deteriorating Underground remains typical of the way in which devolved administrations can come into conflict with central government. The Blair government remained committed to PPP, despite having the unions, most of the other parties and the voters of London opposed to the semi-privatisation of the Underground. In July 2001 Kiley was sacked from his position at London Transport for opposing the government and two weeks later Livingstone and Kiley lost out in a judicial review which stated that the government had the right to insist on PPP funding for the Tube. However, Kiley remained as traffic commissioner and Livingstone was talking of an appeal.

Another controversial transport measure has been congestion charging for Central London. Most other major European cities place some sort of restriction on private motor vehicles and the proposed GLA solution was to charge £5 a day for motorists to enter an inner zone as of 2003. This is potentially an unpopular policy that will depend on the Transport for London agency's ability to improve public transport facilities in that inner zone if it is to work.

Conclusion

There are conflicting views as to what future there may be for English devolution. Immediately prior to the 2001 election the government had seemed very much in favour, and John Prescott in particular seemed to be promising that legislation for English devolution would be introduced in the post-election period. But the issue seemed to fade once the election was over; particularly since John Prescott's role seemed to change and be reduced in influence. However, the network of regional government offices and their advisory councils remains in place as a possible basis for devolution.

The other alternative is an extension of the London model. Birmingham and Liverpool are just two of the major provincial cities that have expressed an interest in creating strategic authorities made up of an elected mayor and assembly. On the other hand it is by no means clear whether the pattern established by the GLA is a form of devolved government or whether it is merely a reformed means of local government. David Clark, special adviser to Robin Cook at the Foreign and Commonwealth Office (FCO) until May 2001, let it be known that neither the Blair government nor the Civil Service were in any doubt as to the nature of the Greater London Authority. '. . . an internal advice note stressed that the GLA should not be considered a devolved administration on the lines of those in Scotland, Wales and Northern Ireland. The GLA was to be treated as a strategic form of local government' (Clark, 14 August 2001).

Notes

1 *Hansard*, Vol. 939, Cols. 122–3, 14 November 1977 (quoted in Pilkington, 1997, p. 275).
2 In the Midlothian campaign of 1879 Gladstone declared: 'If we can make arrangements under which Ireland, Scotland, Wales, *portions of England*, can deal with questions of local and special interest to themselves more efficiently than parliament now can, that, I say, will be the attainment of a great national good' (quoted in Bogdanor, 2001).
3 The supplementary voting system is a variation of the alternative vote, developed for the Labour party in 1990 by the Plant Committee for possible future use if the electoral system for Westminster were to be reformed. An absolute majority voting system rather than proportional, voters list the candidates in order of preference and, after the first ballot, if there is no outright winner, all but the top two candidates are eliminated and the second preference of these eliminated candidates redistributed until a winner is found.
4 Interestingly enough, the same division of union votes into those that balloted their membership first and those that did not was also true of the election of Alun Michael as Labour leader in Wales.

10

Conclusion:
where do we go from here?

For a development that had been so long in the preparation, devolution for Scotland and Wales, when it happened, came remarkably quickly. The whole process of referendums, consultative documents, legislation and elections leading to the official opening of the Scottish Parliament and Welsh Assembly was completed in two years and little more than a week from the date of Labour's election victory. In Northern Ireland the process was a little more protracted but then there were special reasons for that.

There were those who protested that the process had been too hurried and that therefore the result was bound to be flawed. It was inevitable that, in their first year, the devolved administrations had many critics: we noted earlier the belief of a commentator that the Welsh would have preferred bubonic plague to the Assembly. Yet, when those two years were up it became very clear that, no matter how defective those devolved structures that had been put in place might be and no matter how critical some people might be, the tangible benefits were also beginning to be evident and it was equally clear that the inhabitants of the devolved territories would not willingly give up the benefits they were now beginning to see. An obvious example of the anomalous marriage of condemnation and approval can be found in the attitude of Ian Paisley's Democratic Unionist Party in Northern Ireland. The party is totally opposed to the Good Friday Agreement and its representatives refuse to participate to the full in power-sharing, neither of the two DUP ministers attending any meetings of the executive at which Sinn Fein might be present. Nevertheless, DUP members have sat quite happily on Assembly committees – despite those committees having SF members – and there is every indication that the DUP very much enjoys its share of power and its executive role, taking great pride and claiming full credit for its part in securing free travel for pensioners.

Alongside this growing sense of approval is an acknowledgment that the politics of devolution are very different from the national politics of the UK parliament. It is certainly the case that those who expected the devolved assemblies to be mere microcosms of Westminster have been surprised: whether that

181

surprise is pleasurable or disagreeable varies according to the perspective of the observer. Those people who argued for constitutional reforms as being the best way forward to a completely different attitude towards the nature of political life have proved to be right in their expectations.

Devolved government is more consensual

This does not apply in Northern Ireland where power-sharing between parties representing the two communities is structurally enshrined in the constitutional settlement. But elsewhere – in Scotland, Wales and to a lesser extent in London, the parties have learned to work together and have joined together in coalition administrations. This is partly as a consequence of the electoral system since it is well known that proportional representation militates against one-party domination and leads inevitably to compromise and coalition. It can also be attributed to the layout of the new assemblies that breaks away from the face-to-face confrontation across a central divide that is typical of Westminster and which emphasises the adversarial nature of UK politics. But there is also the possibility that local loyalties supersede party affiliations and that Scots and Welsh of whatever party feel closer to their fellow Scots or Welsh in opposition to English or Westminster attitudes than they do to their party colleagues elsewhere in the UK.

Devolved assemblies are more concerned with regional matters than with UK policy issues

Again this is seen less in Northern Ireland where the political parties are different from those at Westminster, but the administrations in Scotland, Wales and Greater London, although nominally Labour, have shown themselves as being prepared to pass measures that are completely opposed to decisions of the Labour government at Westminster. This is most clearly seen in Scotland, where the Scottish Parliament has legislative powers, and in this respect we have seen the Scottish executive lay down its own independent position on such matters as student loans, teachers' pay and care for the elderly, but the independent stance can also be seen in Wales where the Assembly created a Children's Commissioner for Wales, and free welfare benefits such as bus travel for the elderly, eye-tests for ethnic minorities and prescriptions for students were made more widely available than they are in England. And, of course, there is the example of London where the mayoral administration is prepared to take the Westminster government to court over the matter of the proposed public–private-partnership funding for the London Underground.

Parties in the devolved regions resent the centralising control of Westminster

This has been seen most obviously where central party headquarters have sought to impose their own candidate for the leadership of the devolved party rather than listen to local grassroots opinion. The Labour government fought hard and long to prevent Rhodri Morgan from becoming leader in Wales. And when their chosen candidate, Ron Davies, was disgraced they imposed Alun Michael on a reluctant Welsh party: only to have him finally resign and concede the victory to Morgan. Much the same thing happened in London where Labour was determined to keep Ken Livingstone from becoming mayor, imposing Frank Dobson as the party's nominee and forcing Livingstone to stand as an independent; once again leading to a defeat for the central party. Nor is this true only of Labour, as witness the attempts made by Conservative Central Office to deny the London mayoralty to Steven Norris, while in Scotland Conservatives were so displeased at the way the UK party was performing north of the border that they threatened to secede from London and form themselves into a separate and independent Scottish Conservative party.

Party allegiances are different at the devolved level and give rise to anomalous voting patterns

It is clear that the people see their devolved administrations and the politics associated with the devolved assemblies as being substantively different from the Westminster government and UK politics. Quite apart from the points mentioned above there is the undisputed fact that at election time party allegiances are different, dependent upon whether the elector is considering electing a representative to Westminster or to a devolved assembly. From the evidence of the devolution elections of 1999, the general election of 2001 and some by-elections it is clear that the nationalist parties do far better in elections for the devolved assemblies than they do in elections for Westminster. In Scotland the SNP lost one seat and came close to losing another in the 2001 general election while in Wales Plaid Cymru lost Ynys Môn and failed to gain a seat in the Valleys as they had done in elections to the Welsh Assembly. Yet at Holyrood and Cardiff Bay the SNP and Plaid Cymru remain the main opposition to Labour–Lib Dem coalitions. A similar anomaly can be seen in Northern Ireland where the moderate unionist and nationalist parties, the UUP and SDLP, both lose out to their more extreme counterparts, the DUP and Sinn Fein.

Where to next?

The factors mentioned above make it very clear that, no matter what dissatisfactions are still expressed over the devolution process, that process is here to stay. That can clearly be seen in Northern Ireland where even those denouncing the Good Friday Agreement and demanding its abolition, nevertheless insist that they want the Northern Ireland Assembly to remain.

As to where the devolution process goes from here the answer would seem to be that some matters that remained unresolved or ignored in the original settlement should now be resolved and put in place. Those matters seem to fall under three areas:

- In Wales there is a growing sense of having been fobbed off with half a settlement. Ron Davies, Rhodri Morgan and Lord Elis-Thomas, as Presiding Officer of the Assembly, have all complained that the Assembly was not given sufficient powers. As Elis-Thomas said, '. . . we have the least that could be established at the time . . . it is time we looked for more'.[1] By more, legislative powers are meant. The original settlement granted only executive devolution to Wales, requiring the Assembly to submit proposals to Westminster for primary legislation. It is possible that Wales will ultimately gain the right to pass primary legislation but this is unlikely until executive devolution has been seen to fail, probably because Westminster cannot find time in its legislative programme for purely Welsh legislation.
- The hole in the centre of devolution continues to be about what is to be done with the 85 per cent of the UK population which lives in England. That predominance of England over the other parts of Great Britain probably rules out the practicability of an English parliament to match the Scottish Parliament and Welsh Assembly. The mechanisms have been put into place for the creation of eight or nine English regional assemblies, each of which would represent a population similar to that of Scotland or Wales. However, despite the earlier enthusiasm of John Prescott the government seems to be in no hurry to move this process forward. On the other hand, the European dimension in British politics is likely to play an important part: 'The impetus towards devolution is also pushed further by the activities of the European Union. Not only have its Structural Funds provided material incentives for regional cooperation, the example of strong successful European regions can be witnessed by British local government councillors through their participation in bodies like the Committee of the Regions' (Deacon *et al.*, 2000, p. 32). As suggested in that passage, however, the answer for the English regions does not have to be devolved regional government but is equally as likely to be satisfied by a reformed and strengthened organisation of local government.
- No matter what the solution for England, there is a very real need for the Westminster Parliament to be reformed in the light of devolution. The most obvious measure anomaly is the over-representation of Scotland, Wales and Northern Ireland if they are to retain their devolved administrations and the Boundary Commissions' reviews need to pursue this as a matter of some urgency. Then we have the so-called West Lothian or English Question, asking about the dubious right of MPs from one part of the UK to debate and vote on legislation that is exclusively the concern of another part, which can probably best be answered by:
  - a re-structuring of the standing committee structure at Westminster. Legislation that is purely English in nature would be passed by the UK par-

liament under normal procedures but the time-consuming committee stage would be heard by a committee with English members only.
- Select committees could also be given a regional basis.
- Finally, the secretaries of state for Scotland, Wales and Northern Ireland would be replaced by just one minister who would coordinate the actions of Westminster and the devolved assemblies.

Note

1   *Wales – A New Constitution*, a speech made by Lord Elis-Thomas at Cardiff University, 2 March 2000.

Appendix 1

Results of the referendum of 11 September 1997 in Scotland

In Scotland the SNP abandoned its '*nothing less than full independence*' stance and supported devolution. Labour, Lib Dems and SNP worked well together for a 'yes-yes' vote, leaving the Tories, with no Scottish MPs, as the only supporters of a weak '*just say no*' campaign. Only Tam Dalyell, poser of the West Lothian Question, opposed devolution from the Labour side. In the event, over 60 per cent voted in the referendum and, although 10 per cent less voted 'yes' for taxation powers, only two areas – Orkney and Dumfries and Galloway – voted 'no'. Over 70 per cent of the total vote said yes to the parliament.

Results for Scotland by local government area

The first of the two figures given is a 'yes' vote for a devolved parliament, the second is a 'yes' vote for tax-varying powers. Votes are expressed as percentages.

Aberdeen	71.77	60.34	Inverclyde	77.98	67.19
Aberdeenshire	63.88	52.27	Midlothian	79.88	67.72
Angus	64.66	53.43	Moray	67.18	52.70
Argyll and Bute	67.30	56.99	North Ayrshire	76.31	65.68
Clackmannanshire	79.97	68.66	North Lanarkshire	82.55	72.17
Dumfries and Galloway	60.72	48.80	Orkney	57.29	47.42
Dundee	76.00	65.50	Perthshire and Kinross	61.74	51.30
East Ayrshire	81.13	70.48	Renfrewshire	79.06	63.59
East Dunbartonshire	69.77	30.23	Scottish Borders	62.79	50.73
East Lothian	74.19	62.68	Shetland	62.38	51.61
East Renfrewshire	61.65	51.56	South Ayrshire	66.86	56.23
Edinburgh	71.93	61.96	South Lanarkshire	77.81	67.61
Falkirk	79.95	69.19	Stirling	68.47	58.88
Fife	76.08	64.68	West Dunbartonshire	84.89	74.74
Glasgow	83.59	62.05	Western Isles	79.40	68.43
Highland	72.58	62.05	West Lothian	79.57	67.27

Appendix 2

Formula for working out
the winners of regional seats in the
Additional Member System (AMS)

Under AMS the electors vote for constituency representatives on a simple majority first-past-the-post system. They then elect the additional members through voting for parties, so as to make party representation as near proportional as possible. The additional members are elected from party lists according to a simple formula known as the d'Hondt method:

> The number of votes cast for each party list
> is divided by the number of constituency members
> already elected plus 1.

In the Scotland Bill there is a section in which this formula is explained by using as an example the actual votes cast for the four main Scottish parties in the 1997 election for the Euro-constituency of North-East Scotland, which was due to be represented in the Scottish Parliament by 9 constituency MSPs and 7 additional members.

In the constituency vote

Labour won 113,021 votes	and elected 5 MSPs
SNP won 95,493 votes	and elected 2 MSPs
Liberal Democrats won 69,164 votes	and elected 2 MSPs
Conservatives won 82,079 votes	and elected 0 MSPs

In the first division

Labour's 113,021 is divided by 5 + 1	= 18,837
SNP's 95,493 is divided by 2 + 1	= 31,831
Lib Dems' 69,164 is divided by 2 + 1	= 23,054
Conservatives' 82,079 is divided by 0 + 1	= 82,079

Of these the Conservatives have the largest share and they receive the first added member.

In the second division

Conservative votes are now divided by $1 + 1$, giving a share of $41,039$

This is still larger than the SNP and the Conservatives get a second additional member.

In the third division

Conservative votes are now divided by $2 + 1$, giving a share of $27,359$

This is less than the SNP share so the SNP received the third additional member.

In the fourth division

The SNP vote is now divided by $3 + 1$, giving a share of $23,873$

This is once again below the Conservatives and it is they who get the fourth added member.

In the fifth division

The Conservative vote is now divided by $3 + 1$, giving a share of $20,519$

The largest vote is now the SNP and they get the fifth additional member.

In the sixth division

The SNP vote is now divided by $4 + 1$, giving a share of 19098

The Liberal Democrats now have the largest share and get the sixth additional member.

In the seventh and final division

Once again the Conservative share is largest and they take the last additional place.

Overall the distribution of seats is		
	Constituency	**Regional list**
Labour	5	0
SNP	2	2
Liberal Democrat	2	1
Conservative	0	4

Appendix 3

Cabinets of the Scottish executive

Cabinet appointed by Donald Dewar, May 1999

First Minister – Donald Dewar
Deputy First Minister and Justice – Jim Wallace (Lib Dem)
Minister for Enterprise and Lifelong Learning – Henry McLeish
Minister for Communities – Wendy Alexander
Minister for Children and Education – Sam Galbraith
Minister for Transport and the Environment – Sarah Boyack
Minister for Rural Affairs – Ross Finnie (Lib Dem)
Minister for Finance – Jack McConnell
Minister for Health and Community Care – Susan Deacon
Minister for Parliament – Tom McCabe
Lord Advocate – Lord Hardie QC*

* Lord Hardie resigned to become a judge in January 2000 and was replaced by Colin Boyd

Cabinet appointed by Henry McLeish, October 2000

First Minister – Henry McLeish
Deputy First Minister and Minister for Justice – Jim Wallace (Lib Dem)
Minister for Education, Europe and External Affairs – Jack McConnell
Minister for Enterprise and Lifelong Learning – Wendy Alexander
Minister for Environment – Sam Galbraith
Minister for Finance and Local Government – Angus MacKay
Minister for Health and Community Care – Susan Deacon
Minister for Parliament – Tom McCabe
Minister for Rural Development - Ross Finnie (Lib Dem)
Minister for Social Justice – Jackie Baillie
Minister for Transport – Sarah Boyack

Sources: Robert Hazell (ed.), *The State and the Nations*, Imprint Academic, 2000 and the Report of the Constitution Unit, November 2000 – www.ucl.ac.uk/constitutionunit

These appointments were bound to change as a result of the resignation of Henry McLeish in November 2001.

Appendix 4

Results of the referendum of 18 September 1997 in Wales

Without either legislative or tax-varying powers, the Welsh Assembly could be seen as no more than an expensive talking shop. Many Labour party members, including half a dozen MPs, were strongly opposed and campaigned for a 'no' vote. After the vote, with a low turnout of only 50 per cent, the country divided in half, east and west. The largely English-speaking areas – along the Welsh Marches, in the north-east near Liverpool, in Pembrokeshire and around Cardiff – voted 'no'. The largely Welsh-speaking Plaid Cymru heartland of the west, and the loyal Labour South Wales Valleys, voted 'yes'. The 'no' camp led throughout, until the very last declaration when a massive 'yes' vote in Carmarthen gave a majority of just 0.6 per cent to the pro-devolution campaign.

Turnout	0.12 per cent
Yes	559,419 (50.3 per cent)
No	552,698 (49.7 per cent)
Majority for Yes	6,721 (0.6 per cent)

Only a little over 25 per cent of the Welsh electorate voted in favour of devolution.

Yes		No	
Ynys Môn	1.80	Torfaen	0.32
Swansea	3.92	Wrexham	9.44
Bridgend	8.78	Cardiff	11.26
Caerphilly	9.40	Pembrokeshire	14.42
Blaenau Gwent	12.18	Powys	14.68
Merthyr Tydfil	16.42	Conwy	18.16
Rhondda Cynon Taff	16.94	Denbighshire	18.96
Ceredigion	18.40	Flintshire	23.60
Gwynedd	28.17	Newport	25.14
Carmarthenshire	31.08	Vale of Glamorgan	28.92
Neath Port Talbot	33.10	Monmouthshire	35.80

Note: The figures given are the percentage leads over the opposing view.

191

Appendix 5

The electoral regions and districts of Wales

Wales is divided into five electoral regions based on European parliamentary constituencies. Each region is then divided into a variable number of Westminster Parliamentary constituencies. In elections to the Welsh Assembly, each Westminster consituency elects one Assembly member by first past the post, while each European consituency elects four top-up members from a regional list. The proportion of Assembly seats allocated to each region is intended to reflect the proportion of the Welsh electorate living in that region.

European constituency	Proportion of Welsh electorate	Number of Assembly seats
North Wales	21.6%	13 (21.7%)
Mid and West Wales	18.2%	12 (20%)
South Wales West	17.9%	11 (18.3%)
South Wales Central	21.6%	12 (20%)
South Wales East	20.6%	12 (20%)

Source: Figures taken from the *Government of Wales Act 1998* (Welsh Assembly, www.wales. gov.uk).

Note: Each region is divided as follows: North Wales (Ynys Môn, Caernarfon, Conwy, Clwyd West, Vale of Clwyd, Clwyd South, Delyn, Alyn and Deeside, Wrexham); Mid and West Wales (Meirionnydd Nant Conwy, Ceredigion, Preseli Pembrokeshire, Carmarthen West and South Pembrokeshire, Carmarthen East and Dinefwr, Llanelli, Montgomeryshire, Brecon and Radnorshire); South Wales West (Gower, Swansea East, Swansea West, Neath, Aberavon, Bridgend, Ogmore); South Wales Central (Vale of Glamorgan, Pontypridd, Rhondda, Cynon Valley, Cardiff North, Cardiff West, Cardiff Central, Cardiff South and Penarth); South Wales East (Newport East, Newport West, Monmouth, Torfaen, Islwyn, Caerphilly, Blaenau Gwent, Merthyr Tydfil and Rhymney).

Appendix 6

Membership of the
Welsh Assembly executive

Cabinet appointed by Rhodri Morgan, 2000

First Minister – Rhodri Morgan
Deputy First Minister and Minister for Economic Development – Michael German
Minister for Education and lifelong Learning – Jane Davidson
Minister for Assembly Business (Whip) – Andrew Davies
Minister for the Environment – Sue Essex
Minister of Finance, Local Government and Community – Edwina Hart
Minister of Health and Social Services – Jane Hutt
Minister for Rural Affairs (Agriculture and Fisheries) – Carwyn Jones
Minister for Culture, Sport and the Welsh Language – Jenny Randerson

It is interesting to note the gender balance within the executive, with five out of nine ministers being women.

Note that most accounts use the term 'secretary' for the ministerial positions within the Assembly but in this version promoted by the Assembly itself, the term 'minister' is used.

Source: Welsh Assembly website, www.wales.gov.uk

Appendix 7

The single transferable vote (STV) electoral system

A system of voting developed by the British Electoral Reform Society as long ago as 1910 and proposed to the 1917 Speaker's Conference on Electoral Reform, STV was the electoral system used for the four university seats which existed between 1918 and 1949 as well as being adopted for the proposed Irish parliament of 1920. Its use in Northern Ireland elections was abandoned for local government in 1922 and for elections to Stormont in 1929, in order to safeguard the Protestant ascendancy. The system was recommended for devolved assemblies by the Kilbrandon Commission but was discounted in 1997, in favour of the Additional Member System, for the Scottish Parliament and Welsh assembly. After 1922, STV had continued to be used in succession by the Irish Free State, Eire and the Republic of Ireland for all elections. After 1972, it was re-adopted for all non-Westminster elections in Northern Ireland in order to preserve proportional representation for the sectarian communities

At the heart of STV is a multi-member constituency, electing up to six members to the parliament or elected body. For example, in elections to the Northern Ireland Assembly voting takes place in the eighteen Westminster consituencies, each of which elects six members. Electors are faced with a long list of names since each party may nominate as many candidates as there are vacancies to be filled. The voter then places candidates in order of preference by writing 1, 2, 3 and so on alongside their names.

In counting the votes, the aim is to reach a quota calculated by *dividing the total number of votes cast by one more than the number of seats available, plus one*. For example, if 40,000 votes were cast in a constituency where three seats were available, the quota would be 40,000 divided by 3 + 1 plus one: i. e. 10,001. Any candidate reaching the quota with first preference votes is elected but very few are elected on the first count: in the June 1998 elections only one fifth of Assembly seats were decided by first preference votes. There is a complex procedure for achieving the full number of members, involving the redistribution of first preference votes surplus to the quota, as well as redistributing second preference votes from those eliminated candidates who received the fewest first preference votes, so as to eliminate wasted votes both in the sense of candidates who got more votes than were needed as well as candidates who got too few votes to count. This process of redistributing votes goes on until the necessary number of constituency members is elected.

Appendix 8

The Northern Ireland Assembly
– party representation, June 1998

The chief merit of STV as far as Northern Ireland is concerned is not only that there is representation proportional to the size of the various sectarian communities but that the multi-member constituencies ensure that electors from either side of the sectarian divide will have a representative with whom they can identify. Of the eighteen constituencies in the Northern Ireland Assembly there is only one that does not have both unionist and nationalist MLAs (the exception is the entirely nationalist West Belfast).

In the lists that follow the letters in parenthesis after the constituency name represent the party which held the Westminster seat at the 1997 general election.

North Belfast (UUP)

UUP	1
SDLP	1
DUP	1
SF	1
UUAP	1
PUP	1

South Belfast (UUP)

UUP	2
SDLP	2
DUP	1
NIWC	1

East Belfast (DUP)

UUP	2
DUP	2
PUP	1
Speaker (Lord Alderdice)	

West Belfast (SF)

SDLP	2
SF	4

North Antrim (DUP)

UUP	2
SDLP	1
DUP	3
Alliance	
WIUP	1

South Antrim (DUP)

UUP	2
SDLP	1
DUP	1

East Antrim (UUP)		*North Down (UKUP)*	
UUP	2	UUP	3
SDLP	1	Alliance	1
DUP	1	UKUP	1
Alliance	1	NIWC	1
Independent Unionist			

South Down (SDLP)		*Strangford (UUP)*	
UUP	1	UUP	2
SDLP	3	DUP	2
DUP	1	Alliance	1
SF	1	NIUP	1

Lagan Valley (UUP)		*Upper Bann (UUP)*	
UUP	2	UUP	2
SDLP	1	SDLP	1
DUP	1	DUP	1
Alliance	1	SF	1
NIUP	1	UUAP	1

East Derry (UUP)		*Foyle (SDLP)*	
UUP	2	SDLP	3
SDLP	2	DUP	1
DUP	1	SF	2
UUAP	1		

Mid Ulster (SF)		*Newry and Armagh (SDLP)*	
UUP	1	UUP	1
SDLP	1	SDLP	2
DUP	1	DUP	1
SF	3	SF	2

West Tyrone (UUP)		*Fermanagh and South Tyrone (UUP)*	
UUP	1	UUP	2
SDLP	2	SDLP	1
DUP	1	DUP	1
SF	2	SF	2

Appendix 9

Ministers and committees of the Northern Ireland Assembly

The executive and departmental statutory committees

In the list that follows the name of the minister is followed by party allegiance and the post held – which is also the name of the departmental committee headed by the ministers. In parentheses after the name of the committee are the party allegiances of the chair and deputy chair of the committee.

Note that these are the initial allocations made as of 29 November 1999. Changes were made later.

David Trimble (UUP) – First Minister
Seamus Mallon (SDLP) – Deputy First Minister
Brid Rodgers (SDLP) – Agriculture and Rural Development (DUP, UUP)
Michael McGimpsey (UUP) – Culture, Arts and Leisure (SDLP, SF)
Martin McGuinness (SF) – Education (UUP, DUP)
Reg Empey (UUP) – Enterprise, Trade and Investment (SF, Alliance)
Sam Foster (UUP) – Environment (DUP, SDLP)
Mark Durkan (SDLP) – Finance and Personnel (SF, UUP)
Bairbre de Brun (SF) – Health, Social Services and Public Safety (SDLP, SDLP)
Sean Farren (SDLP) – Higher and Further Education, Training, Employment (UUP, DUP)
Peter Robinson (DUP) – Regional Development (SDLP, UUP)
Nigel Dodds (DUP) – Social Development (UUP, SF)

Standing committees

The list that follows lists the six standing committees set up on 29 November 1999. In parentheses are the party allegiances of the chair and deputy chair initially appointed.

Audit (SDLP, PUP)
Procedure (SF, UUP)
Business (Speaker, Alliance)
Public Accounts (UUP. SF)
Committee of the Centre (DUP, DUP)
Standards and Privilege (SDLP, UUP)

Appendix 10

Members of the Standing Committee on (English) Regional Affairs (as convened 10 May 2001)

There were fifteen members, although of the Conservative members, only Anthony Steen actually attended. All members sit exclusively for English constituencies.

Chair: John McWilliam (Blaydon)
Joe Ashton (Bassetlaw)
Candy Atherton (Falmouth and Camborne)
Karen Buck (Regent's Park and Kensington, North)
David Chidgey (Eastleigh)
Louise Ellman (Liverpool Riverside)
Nigel Evans (Ribble Valley)
Christopher Fraser (Mid-Dorset and North Poole)
Andrew George (St Ives)
Denis Murphy (Wansbeck)
Ian Pearson (Dudley, South)
Lawrie Quinn (Scarborough and Whitby)
Anthony Steen (Totnes)
Derek Wyatt (Sittingbourne and Sheppey)

Source: UCL Constitution Unit, May 2001.

Appendix 11

The GLA assembly members, 6 May 2000

Labour

Trevor Phillips (Barnet and Camden) elected chair of the assembly
John Biggs (City and East)
Len Duvall (Greenwich and Lewisham)
Nicky Gavron (Enfield and Haringey)
Lord (Toby) Harris (Brent and Harrow)
Meg Hillier (North East–Hackney, Islington and Waltham Forest)
Val Shawcross (Lambeth and Southwark)
Samantha Heath (London list)
David Lammy (London list)

Conservative

Tony Arbour (South West–Hounslow, Kingston and Richmond)
Richard Barnes (Ealing and Hillingdon)
Angela Bray (West Central–Hammersmith, Kensington, Chelsea, Westminster)
Roger Evans (Havering and Redbridge)
Elizabeth Howlett (Merton and Wandsworth)
Bob Neill (Bexley and Bromley)
Andrew Pelling (Croydon and Sutton)
Eric Ollerenshaw (London list)

Liberal Democrats

Lady (Sally) Hamwee (London list) elected deputy chair of the assembly
Louise Bloom (London list)
Lynne Featherstone (London list)
Lord (Graham) Tope (London list)

Green Party

Victor Anderson (London list)
Darren Johnson (London list)
Jenny Jones (London list)

Bibliography

Books and articles

Adonis, Andrew, *Parliament Today,* Manchester University Press, Manchester, 1993.

Alder, John, *Constitutional and Administrative Law* (2nd edn), Macmillan, Basingstoke, 1994.

Aughey, Arthur and Duncan Morrow (eds), *Northern Ireland Politics*, Longman, Harlow, 1996.

Bogdanor, Vernon, *Devolution in the United Kingdom*, Opus, Oxford, 1999.

Bogdanor, Vernon, 'England may get its turn', *Guardian*, 23 April 2001.

Bradbury, Jonathan, 'English Regional Government', *Politics Review*, April 1996.

Bradbury, Jonathan, '*Yr Ie Bychan* – the little yes', *Politics Review*, April 1998.

Brogan, Hugh, *Longman History of the United States*, Longman Group, Harlow, 1985.

Budge, Ian, Ivor Crewe, David McKay and Ken Newton, *The New British Politics*, Addison Wesley Longman, Harlow, 1998.

Cannon, Jon (ed.), *The Oxford Companion to British History*, Oxford University Press, Oxford, 1997.

Clark, David, 'A people's convention for London', *Guardian*, 14 August 2001.

Cole, John, *As it Seemed to Me*, Weidenfeld & Nicolson, London, 1995.

Cole, Michael, 'The changing governance of London', *Talking Politics*, Summer 2000.

Cook, Chris and John Ramsden (eds), *By-elections in British politics*, UCL Press, London, 1997.

Cooper, Marc-Philippe, 'Understanding subsidiarity as a political issue in the European Community', *Talking Politics*, Spring 1995.

Coxall, Bill and Lynton Robins, *Contemporary British Politics* (2nd edn), Macmillan, Basingstoke, 1995.

Cunningham, Michael, *British Government Policy in Northern Ireland 1969–89, its Nature and Execution,* Manchester University Press, Manchester, 1991.

Cunningham, Michael, 'British Government Policy in Northern Ireland', *Politics Review*, September 1992.

Davies, Norman, *The Isles, a History*, Macmillan, London, 1999.

Deacon, Russell, Dylan Griffiths and Peter Lynch, *Devolved Great Britain: The New Governance of England, Scotland and Wales*, Sheffield Hallam University Press, Sheffield, 2000.

Deacon, Russell, '"Early Days" The first year of the National Assembly for Wales (1999–2000)', *Talking Politics*, April 2001.

Evans, Mark, *Devolution to Scotland and Wales: Is 'Power Devolved Power Retained'?* in Steve Lancaster (ed.) *Developments in Politics Vol. 10*, Causeway Press, Ormskirk, 1999.

Falconer, Peter and Alistair Jones, 'Electing a Scottish Parliament', *Talking Politics*, Winter 1999.

Falkus, Malcolm and John Gillingham (eds), *Historical Atlas of Britain*, Grisewood & Dempsey, London, 1981.

Freedland, Jonathan, 'Livingstone's London', *Guardian*, 4 May 2001.

Griffin, Brian, 'A force divided – policing Ireland 1900–60', *History Today*, October 1999.

Griffiths, Dylan, 'The Welsh Assembly', *Talking Politics*, Winter 2000.

Hassan, Gerry, 'The Almanac of Scottish Politics', *Guardian*, 22 March 2001.

Hazell, Robert, 'Constitutional futures', *Talking Politics*, Spring 1999.

Hazell, Robert (ed.), *The State and the Nations*, Imprint Academic, Thorverton, 2000.

Hazell, Robert, 'A purely English parliament?', *Guardian*, 3 January 2001.

Henderson, Ailsa and Amanda Sloat, 'New Politics in Scotland? A profile of MSPs', *Talking Politics*, Summer 1999.

Henderson, Ailsa and Amanda Sloat, 'New Politics in Scotland? Evidence from Holyrood', *Talking Politics*, Winter 2000.

Hetherington, Peter, 'Prescott gets half a cake', *Guardian*, 20 November 1998.

Hetherington, Peter, 'The benefits of regionalism', *Guardian*, 31 January 2001.

Hetherington, Peter, 'Scots and Welsh face subsidy axe', *Guardian*, 24 April 2001.

Hopkins, Stephen, 'The Good Friday Agreement in Northern Ireland', *Politics Review*, February 1999.

Hunt, Steven, 'Peace in our times? Prospects and dilemmas after the Northern Ireland Assembly election results', *Talking Politics*, Winter 1999.

Jackson, Alvin, 'The Irish Act of Union', *History Today*, January 2001.

Jones, Bill (ed.), *Political Issues in Britain Today* (3rd edn), Manchester University Press, Manchester, 1989.

Jones, Bill and Dennis Kavanagh, *British Politics Today* (2nd edn), Manchester University Press, Manchester, 1994.

Judge, D., *The Parliamentary State*, Sage, London, 1993.

Keegan, Victor and Martin Kettle (eds), *The New Europe*, Fourth Estate, London, 1993.

Kingdom, John, *Government and Politics in Britain*, Polity Press, Cambridge, 1991.

Lynch, Peter, 'Labour, devolution and the West Lothian question', *Talking Politics*, Autumn 1996.

Lynch, Peter, 'Devolution and a new British political system', *Talking Politics*, Winter 1997/98.

Lynch, Peter, 'The Road to a Scottish Parliament', *Politics Review*, April 1998.

Lynch, Peter, 'Petitioning the Scottish Parliament: an experiment in citizen participation', *Talking Politics*, April 2001.

Lynch, Peter and Steven Birrell, 'Grievances galore', *Guardian*, 7 May 2001, p. 13.

Mackie, J. D. *A History of Scotland*, Penguin, Harmondsworth, 1964.

Mattingley, H. (trans.), *Tacitus on Britain and Germany*, Penguin, Harmondsworth, 1948.

Mitchell, James, 'Reviving the union state?', *Politics Review*, February 1996.

Mitchell, James, *Devolution in the United Kingdom – revision notes*, Politics Association Resource Centre, Manchester, 1999.

Moran, Mike, 'Reshaping the British state', *Talking Politics*, Spring 1995.

Morgan, Kenneth O., 'Divided we stand', *History Today*, May 1999.

Nairn, Tom, *After Britain, New Labour and the Return of Scotland*, Granta, London, 2000.

Neunreither, K., 'Subsidiarity as a guiding principle for European Community activities', *Government and Opposition*, Vol. 28, No. 2, Spring 1993, pp. 207–18.

Norton, Philip (ed.), *The Consequences of Devolution*, Hansard Society, London, 1998.

Pilkington, Colin, *Representative Democracy in Britain Today*, Manchester University Press, Manchester, 1997.

Pilkington, Colin, *The Politics Today Companion to the British Constitution*, Manchester University Press, Manchester, 1999.

Pilkington, Colin, *The Civil Service in Britain Today*, Manchester University Press, Manchester, 1999a.

Pilkington, Colin, *Britain in the European Union Today* (2nd edn), Manchester University Press, Manchester, 2001.

Prebble, John, *The Lion in the North*, Secker & Warburg, London, 1971.

Preston, Peter, 'The break-up of Britain', *Guardian*, 23 April 2001.

Robins, Lynton and Bill Jones (eds), *Debates in British Politics Today*, Manchester University Press, Manchester, 2000.

Philip, Schlesinger, David Miller and William Dinan, *Open Scotland? Journalists, Spin Doctors and Lobbyists*, Polygon at Edinburgh University Press, Edinburgh, 2001.

Seldon, Anthony, 'Northern Ireland', in Bill Jones (ed.), *Politics UK* (2nd edn), Harvester Wheatsheaf, Hemel Hempstead, 1994.

Sell, Geoffrey, 'Scottish Nationalism in the 1990s', *Talking Politics*, Spring 1998.

Steinberg, S. H. and I. H. Evans, *Steinberg's Dictionary of British History* (2nd edn), Edward Arnold, London, 1970.

Stenton, Frank, *Anglo-Saxon England* (2nd edn), Clarendon Press, Oxford, 1947.

Stoker, Gerry, Brian Hogwood and Udo Bullman, 'Do we need regional government?' *Talking Politics*, Spring 1996.

Taylor, A. J. P. *The Struggle for Mastery in Europe 1848–1918*, Oxford University Press, Oxford, 1954.

The Scotland Bill, Scottish Office, 1998.

TEU, *Treaty on European Union*, Office for Official Publications of the European Communities, Luxembourg, 1992.

White Paper: *Scotland's Parliament*, Cm 3658, 1997.

White, Michael, 'How the mayor has performed . . .', *Guardian*, 4 May 2001.

Wober, J. M., *Watching parliament on TV – Views from Scotland, England, Wales and Northern Ireland*, Hansard Scottish Parliament Programme, Edinburgh, 2000.

Young, Hugo, *One of Us*, Macmillan, London, 1989.

Internet websites

General

The Constitution Unit, University College of London, produces four reports each quarter on the progress and development of devolution in respectively Scotland, Wales, Northern Ireland and England. The reports are posted on the internet in May, August, November and February each year and can be read at www.ucl.ac.uk/constitutionunit.

The reports are found on the *Nations and Regions* pages, where information can be found on how to receive the relevant reports by e-mail.

Directory of politics related websites compiled by Keele University: www.psr.keele.ac.uk

Guide to sites related to devolution on the internet: www.geocities.com/Athens/Ithaca

British government

HMSO: www.hmso.gov.uk
Open government: www.open.gov.uk

Scotland

Scottish Executive: www.scotland.gov.uk
Scottish Office: www.scottish.secretary.gov.uk
Scottish Parliament: www.scottish.parliament.uk
Scottish Petitions Committee: www.scottish.parliament.uk/parl_bus/petitions.html
Scottish Politics (from an SNP standpoint): www.alba.org.uk

Wales

Welsh Assembly: www.wales.gov.uk

Northern Ireland

Northern Ireland Office: www.nio.gov.uk
Northern Ireland Assembly: www.ni.assembly.gov.uk

Index